I0803100

The Campus History Series

WHEELING JESUIT UNIVERSITY

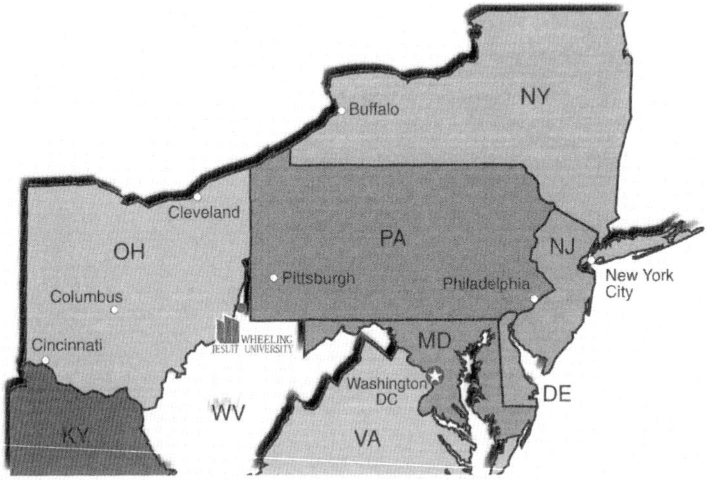

Mileage to Wheeling Jesuit University

Akron, OH	100	Harrisburg, PA	260
Baltimore, MD	290	Huntington, WV	230
Boston, MA	615	Johnstown, PA	145
Buffalo, NY	255	New York, NY	450
Cincinnati, OH	240	Parkersburg, WV	110
Charleston, WV	180	Philadelphia, PA	360
Cleveland, OH	155	Pittsburgh, PA	60
Columbus, OH	135	Toledo, OH	275
Detroit, MI	330	Trenton, NJ	360
Erie, PA	190	Washington, DC	300
Fairfield, CT	460	Youngstown, OH	85

Wheeling's Centrality. This map or variations of it were used in the Wheeling Jesuit University academic catalog and in much of the college's promotional literature to show how accessible the college was to major urban centers. (Courtesy of Wheeling Jesuit University.)

On the Front Cover: Students in this 1978 graduation ceremony at Oglebay Park are still holding their hoods, so they have not yet crossed the stage to pick up their diplomas. Those wearing cords are in an honor society. (Courtesy of Wheeling Jesuit University.)

On the Cover Background: The wraparound picture shows Donahue Hall after it was remodeled inside and out in 1987. The new exterior received mainly decorative alterations, but the inside was extensively changed to increase privacy and reduce noise. (Courtesy of Wheeling Jesuit University.)

The Campus History Series

WHEELING JESUIT UNIVERSITY

JOSEPH A. LAKER

ARCADIA PUBLISHING

ISBN 978-0-7385-9221-3

Published by Arcadia Publishing
Charleston, South Carolina

Printed in the United States of America

Library of Congress Catalog Card Number: 2011936491

For all general information, please contact Arcadia Publishing:
Telephone 843-853-2070
Fax 843-853-0044
E-mail sales@arcadiapublishing.com
For customer service and orders:
Toll-Free 1-888-313-2665

Visit us on the Internet at www.arcadiapublishing.com

This photographic history of Wheeling Jesuit University is dedicated to my faculty colleagues—especially Margaret Geroch—who have inspired me with their idealism, nurturing of their students, intellectual stimulation, and fellowship.

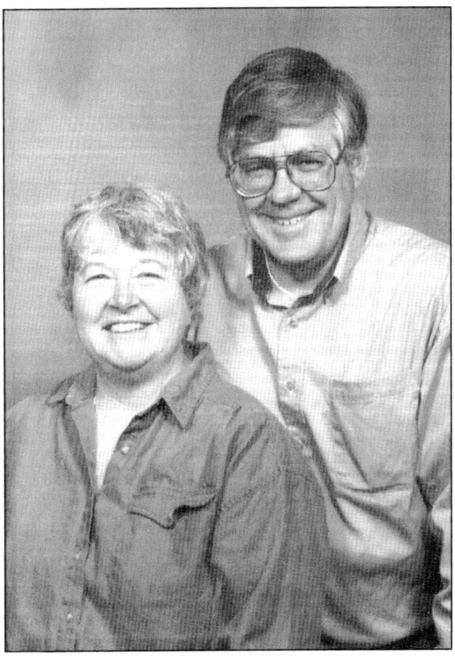

Joe and Margaret. The author, Dr. Joseph Laker, and his wife, Margaret Geroch, were longtime colleagues at Wheeling Jesuit. Dr. Laker was a professor of history, and Geroch was an associate professor of math and computer science.

CONTENTS

Acknowledgments

When I suggested doing a pictorial history of Wheeling Jesuit, Pres. Richard Beyer was immediately supportive, and James Holt, vice president for institutional advancement, expressed enthusiasm for the project. There are so many people that I have to thank for lending me pictures, offering suggestions, and providing me with information that I am sure I will miss someone, but some of these people include Carol Cannon; Joan Carrigan; Tim Dilworth; Erin Burns; Mary Moore; Chris Rouhier; David Fluharty; Katherine Vorhees; John Whitehead; Judy Paulhus; WJU president emeritus Thomas Acker, SJ; Joe Sanders, SJ; and Don Mercer. In addition, Jimmy Brogan of Campus Ministry lent photographs to me, Rob Kulpa of Student Affairs let me borrow pictures and the most recent copies of the *Manifest*, Kelly Klubert and Maureen Zambito provided pictures and information on alumni, Ryan Rutkowski gave me access to the archives of the Catholic Diocese of Wheeling-Charleston, and the Charles F. Gruber Company took some of the beautiful older pictures I found in the college archives.

Indeed, all the members of the Wheeling Jesuit community responded with support. Paul Orr, archivist and college historian, was most helpful in directing me to photographs and materials in the Wheeling Jesuit archives, and Kelly Mummert and her staff at the Bishop Hodges Library not only gave me access to their collection of photographs and other materials but were gracious in adjusting to my comings and goings. Thanks also go to Joseph Buch, who helped me write the book proposal with Arcadia. John Wack helped by identifying people in old photographs and agreeing to read the text. The succession of editors that I have had at Arcadia all proved to be understanding and encouraging.

Finally, I need to give special thanks to two people—Blake Williams and Margaret Geroch. Blake's expertise in scanning, sending e-mails, and all things technical greatly facilitated my finishing of the book; he gave his time unstintingly. Margaret assisted by reading and critiquing the text, encouraging me at every turn, and putting up with my crankiness when things did not go smoothly.

Unless otherwise noted, all photographs in this book are courtesy of Wheeling Jesuit University.

Introduction

When Wheeling College was officially incorporated on September 26, 1954, Wheeling was a thriving, small industrial city in the northern panhandle of West Virginia, approximately 50 miles southeast of Pittsburgh. With a population of about 55,000, the city was home to steel, coal, glass, tobacco factories, mines, and a variety of other firms. Wheeling, once the principal city of western Virginia, was a hotbed of Unionist sentiment during the Civil War. Unionist leaders were integral in breaking Virginia apart and creating the new state of West Virginia in 1863. In the late 19th century, immigrants, attracted by mining and industrial employment, poured into the region. Wheeling was also the home and headquarters of the bishop of the Wheeling diocese of the Roman Catholic Church.

As early as 1848, the bishop of Wheeling, Rev. Richard Whelan, had asked the Society of Jesus (a Catholic religious order also called Jesuit) to open and operate a college in the diocese to meet the higher education needs of Catholics, but the Jesuits initially refused. When Bishop John Swint renewed the request in 1951, the Jesuits responded more favorably, sending a small team to gauge the community needs and level of support for the college and begin planning. Bishop Swint purchased a 61-acre property from the nuns of the Mount de Chantal Visitation Academy and pledged $2,000,000 to help finance the construction of the campus.

The overall theme of this history of the college is community. The transformation of Wheeling College, a small liberal arts institution at its founding, into today's Wheeling Jesuit University will be illustrated by pictures, a few documents, and commentary. How this academic community has operated and adjusted to change is the principal focus of the text.

The first chapter provides a chronological picture of the university's development during the past 57 years by concentrating on the bishops, presidents, and a few key individuals whose support was crucial to the creation and growth of the institution. The bishops and presidents provided the overall vision and leadership to create the kind of school Wheeling Jesuit has become. Above all, its mission was to be Catholic and to serve the needs of the Catholic population of West Virginia and the surrounding region.

The physical environment in which any community operates is of considerable importance. What kind of physical environment has nature provided? What kind of buildings and other facilities have been created to foster to goals of the college's founders? Located in an eastern suburb of Wheeling, the campus is largely self-contained and rather isolated from the larger community. Bounded on the east to the northwest by Wheeling Creek, on the west by the former Mount de Chantal Visitation Academy, and to the south by a high hill that rises up from Washington Avenue, the campus is easily accessible at only two points—where College

Drive enters and leaves the property. Students find stores, restaurants, churches, and bus lines within walking distance, yet operate in a village that is largely their own.

Central to the purpose of creating Wheeling Jesuit University are the academic program and the experiences that administrators and faculty require students to master. The focus here is on how the faculty operate both inside and outside the classroom to create a sense of community amongst themselves and with their students, bringing about intellectual and emotional development. The core courses—which all students must take—provide, in the words of the most recent academic catalog, "all students, regardless of major, with the skills that will enable them to pursue their own integral development and contribute to the common good. In a spirit of free inquiry, it also enables them to articulate a coherent vision of reality and a set of resulting ethical principles." Although the university has greatly expanded its curriculum since its founding, the core experience remains important and helps keep the university close to its liberal arts traditions.

Of almost equal importance to a student's growth and development—and for some students, the most crucial factor—are the experiences they have while studying, playing, and living on campus and participating in numerous off-campus activities created by student development and Campus Ministry administrators, as well as the nonacademic activities they themselves create.

When Wheeling College began its intercollegiate sports program in September 1956, men could compete to play on basketball, tennis, or golf teams, while female students vied for the five spots open for cheerleaders. Intramural sports, including football, basketball, archery, table tennis, and weight lifting, offered students more opportunities. Extracurricular activities did not change much until the early 1980s, when federal law, growing demand by students, and the increasing use of sports as a recruitment tool led to a rapid expansion of facilities, programs, and staff at the intercollegiate level. Today, more than 40 percent of Wheeling Jesuit students are active in eight intercollegiate sports for men and an equal number for women. The 21 coaches have 16 graduate assistants to help them manage the athletic programs at the university. Club sports teams and intramural competitions are still quite popular but play less of a role than they formerly did.

The final chapter concentrates on how Wheeling Jesuit has tried to create and maintain strong support from alumni. It has worked to create a post-commencement community through alumni organizations, reunions, and the bestowal of honors on alumni who have put their education to good use and remain supportive of the institution. A few alumni are pictured, and their accomplishments are commented upon.

In this history of Wheeling Jesuit University, I have used the words *Jesuits* and the *Society of Jesus* interchangeably. The official name of this Catholic religious order, founded in Europe in 1540, is the Society of Jesus, and the word *Jesuit* was a name that once had negative implications. Today, it has lost those negative connotations and is widely used by the Jesuits themselves. In like manner, I have used the three names of the school—Wheeling College, Wheeling Jesuit College, and Wheeling Jesuit University, but I have tried to use the terms correctly to indicate the time of the picture or event that took place.

One

Bishops, Presidents, and Founders

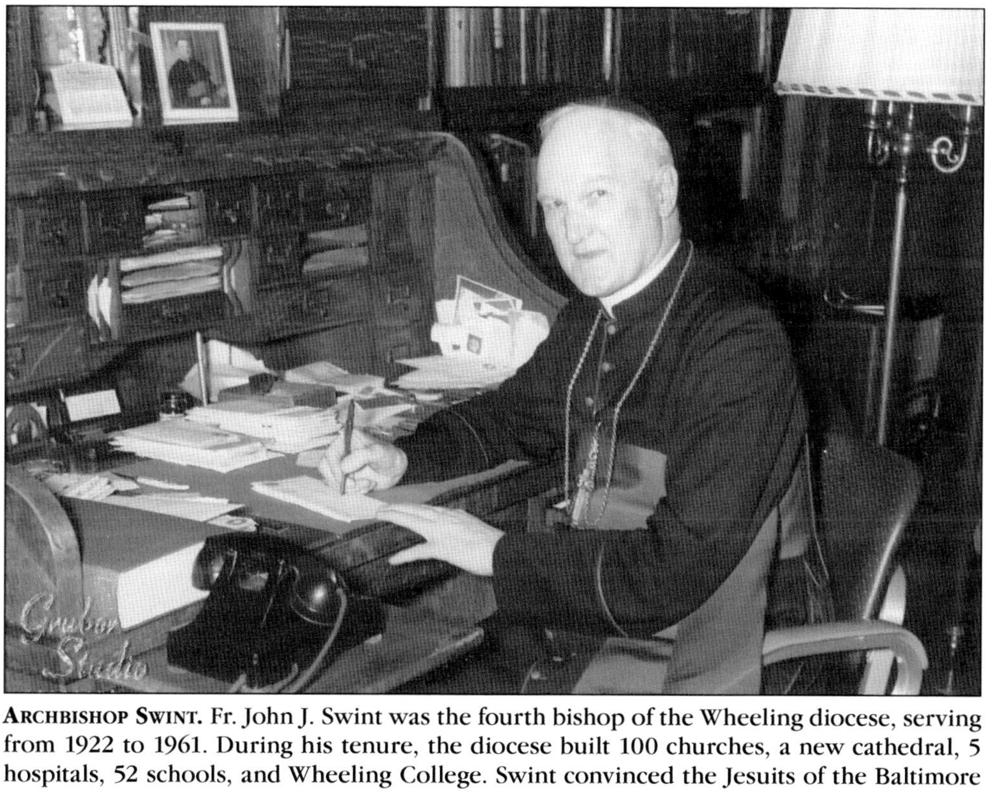

Archbishop Swint. Fr. John J. Swint was the fourth bishop of the Wheeling diocese, serving from 1922 to 1961. During his tenure, the diocese built 100 churches, a new cathedral, 5 hospitals, 52 schools, and Wheeling College. Swint convinced the Jesuits of the Baltimore province to open the college in 1951. Pope Pius XII named Swint an archbishop in 1954. (Courtesy of the Wheeling-Charleston Diocese Archives.)

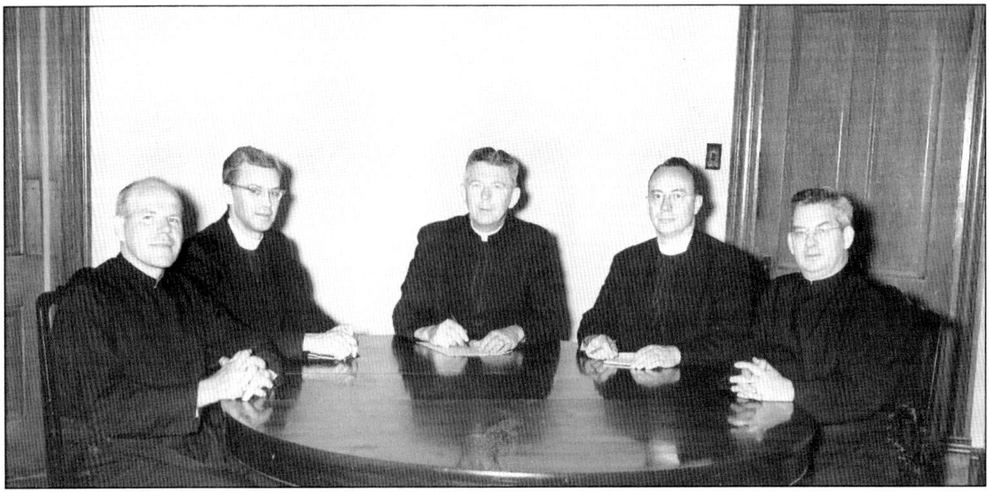

FIRST BOARD OF TRUSTEES. The five Jesuits pictured here are, from left to right, Brother John Michalowicz, Fr. Edward Powers, Fr. Lawrence McHugh, Fr. Clifford Lewis, and Fr. Joseph Drane. They incorporated the college on September 1955 and were the initial trustees. Drane created the academic structure, McHugh was the first president, Lewis handled fundraising and public relations, and Powers selected equipment and furniture for the buildings and kept the books.

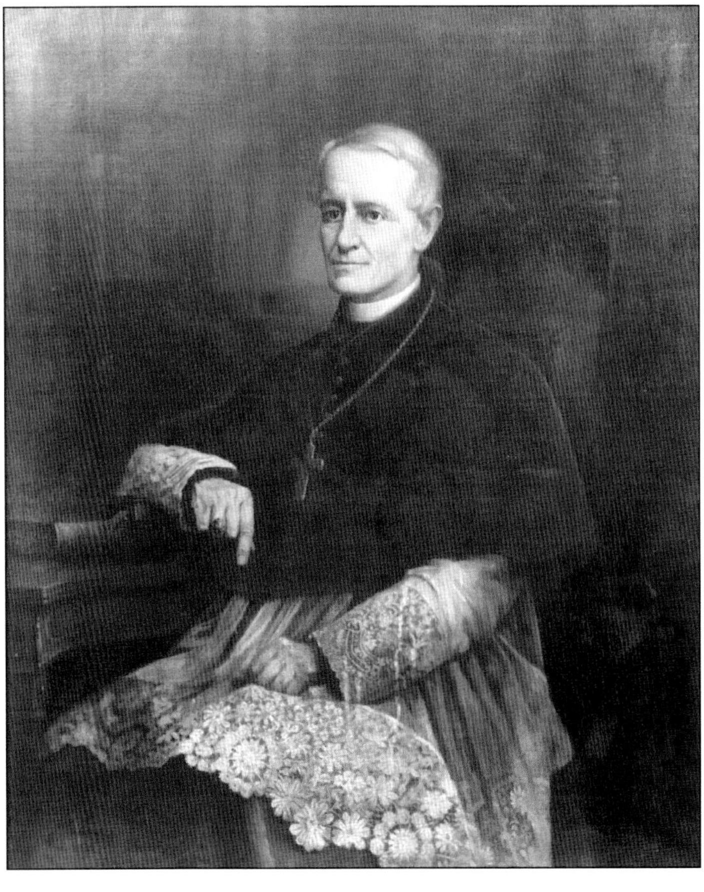

FIRST BISHOP. Rev. Richard Whelan was bishop of the Wheeling diocese from 1850 to 1874. During his tenure, the diocese built 42 churches, 9 schools, 1 orphanage, and 1 hospital. He convinced the Visitation Nuns of Baltimore to open the Mount de Chantal Academy for girls. Although he asked the Society of Jesus (Jesuits) to create a college in Wheeling, his suggestion was turned down. The Jesuit residence on campus is named in his honor, and this official portrait hangs in Whelan Hall.

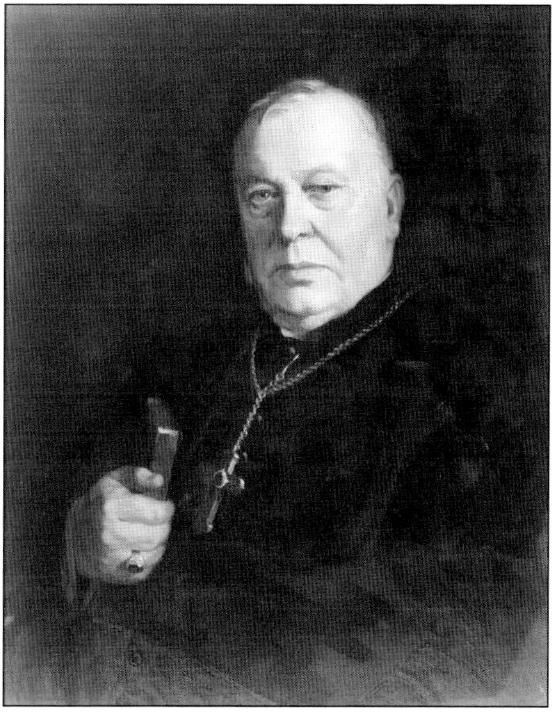

THIRD BISHOP. Rev. Patrick Donahue was bishop from 1894 to 1922. His friendship with wealthy New York benefactress Sara Tracy provided the diocese with funds to buy the land and finance the construction of the first three buildings on campus. The college's main classroom building, Donahue Hall, is named in his honor, and his official portrait hangs near the entrance.

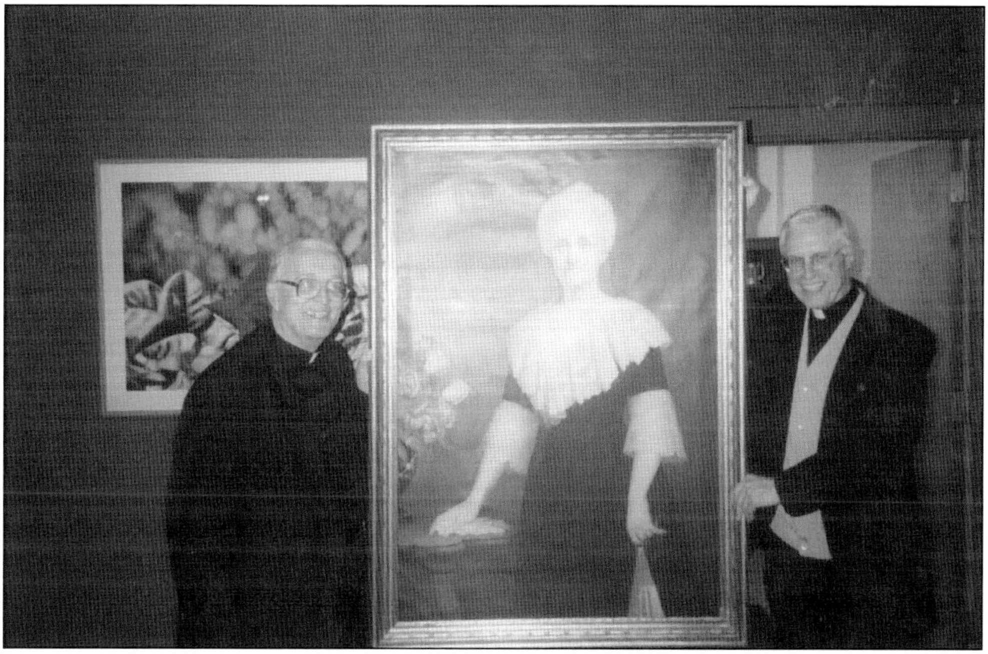

PORTRAIT OF SARA TRACY. This painting hangs in the college's first dormitory for women, which is named in Tracy's honor. Tracy was an heiress who met Bishop Donahue on a ship bound for Europe and was impressed by his victory over an arrogant German officer in an all-night chess match. They became good friends, and Donahue and the Wheeling diocese became heirs to most of her estate. Frs. Joseph Sanders, SJ (left), and Walter Buckius Jr., SJ, blessed and dedicated the portrait on December 6, 2001.

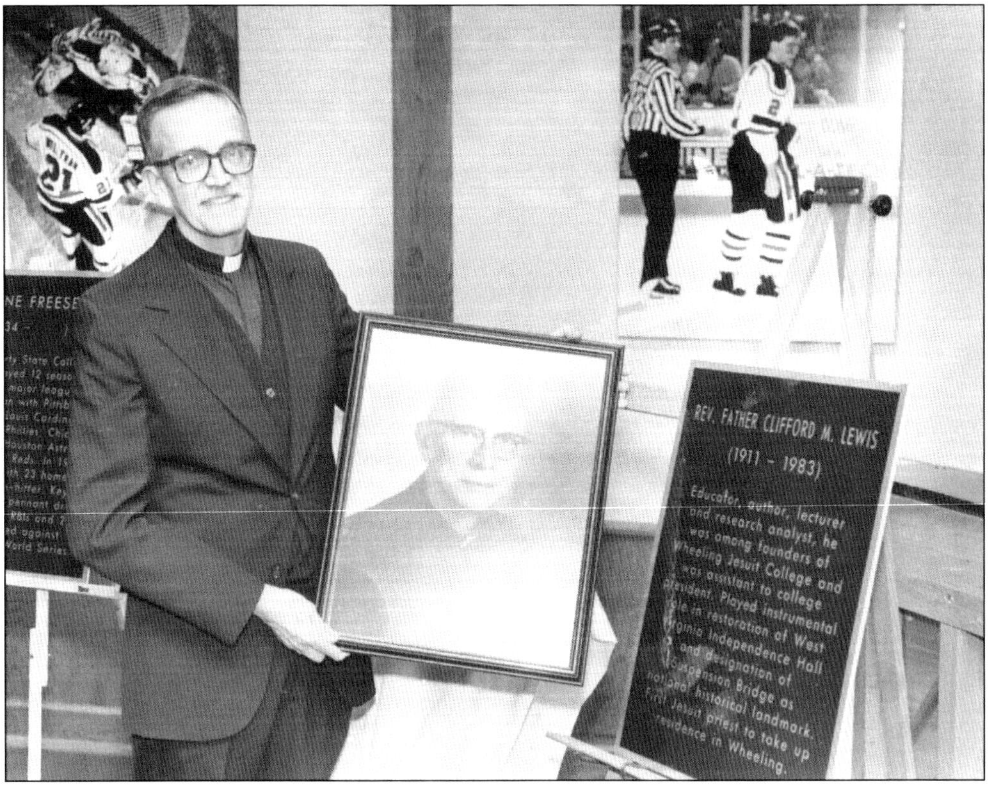

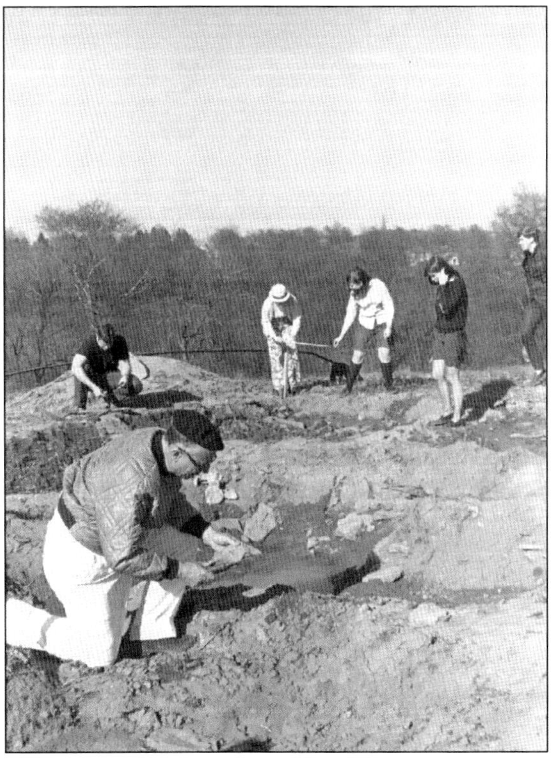

CLIFFORD LEWIS, SJ. Fr. Joseph Hayden, SJ, rector of the Jesuit Community and professor of psychology, holds a portrait of Clifford Lewis, SJ, from when Lewis was inducted into the City of Wheeling's Hall of Fame. Father Lewis, the first Jesuit to visit Wheeling at the founding of the college, played a crucial role in its early development by raising money, doing public relations, teaching history, and coaching the golf team.

ARROWHEADS ON CAMPUS. Fr. Clifford Lewis worked with students on archeological digs on college property during construction in the 1950s, collecting the arrowheads and spearheads now displayed in the case near the main entrance of Donahue Hall. Father Lewis wrote a number of articles on local and frontier history, including a very fine piece on the Wheeling Suspension Bridge that crosses the Ohio River.

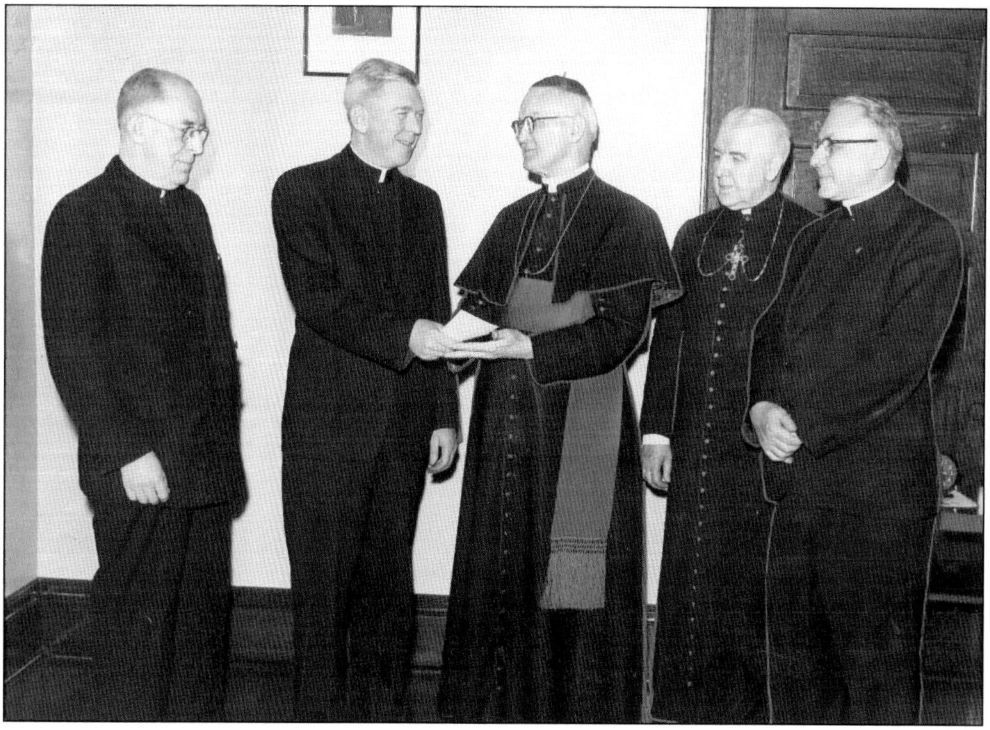

Transferring the Deed. On February 11, 1957, Archbishop John Swint hands the deed of property of the college over to Pres. Lawrence McHugh. From left to right are Msgr. Lee, McHugh, Swint, Fr. McDonnell (auxiliary bishop of Wheeling), and Msgr. Schwertz. (Courtesy of the Wheeling-Charleston Diocese Archives.)

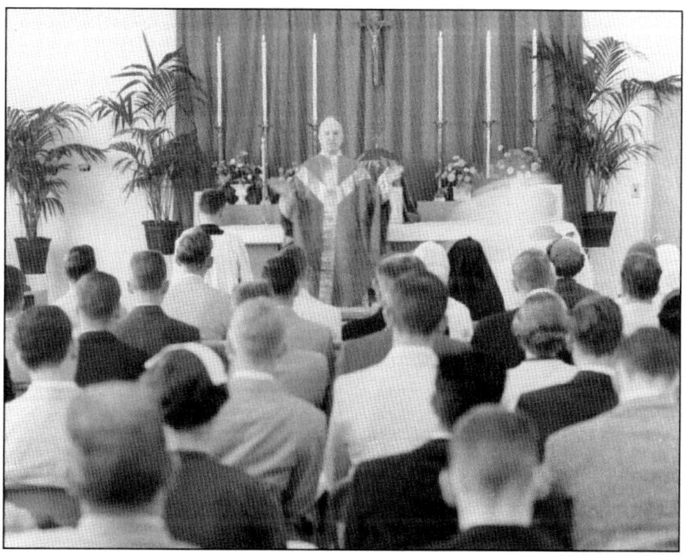

First Mass in Student Chapel. Archbishop Swint celebrates Mass in the small student chapel on the second floor of Donahue Hall. Only about one-third of the student body could be accommodated at one time, so Swint hoped Sunday Mass would be conducted in the gymnasium. The gym was occasionally used for Sunday Mass and school-wide convocations.

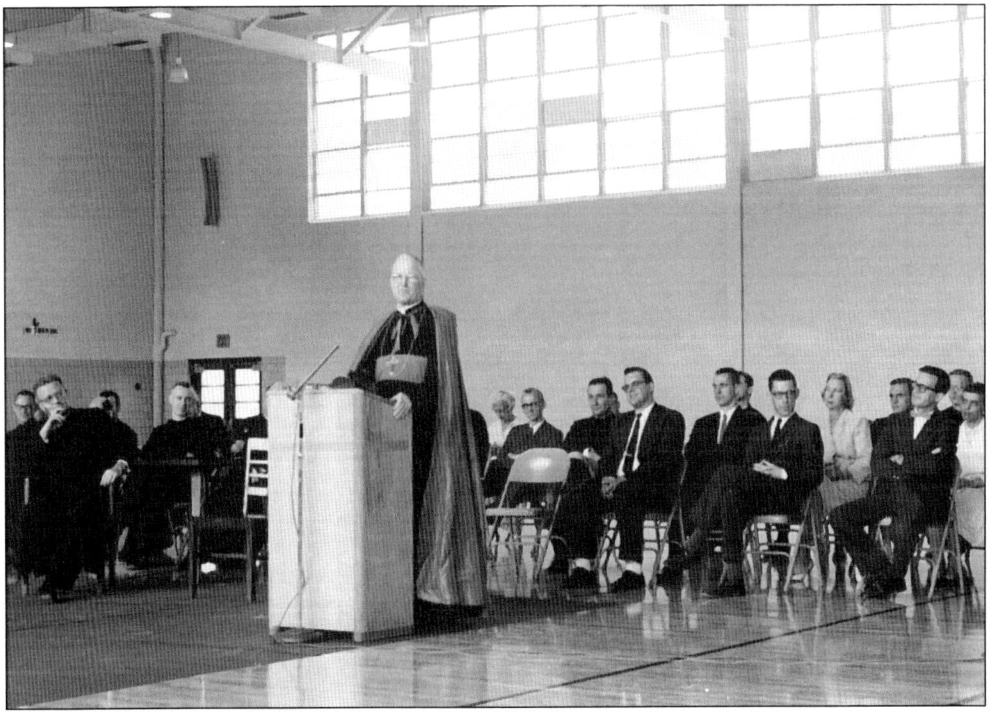

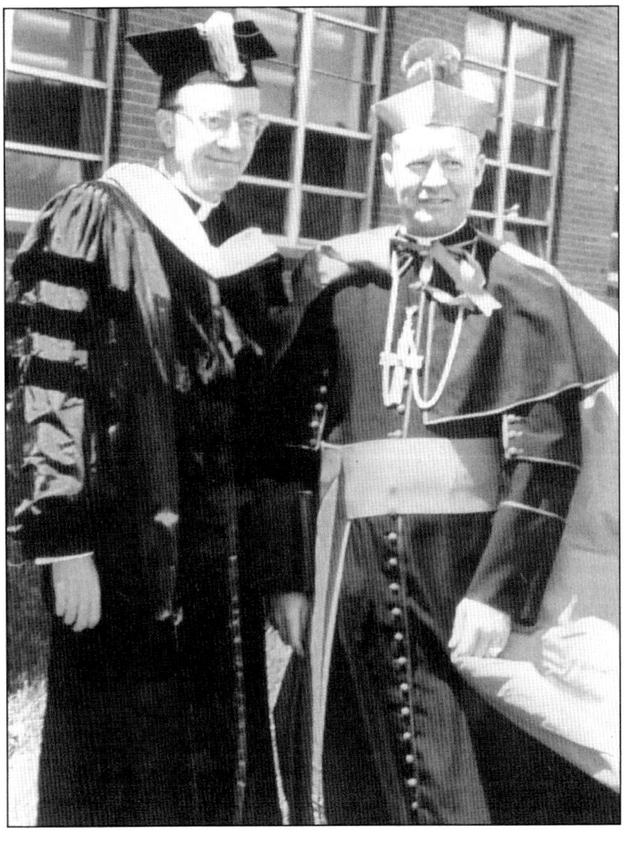

Swint's Last Visit. Archbishop John Swint made his last appearance at Wheeling College in the fall of 1962, shortly before his death. The fall honors convocation was held in the gymnasium, and he was the principal speaker. Archbishop Swint fought hard to see the gym completed, and it was officially opened and dedicated eight days after he passed away.

Fifth Bishop. Bishop Joseph Hodges (right) and Pres. William Troy, SJ, stand in front of Donahue Hall before commencement exercises on May 19, 1963. The fifth bishop of the diocese, Hodges gained approval for the reorganization of its borders so they would coincide with those of West Virginia and for the renaming of the diocese to Wheeling-Charleston. He was bishop from 1962 until 1985.

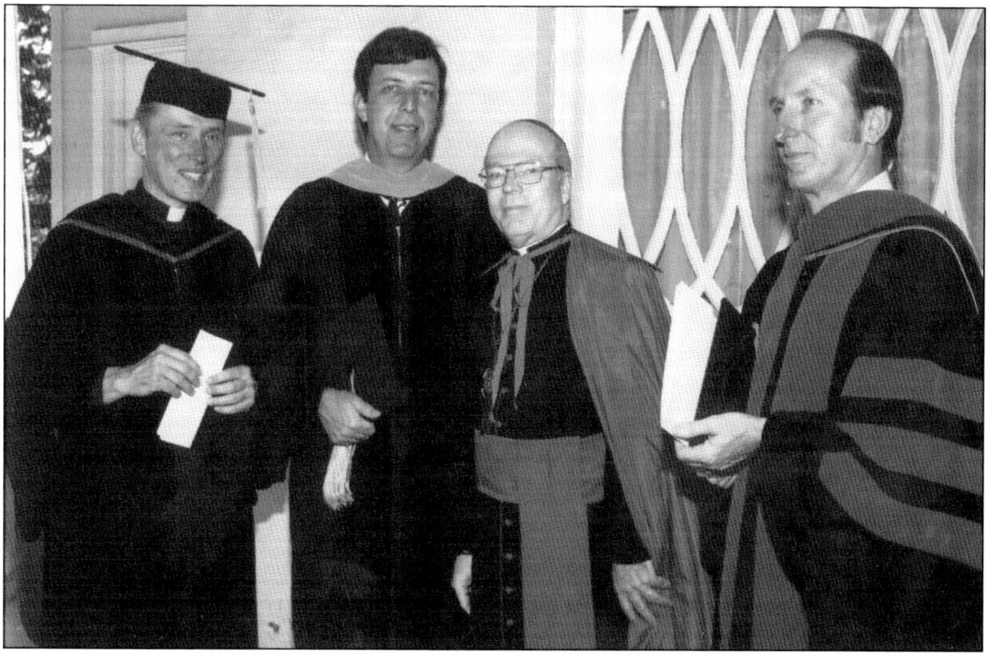

SIXTH BISHOP. Rev. Francis Schulte (third from left) is pictured at the 1986 commencement exercises with faculty members, from left to right, Jim O'Brien, SJ (philosophy), Jim Goodwin (psychology), and Fr. Eugene Lauer (theology). Schulte succeeded Joseph Hodges and served until February 1989, when he was appointed archbishop of New Orleans.

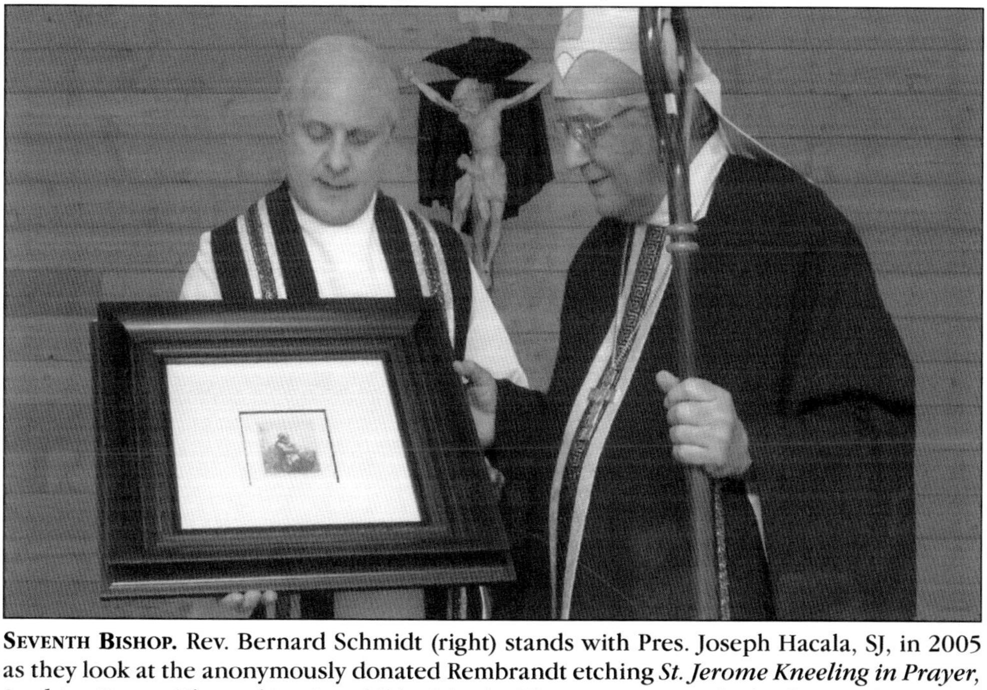

SEVENTH BISHOP. Rev. Bernard Schmidt (right) stands with Pres. Joseph Hacala, SJ, in 2005 as they look at the anonymously donated Rembrandt etching *St. Jerome Kneeling in Prayer, Looking Down*. The etching is exhibited in the library. A native of Wheeling and pastor of St. Michael's Church before his elevation to the episcopacy, Father Schmidt was a strong supporter of the college and its mission.

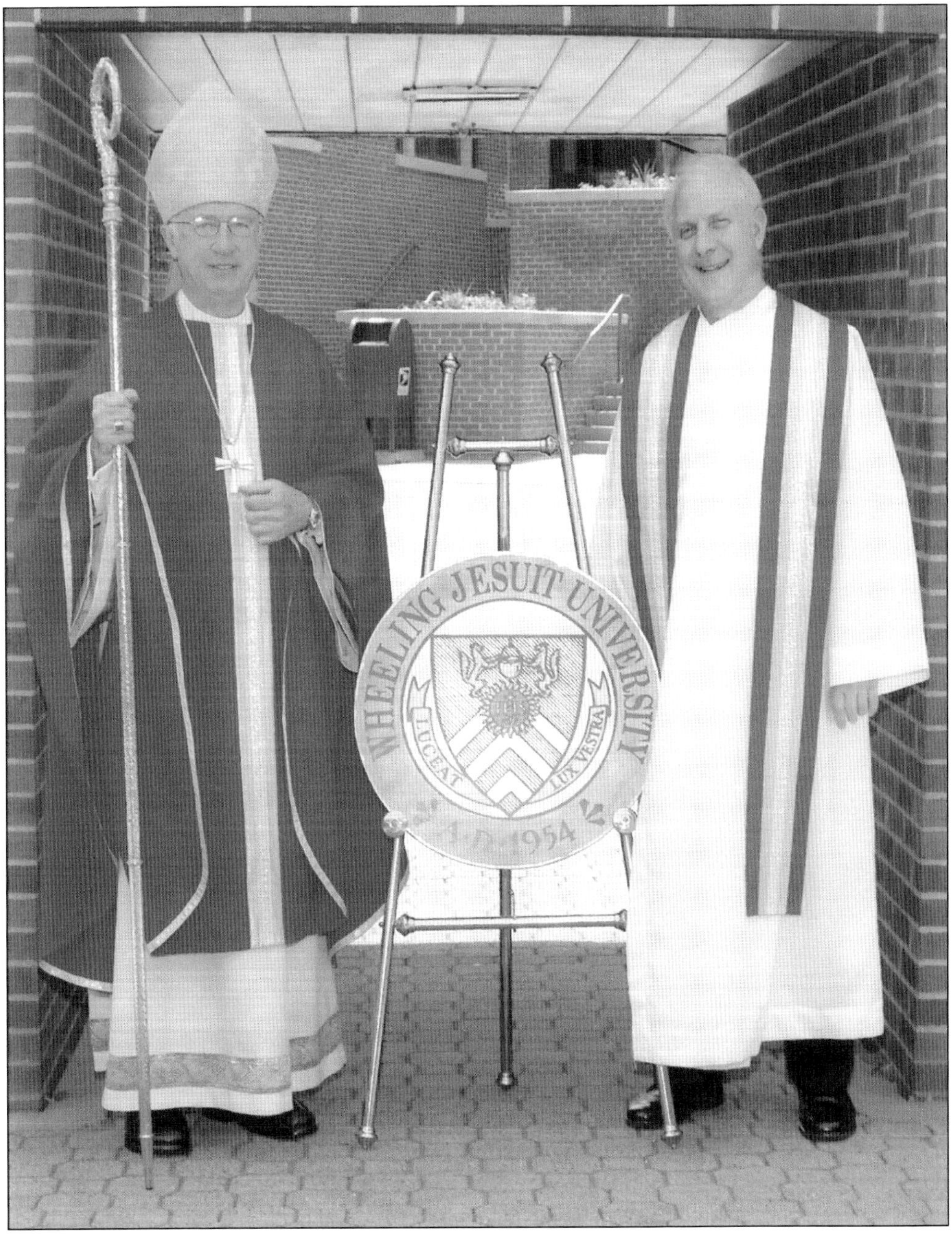

EIGHTH BISHOP. Rev. Michael Bransfield and Pres. Joseph Hacala stand in front of the Chapel of Mary and Joseph after the bishop's celebration of his first Mass in Wheeling Jesuit's chapel on June 1, 2005. Recently, Bishop Bransfield authorized a $1.2 million grant from the diocese to the university to improve its health sciences departments and provide scholarships for graduates of the diocesan high schools.

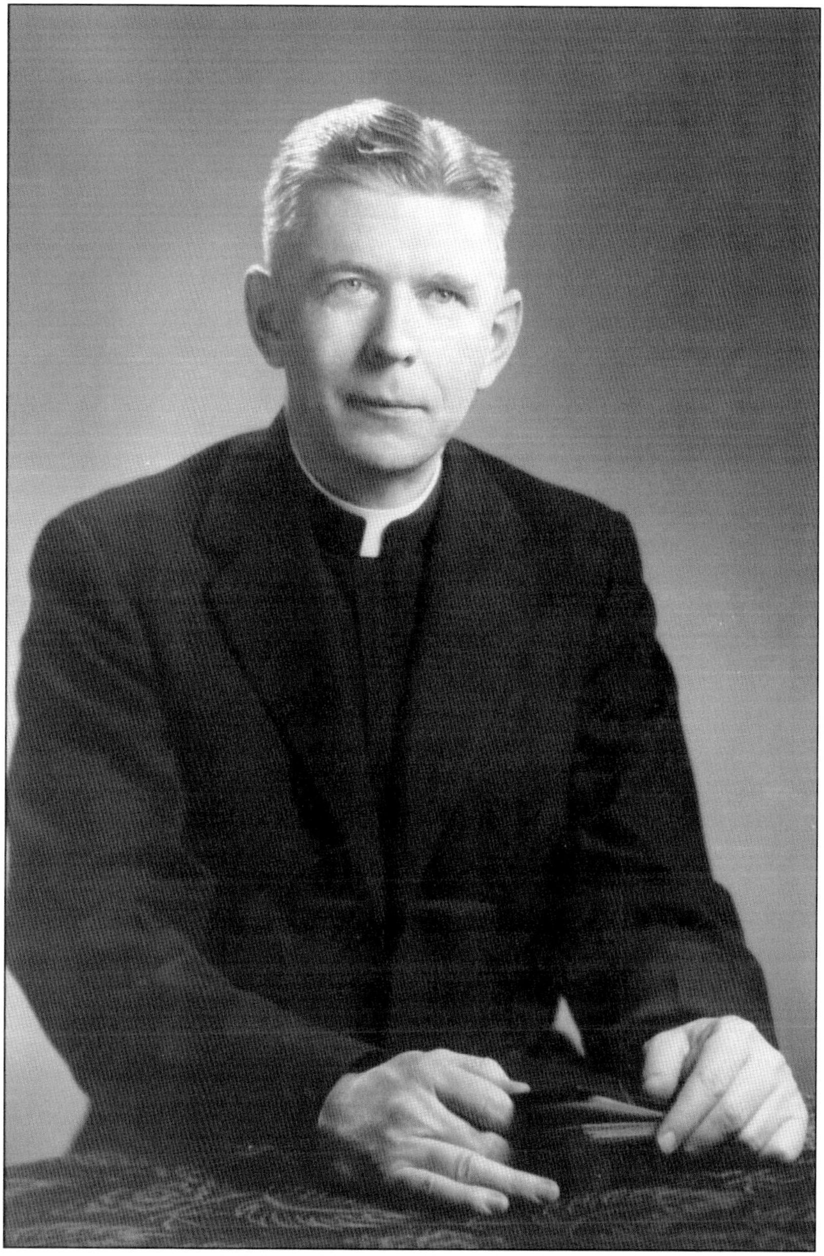

First President. This is the official portrait of Fr. Lawrence McHugh, SJ, who was the college's president from its founding until the summer of 1959. A native of Baltimore, McHugh entered the Society of Jesus in 1922. He studied theology for three years in Vienna, Austria, before being expelled by the Nazis in 1938. After serving as a Navy chaplain during World War II, McHugh became an assistant dean of students at Georgetown University. During his time as president of Wheeling College, he oversaw chartering of the school by the State of West Virginia; creation of the institutional structures; hiring of faculty; the building of Whelan, Swint, and Donahue Halls; and the creation of organizations to provide support from the local community. After leaving Wheeling, he served at St. Joseph's University in Philadelphia. McHugh retired in 1983 and died on April 8, 1988, at the age of 80.

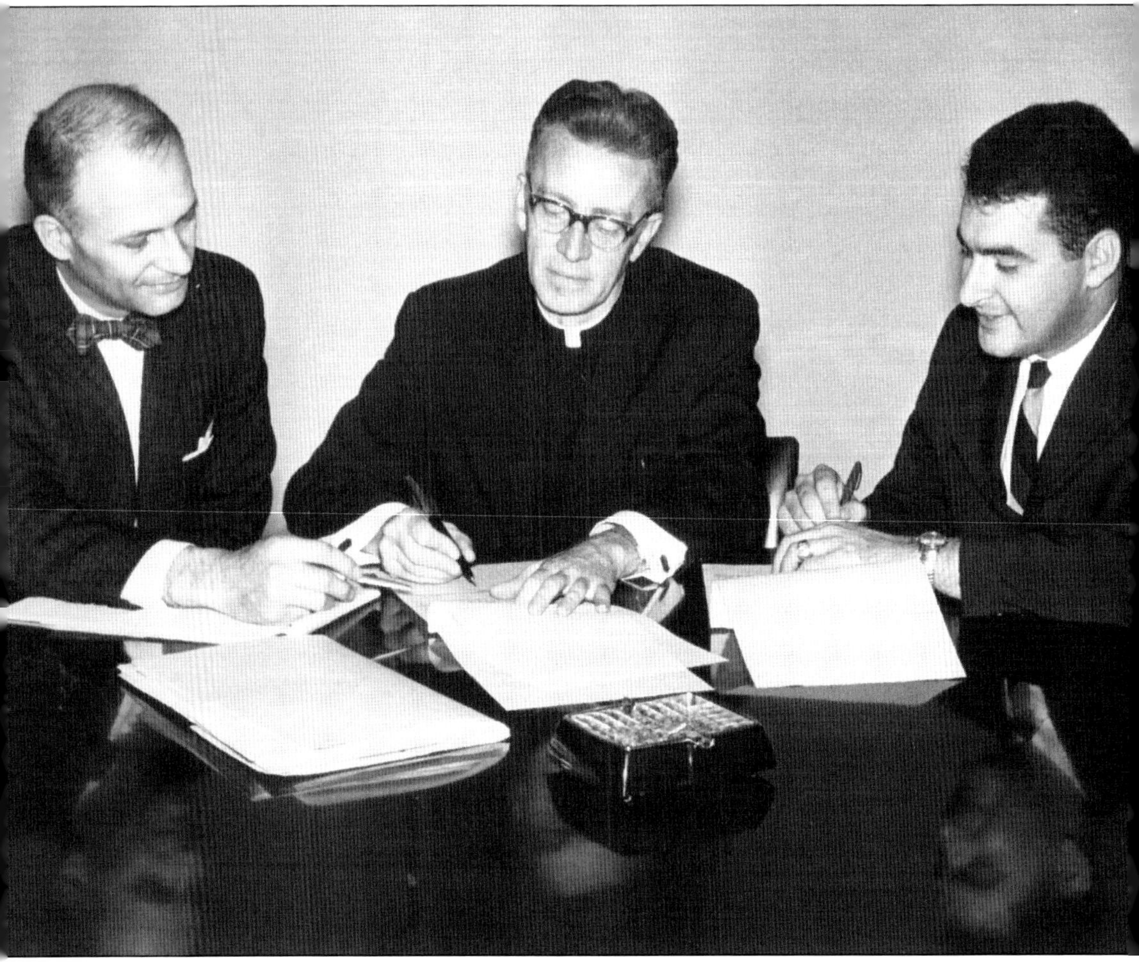

Second President. First academic dean, then president, William Troy, SJ, came to Wheeling College in 1954 after serving as headmaster of Gonzaga High School in Washington, DC. Troy was president of the college from 1959 until 1966. He oversaw the completion of the McHugh and Sara Tracy dorms, the gymnasium, and the construction of three student apartment buildings on the hill. Here, Troy (center) signs the contract to build More Hall with attorney Joseph Gompers (left) and James Braden, president of the Area Company. The college created a summer school in 1960 and developed a $5.3 million capital campaign. Student enrollment quickly rose, which necessitated an increase in faculty and staff. The college received full accreditation by the North Central Association in 1962. Father Troy left the college to serve as the regional headmaster of the Jesuits. He died at the age of 47 the year after he left Wheeling.

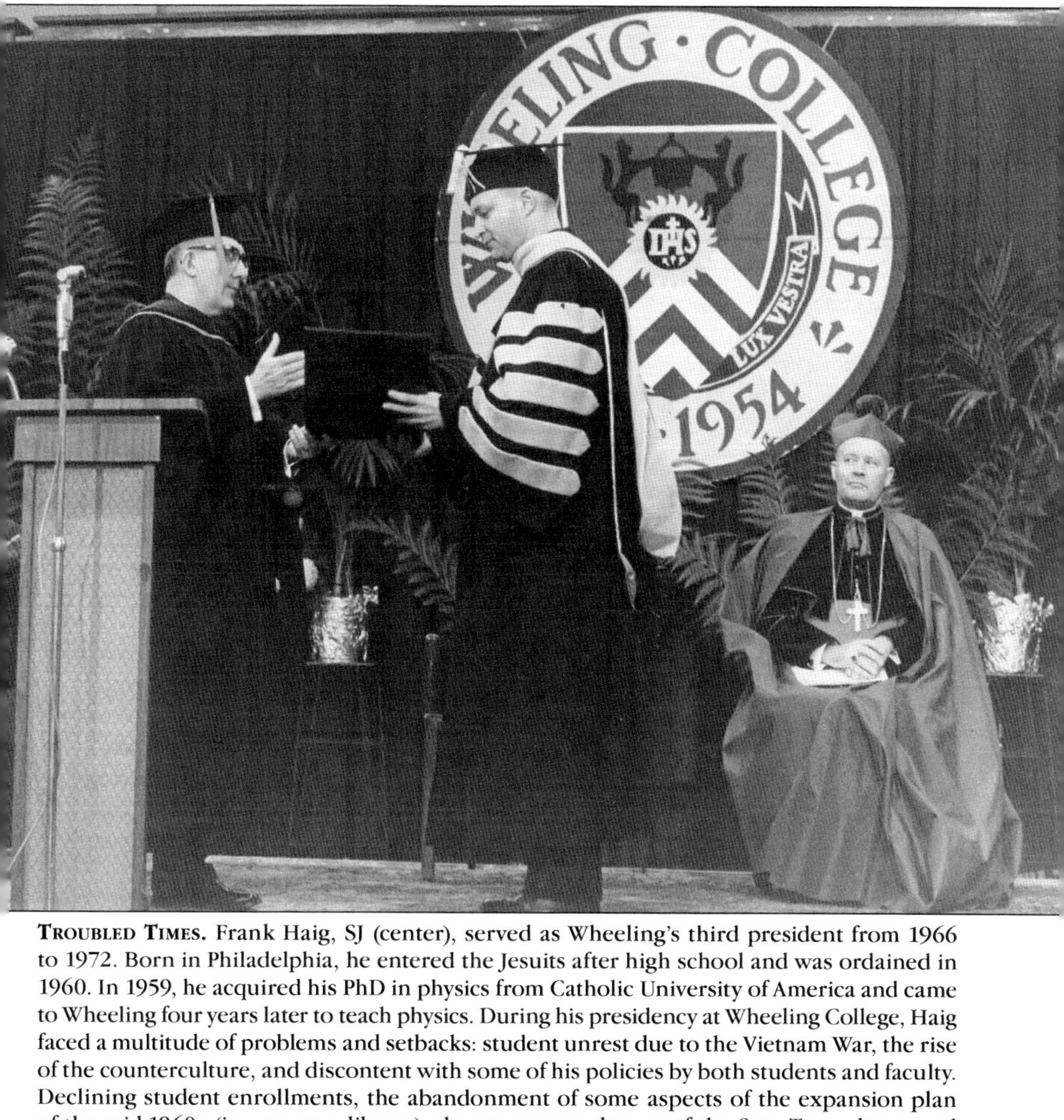

TROUBLED TIMES. Frank Haig, SJ (center), served as Wheeling's third president from 1966 to 1972. Born in Philadelphia, he entered the Jesuits after high school and was ordained in 1960. In 1959, he acquired his PhD in physics from Catholic University of America and came to Wheeling four years later to teach physics. During his presidency at Wheeling College, Haig faced a multitude of problems and setbacks: student unrest due to the Vietnam War, the rise of the counterculture, and discontent with some of his policies by both students and faculty. Declining student enrollments, the abandonment of some aspects of the expansion plan of the mid-1960s (i.e., no new library), the temporary closure of the Sara Tracy dorm, and other cutbacks led to some disaffected faculty leaving and concern about the viability of the college. There were also some positive achievements, including a new system of governance at the college that strengthened the faculty's role in policy-making and the appointment of Dr. Thomas Wack as the first lay academic dean. After leaving Wheeling, Father Haig taught physics at Loyola University in Baltimore and then became president of Le Moyne College in Syracuse, New York, for six years. He returned to Loyola as a faculty member in 1988.

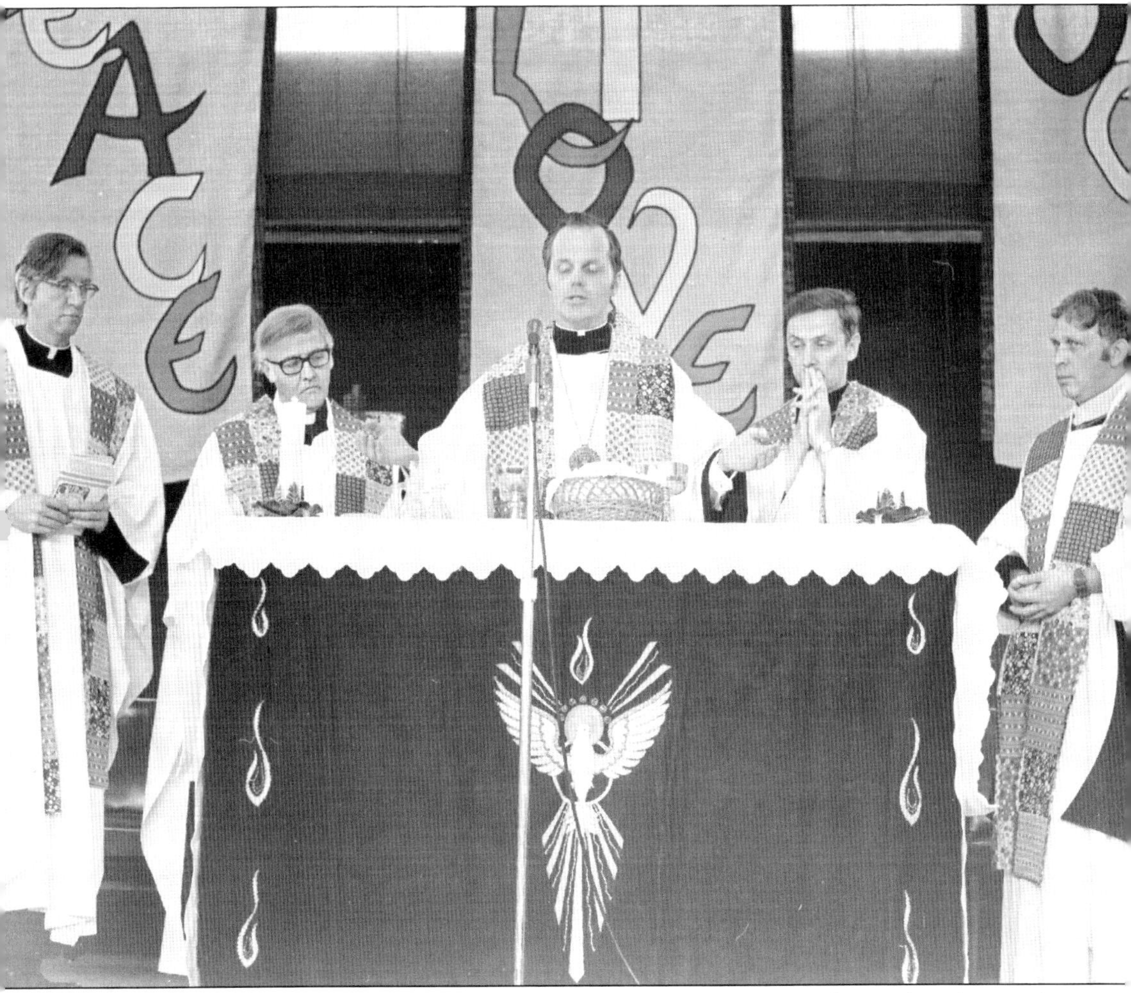

Currie's Inaugural Mass. Charles L. Currie, SJ, was Wheeling College's fourth president, serving from August 1972 until 1982. Born in Philadelphia in 1930, he entered the Jesuits in 1950 and was ordained 13 years later. After studying in Fordham and at Boston College, he went to Catholic University of America and received a doctorate in chemistry. At Wheeling, Father Currie was successful in increasing enrollment, gaining donor support, and starting 12 new academic programs—most importantly, nursing, respiratory therapy, and nuclear medicine. The evening division was also created during his time in office. Upon leaving Wheeling, Currie became president of Xavier University from 1982 to 1986. He then returned to Georgetown, and later taught theology and science at St. Joseph's in Philadelphia. In 1997, he became president of the Association of Jesuit Colleges and Universities and remained at that post for almost 15 years. The priests are, from left to right, Al Jenemann, SJ; Joseph Burke, SJ; Currie; Jim O'Brien, SJ; and Carl Bauer.

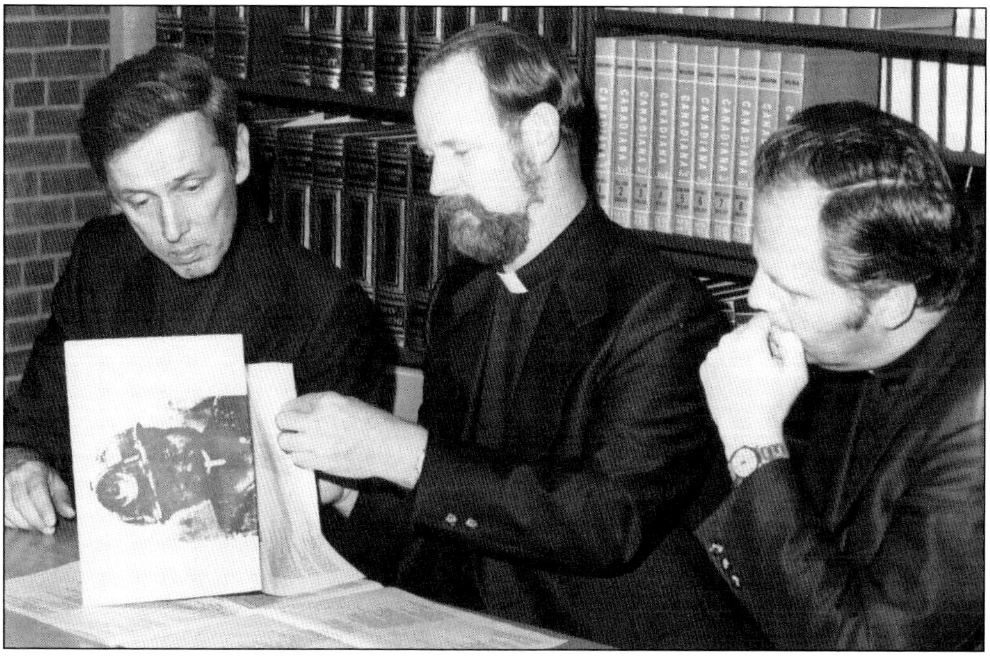

Pastoral Letter. Jim O'Brien, SJ (left), and Charles Currie, SJ (right)—with an unidentified Jesuit in the center—look at the 1975 pastoral letter *This Land is Home to Me*. The bishops of Appalachia promulgated it in 1975 from Sara Tracy lounge. The document called on Catholics to ensure that social justice prevailed in the region.

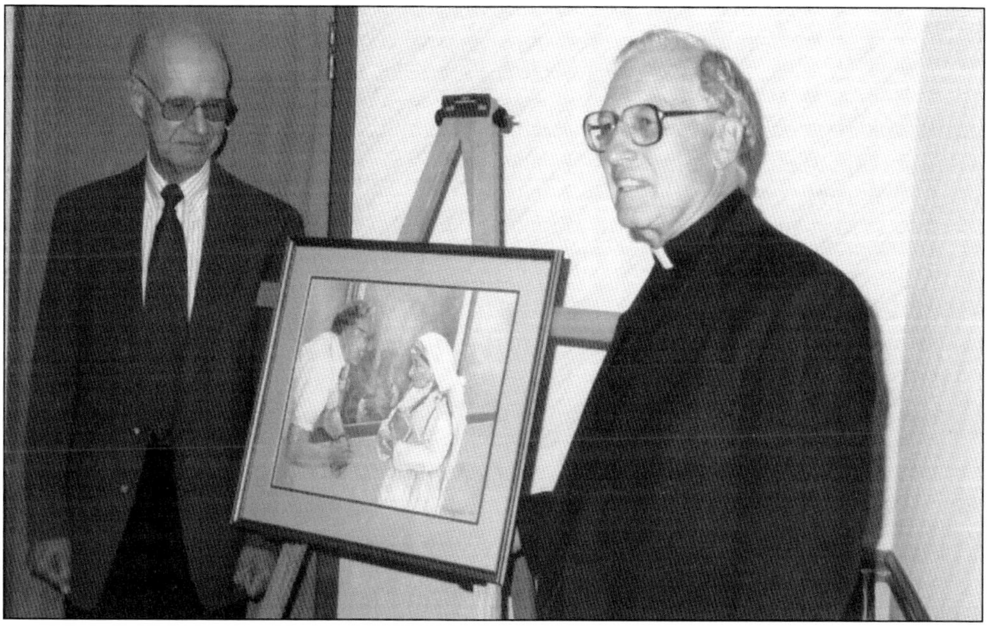

Fifth President. Thomas S. Acker, SJ, oversaw the huge transformation of Wheeling College to Wheeling Jesuit University. New buildings were erected, most of the older buildings were refurbished and/or expanded, new academic programs were created, and a number of federal programs became a part of the university. Here, Acker (right) and Philip Kirby, chairman of the board of directors, look at a portrait of Mother Teresa.

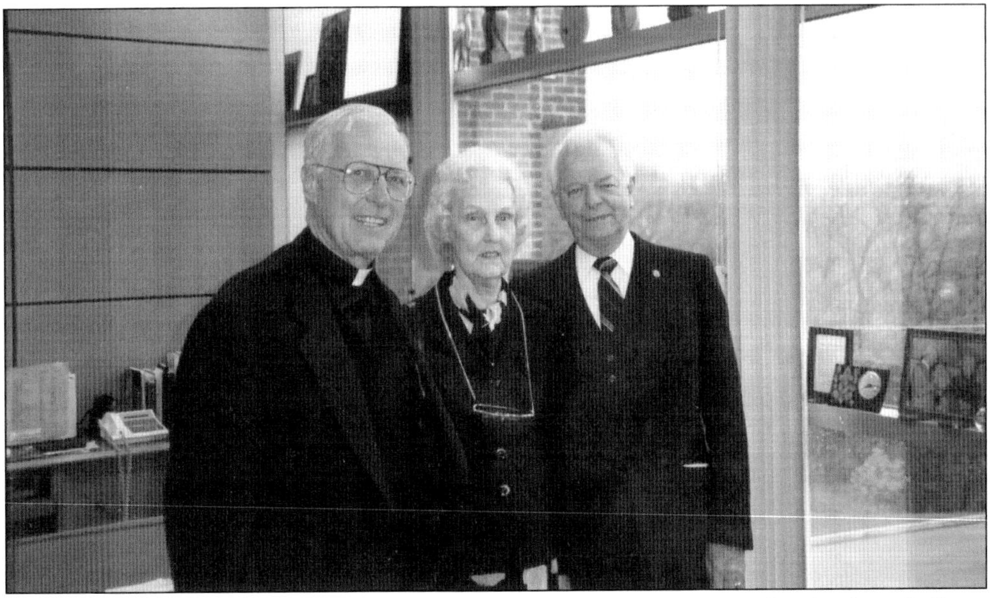

Acker and the Byrds. Sen. Robert C. Byrd had a long association with Wheeling College, but the relationship became closer when Thomas Acker was named president of the school. Senator Byrd was supportive of the university and crucial to the establishment of several federal programs on campus, including the National Technology Transfer Center, the Center of Educational Technology, and the Challenger Center. Here, Acker (left) and Byrd are pictured with Byrd's wife, Erma, in the president's office.

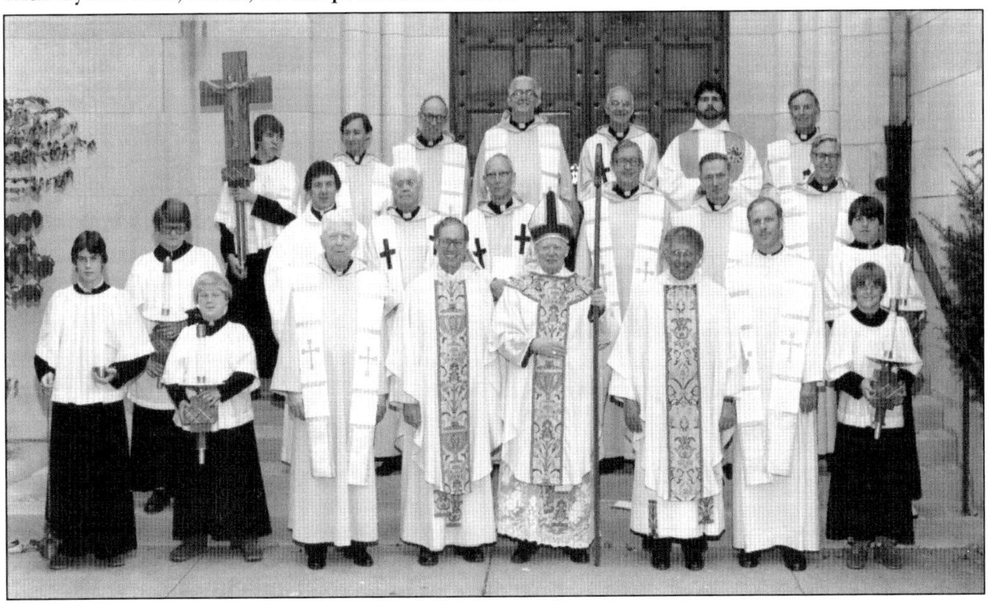

Jesuit Community. The Jesuit community at St. Joseph's Cathedral in the early 1980s included these men. Pictured here are, from left to right (priests only), (first row) Lawrence McHugh, Thomas Acker, Bishop Joseph Hodges, Carl Bauer, and Joseph Hacala; (second row) Burt Valdes, Joseph Kennedy, Clifford Lewis, Albert Jenemann, Jim O'Brien, and Walter Buckius; (third row) Bill O'Brien, Jim Neville, Joe Sanders, Joe Hanzely, Tom Rambert, and Terrence Toland. The non-Jesuits are Bauer, Valdes, and Rambert.

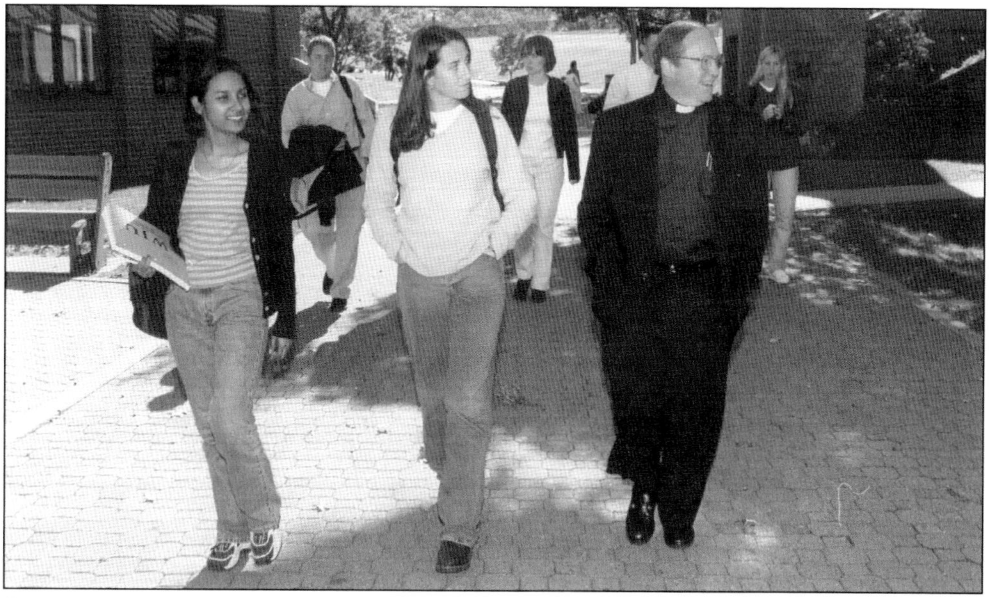

Sixth President. George Lundy, SJ, served from 2000 to 2003. Before arriving at Wheeling Jesuit, Father Lundy was the vice president and provost of the University of Detroit-Mercy for six years. At Wheeling, he focused on improving the salaries of faculty and staff and promoting social justice issues such as ending the death penalty. The Thomas S. Acker, SJ, Science Center opened during his presidency.

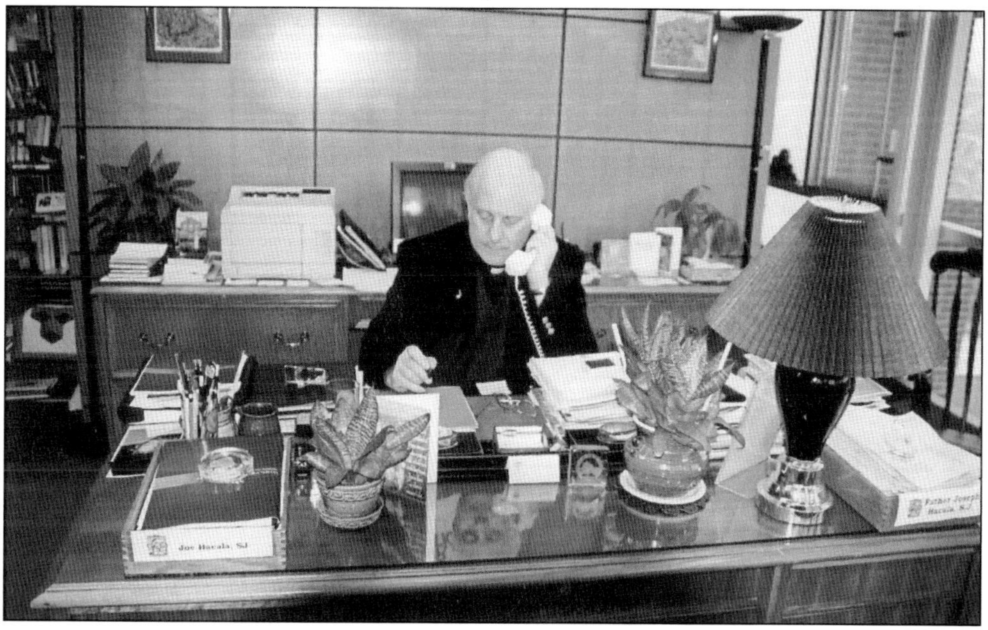

Seventh President. Joseph Hacala had a close relationship with the university for most of his career. Twice rector of the Jesuit community on campus, he served as president from 2003 to 2006. His principal achievements as president included restructuring the university's debt, creating the Clifford M. Lewis, SJ, Appalachian Institute, stressing the need for a service learning component of a Wheeling student's experience, and strengthening the sense of mission and identity at WJU.

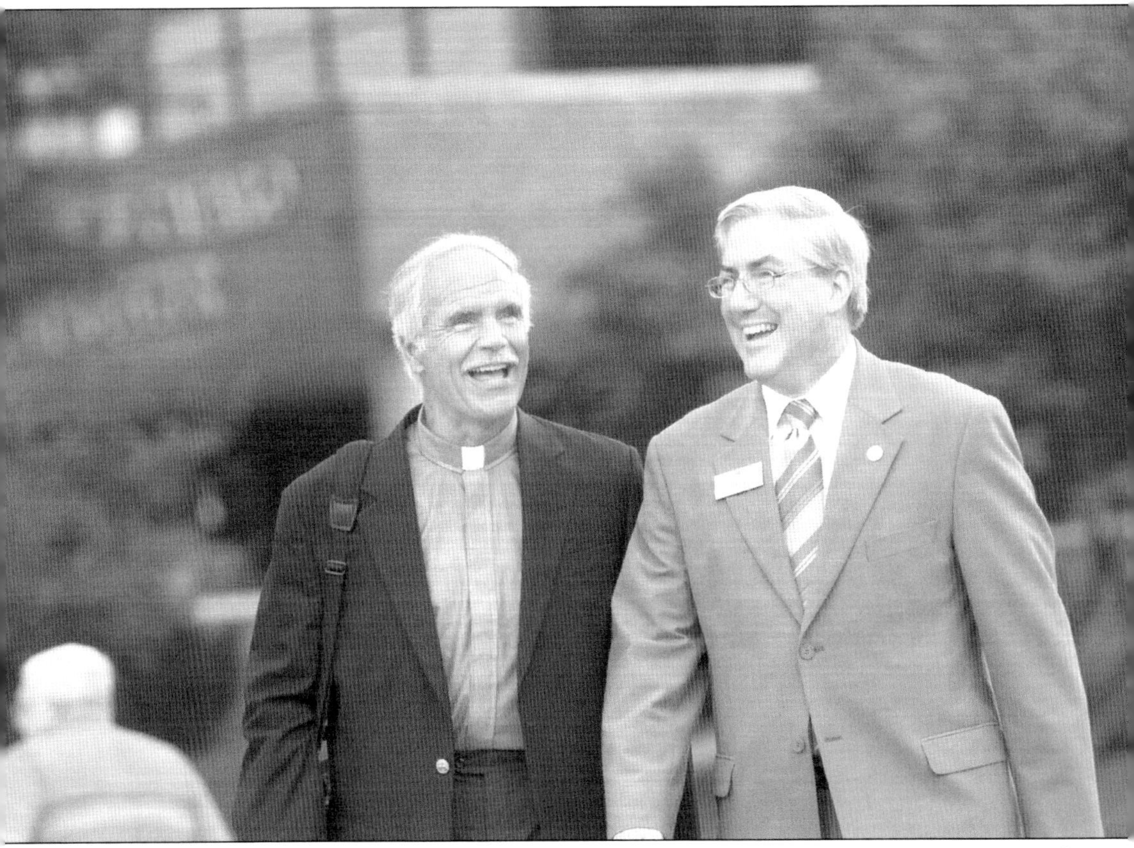

GIULIETTI AND BIRGE. Following Joseph Hacala's death, Jamie Birge (right), vice president for academic affairs, took over as interim president until Wheeling's eighth president, Julio Giulietti, SJ, was chosen in February 2008. Dr. Birge was the first non-Jesuit to serve as head of the institution—even on an interim basis. Giulietti grew up in New York City and was ordained a priest in the Society of Jesus in 1972. He acquired advance degrees in comparative religions and counseling and a doctorate in theology. He worked at a variety of institutions focusing on international programs and higher education, and as director of the Center for Ignatian Spirituality at Boston College. At Wheeling, Father Giulietti sought to bring foreign students to Wheeling, creating agreements that allowed people in other countries to benefit from Wheeling Jesuit's health sciences programs. After leaving Wheeling, Giulietti was appointed director of the Loyola in Vietnam program by Loyola University in Chicago.

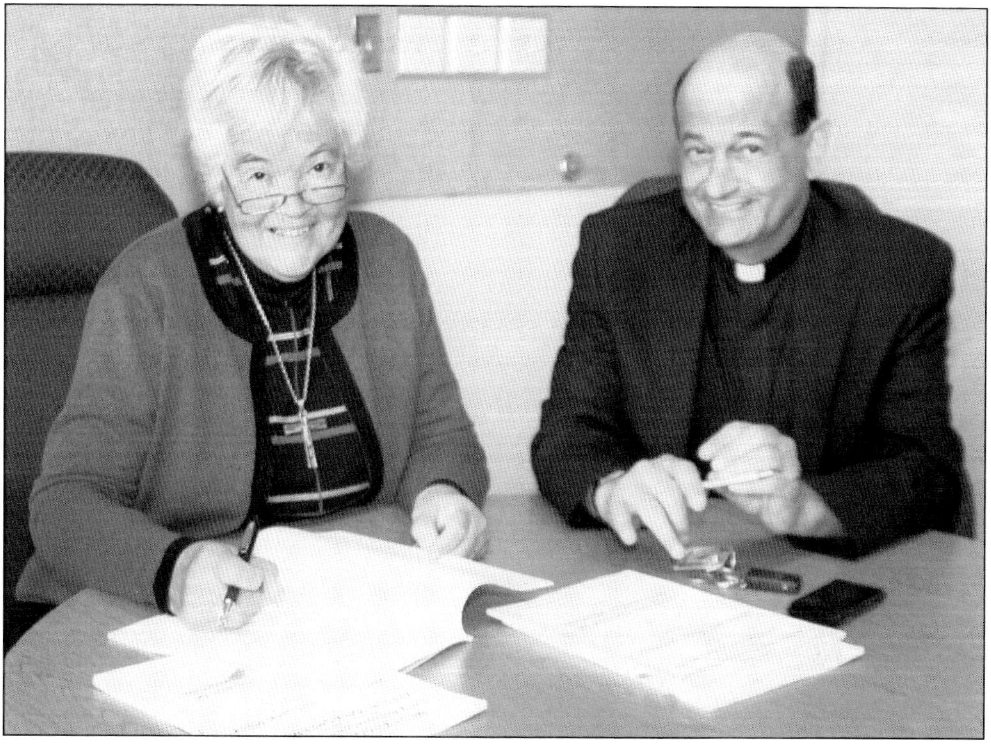

Interim Presidents. When the Wheeling College Board of Trustees dismissed Father Giulietti in August 2009, two persons served as interim presidents. Davitt McAteer, the university's vice president for external programs, served as interim president until Sr. Francis Marie Thrailkill took charge in January 2010. Sister Thrailkill, an Ursuline nun, is pictured with Msgr. David Rubino, of Lake Erie College of Osteopathic Medicine, after reaching an agreement about cooperation between the two institutions.

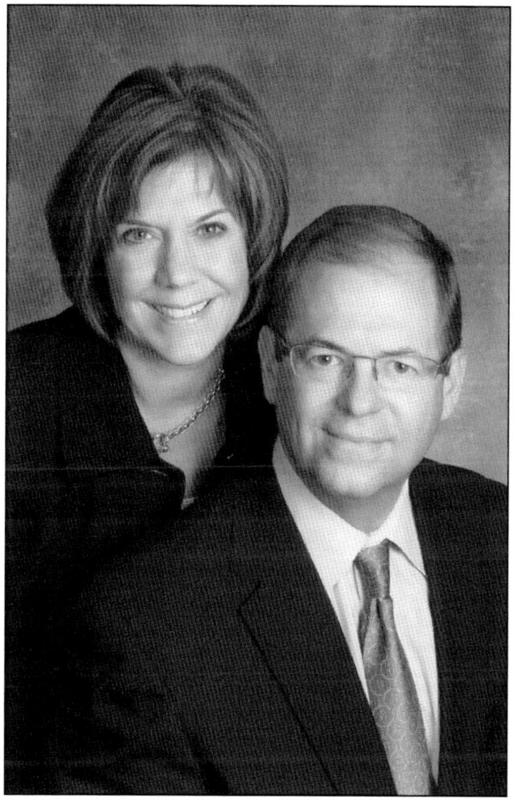

Richard Beyer. On January 2, 2011, Richard Beyer was installed as Wheeling Jesuit's ninth president. The university changed its bylaws to permit a non-Jesuit to serve as president of the university. A businessman, Beyer has long been interested in higher education. He served on the board of trustees of his alma mater, Olivet College, and at several other institutions. Beyer is pictured with his wife, Cindy.

MISSION STATEMENT

EDUCATING FOR LIFE

The Jesuit traditions of educational excellence and service to others guide the programs at Wheeling Jesuit University. By integrating learning, research, and economic development with classical knowledge and Christian revelation, the University seeks to foster competence, creativity and innovation throughout and beyond the campus community. Graduates of the University enter the world of work with socially responsible goals, a lifelong appetite for learning and the desire to make our universe a better place.

EDUCATING FOR LEADERSHIP

To model the Jesuit concern for regional and global neighbors, the University welcomes people of all creeds, races and nationalities to share in the intelligent pursuit of excellence. The University promotes close student-faculty contacts and encourages students to develop their full potential for leadership. Through a grounding in the liberal arts and, above all, the example of Jesus Christ, the University endeavors to produce intelligent, moral leaders who will champion the Jesuit values of faith, peace and justice. Wheeling Jesuit envisions a dynamic leadership role for the University in the lives of its students and in the world at large.

EDUCATING MEN AND WOMEN FOR SERVICE WITH AND AMONG OTHERS

In its faculty and students, its research and outreach, the University is national and international. Yet, as the only Catholic institution of higher learning in West Virginia, Wheeling Jesuit also values its distinctive mission to the immediate area: educating local men and women and returning them to enrich their own communities. Wheeling Jesuit University firmly believes its graduates will enter the professional world prepared to use their God-given talents not solely for personal fulfillment, but as men and women in service with and among others.

Let your light shine

LUCEAT LUX VESTRA

MISSION STATEMENT. A committee chaired by Carol Orts, vice president and special assistant to the president, met for almost a year to write the current mission statement. The board of directors formally approved it in 1994. The committee—made up of Jesuits, administrators, faculty, and students—attempted to clearly articulate the mission of the university, which has not substantially changed since the beginning of the school.

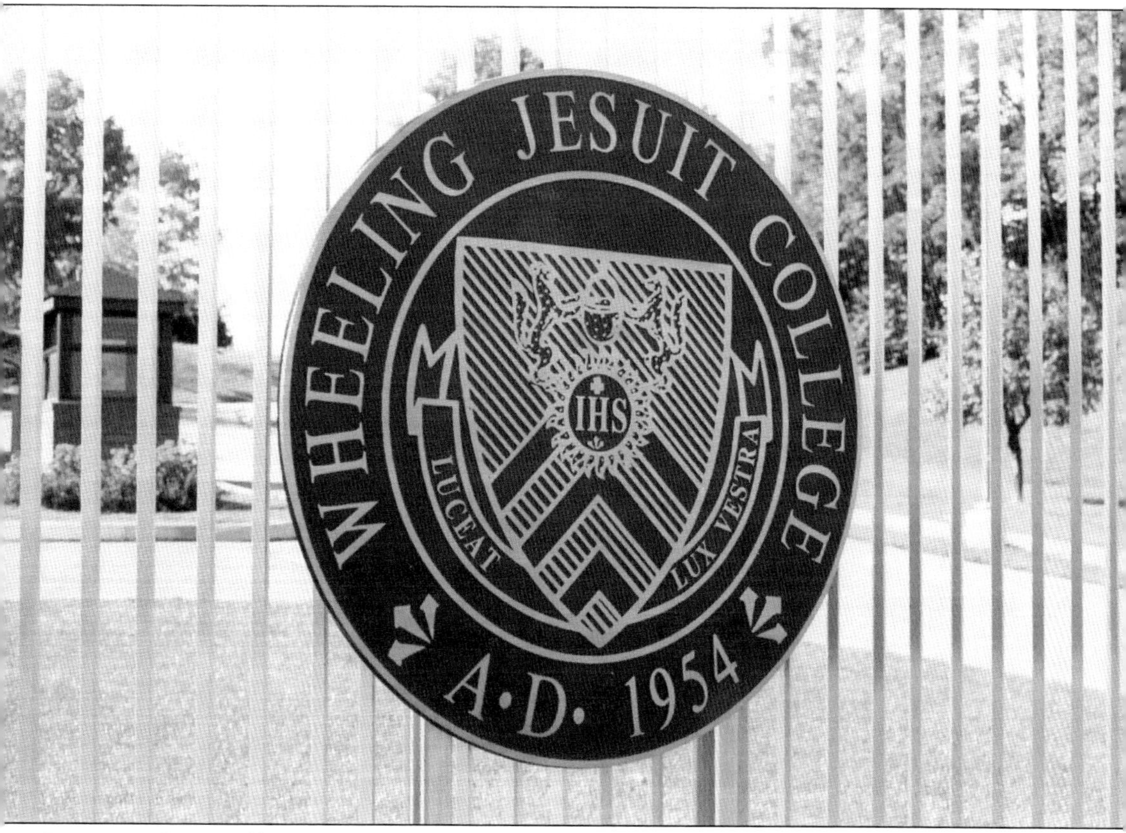

UNIVERSITY SEAL. William F. Ryan designed the WJU seal; the three silver chevrons on a green field come from the coat of arms of the Wheeling-Charleston Diocese. The badge of the Society of Jesus is at the apex of the chevrons, while two wolves grasp a cauldron suspended from a chain. The wolves are from the coat of arms of Ignatius Loyola's family. The blue symbolizes the Marian Year (1954) in which the college was founded. The school's motto, Luceat Lux Vestra ("Let Your Light Shine"), comes from Christ's Sermon on the Mount.

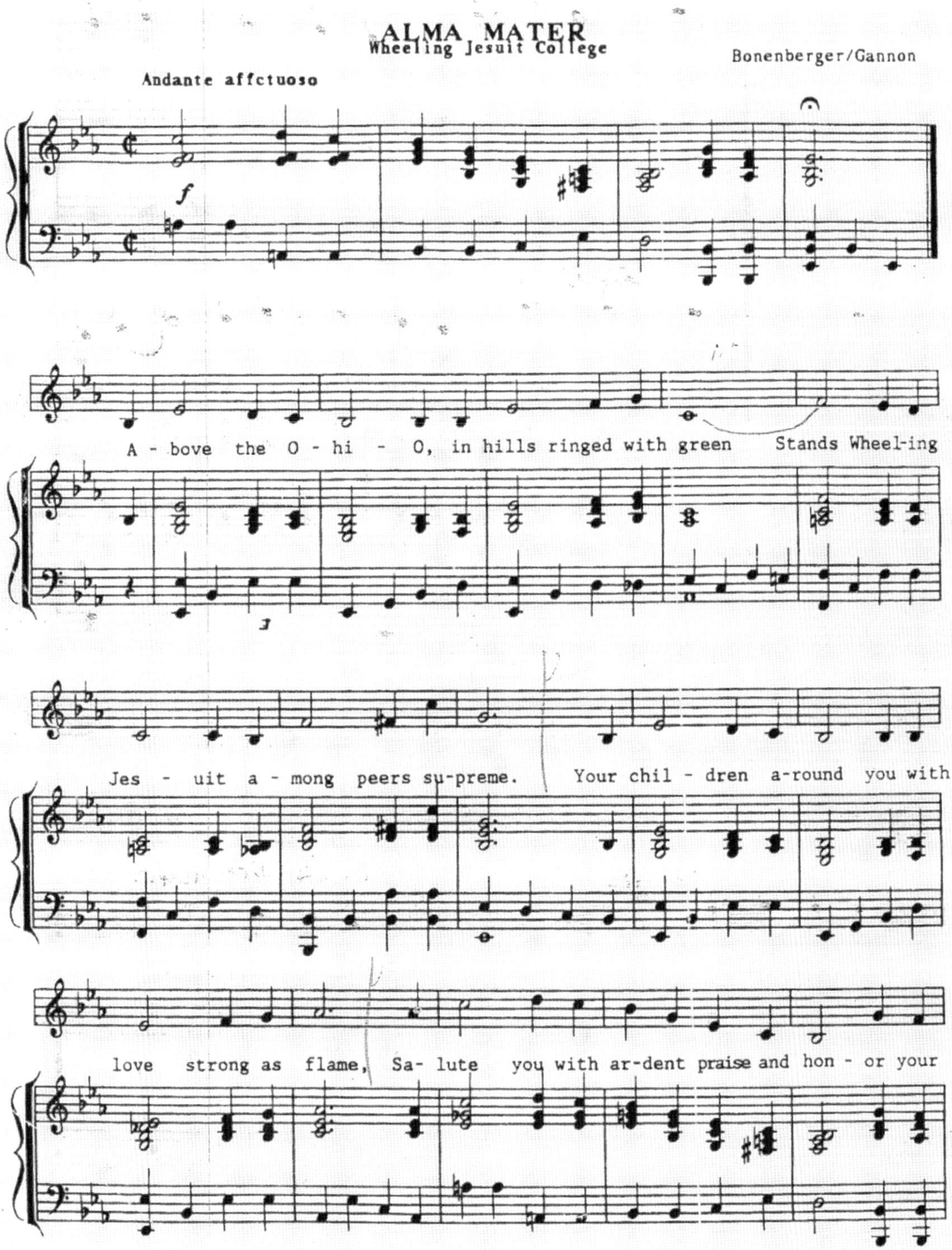

Alma Mater. The song is sung at the most important ceremonial occasions at the university, including opening convocation, honors convocations, graduation, and the installation of new presidents. Fr. Edward Gannon, SJ, wrote the words and music, and Leo J. Bonenberger,

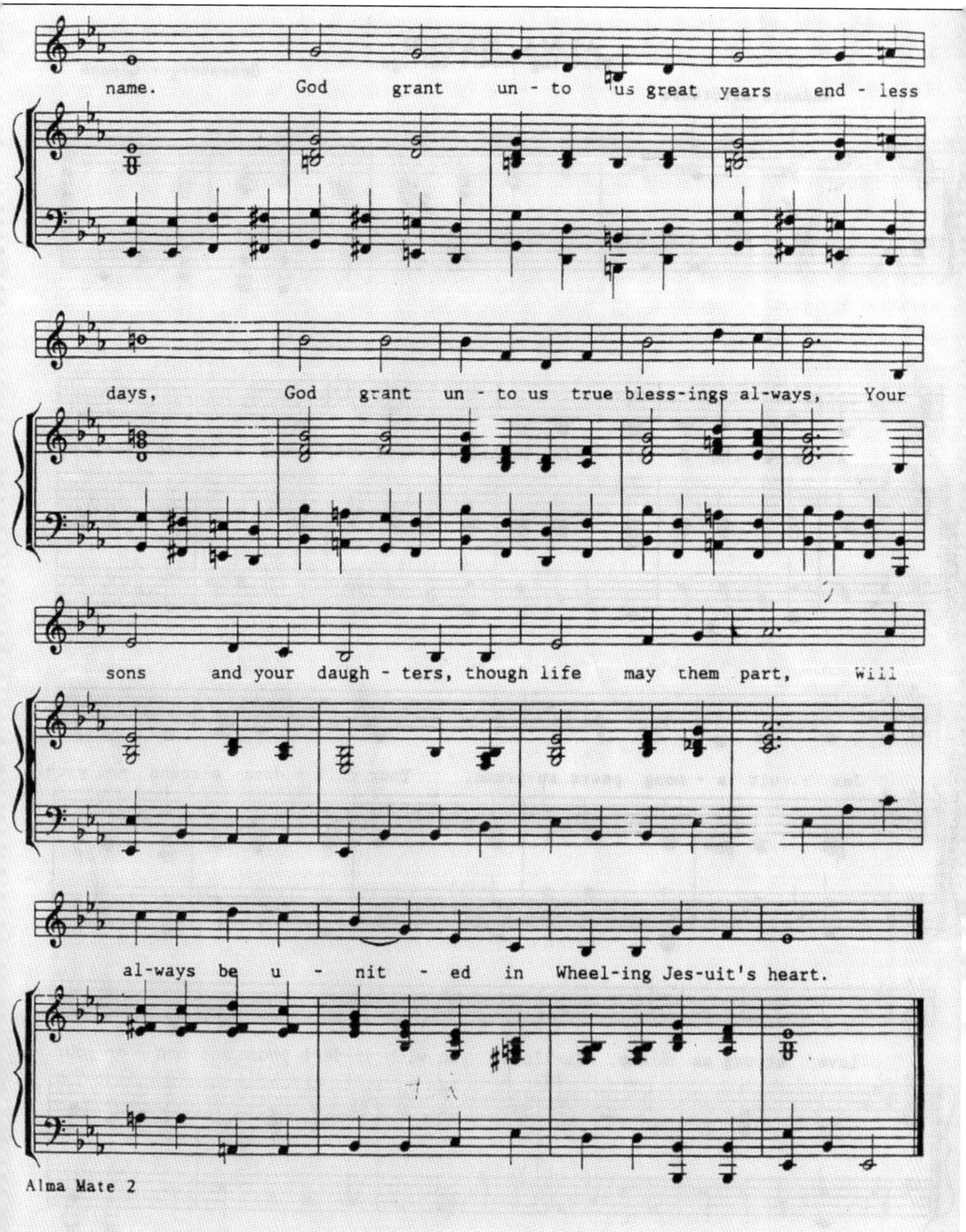

a Wheeling composer, made the arrangement. In April 1993, the alma mater was slightly revised to account for the institution's change from a college to a university.

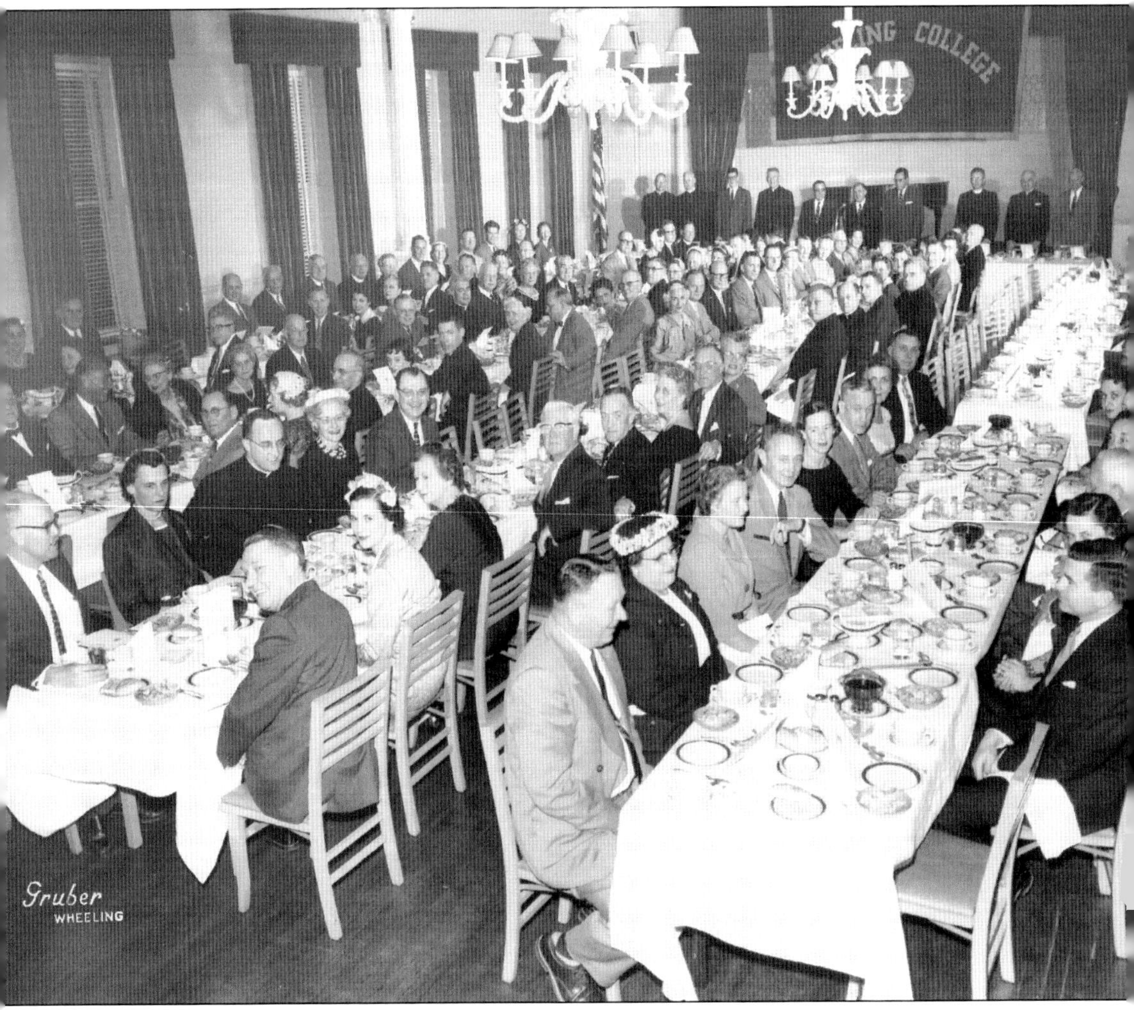

BANQUET IN 1958. To build support in the local community, the college held banquets for influential Wheeling businessmen, lawyers, and city officials. More than 100 guests showed up for this March 28, 1958, event.

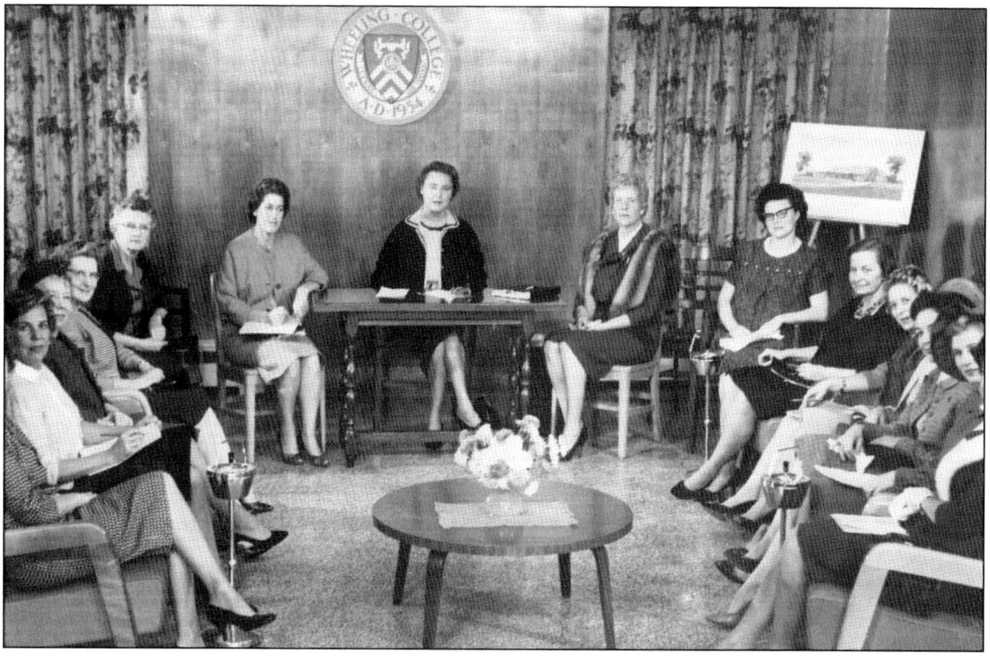

CHARTER GUILD. The woman's auxiliary organization of Wheeling College was founded on January 11, 1955, by 15 women who met in the home of J.W. Woomer. Its goals were to educate members on the purpose and needs of the college, create goodwill for the college, and raise funds. By May of the following year, the guild had 86 members. It continues its work today.

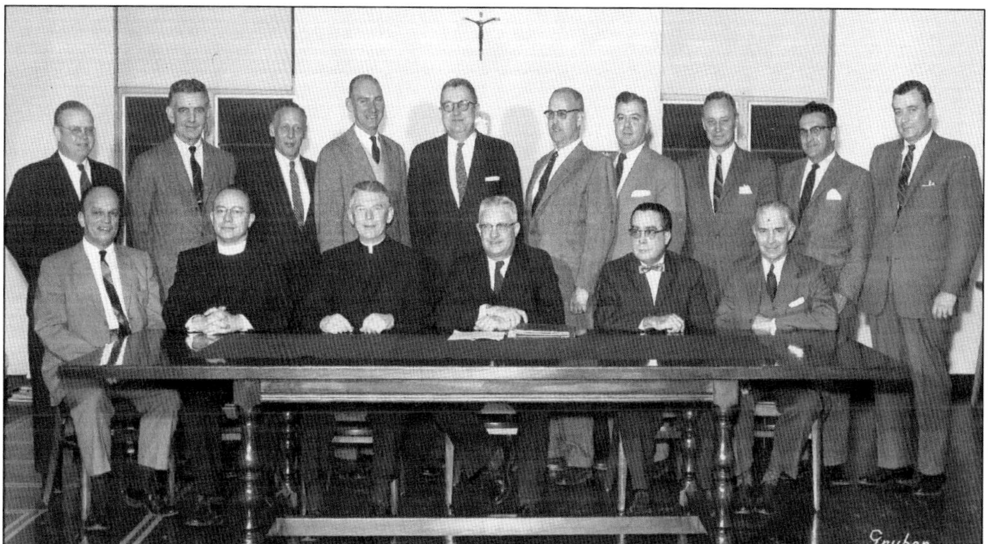

BOARD OF ADVISORS. To gain the support of the local community, Pres. Lawrence McHugh, SJ, asked Fr. Cilfford Lewis, SJ, and 32 businessmen, lawyers, and professionals to join an advisory board. Ten years later, Pres. Frank Haig's board consisted of 20 men, but five of them were college employees. The board met annually in the spring, but had subcommittees that met more often.

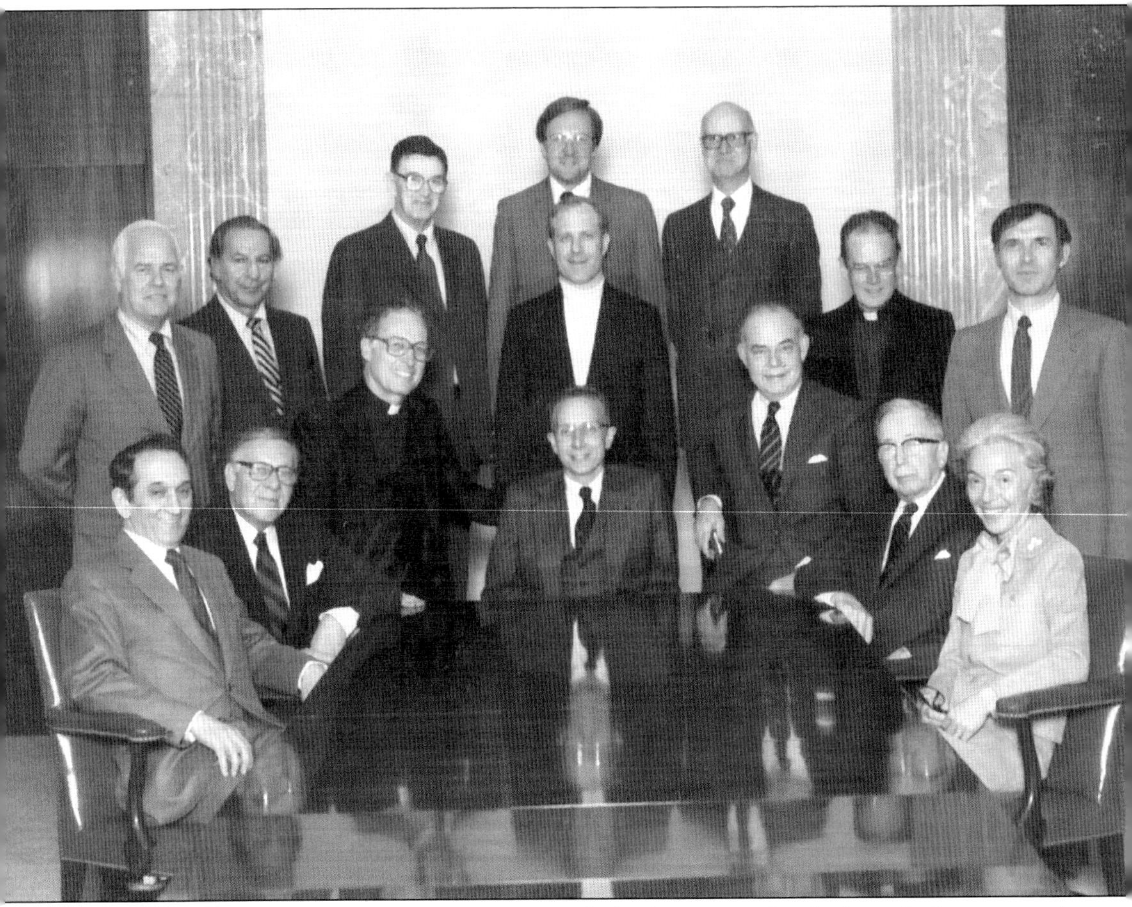

Board of Directors. Until the presidency of Charles Currie, SJ, the board of trustees, who were all members of the Society of Jesus, ultimately governed the college. The president also received counsel from a board of advisors—mostly laymen who were prominent businessmen, lawyers, and professional people. Father Currie created the board of directors, which was composed of a substantial number of both laymen and Jesuits. The board of directors had many of the powers of the board of trustees, but also the range of advice provided by the previous board of advisors. The trustees continue to exist and have final authority, but the advisors disappeared after the board of directors was created. Father Acker is pictured with one of his early boards of directors. There are four Jesuits, two of whom are in suits, one woman, and ten laymen.

Two

Environment of an Academic Community

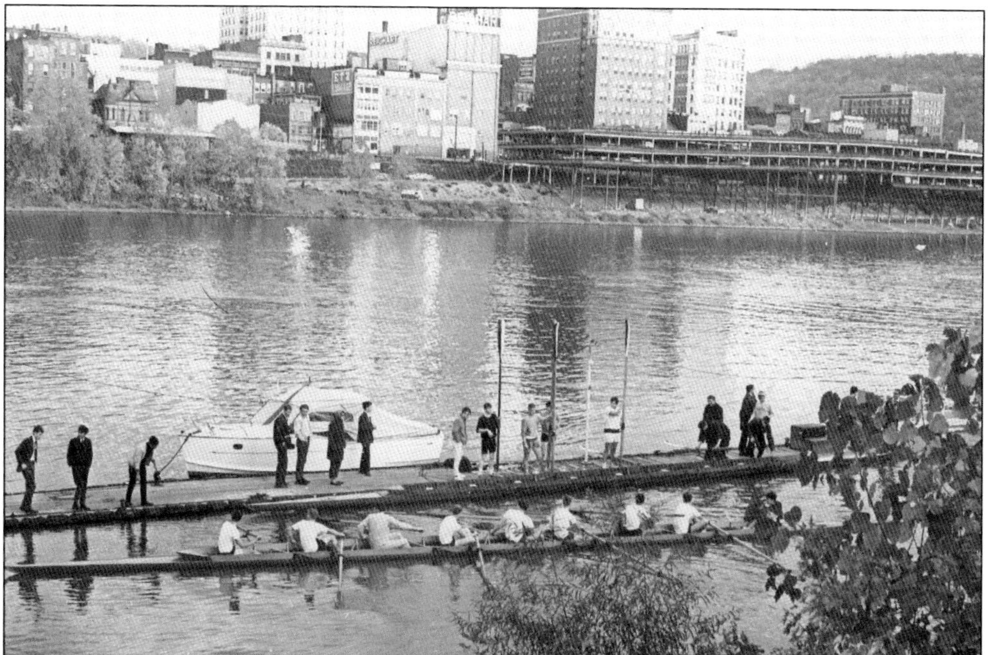

Wheeling in the 1960s. Wheeling College had crew teams in the late 1960s and early 1970s, but the sport failed to draw students. The view of Wheeling from the Ohio side of the river shows the downtown skyline of this small industrial city with a population of around 50,000. The city's principal industries at this time were coal, steel, glass, and tobacco—all enterprises hit by the changing economy of late-20th-century America. In 2011, the population of Wheeling was around 30,000.

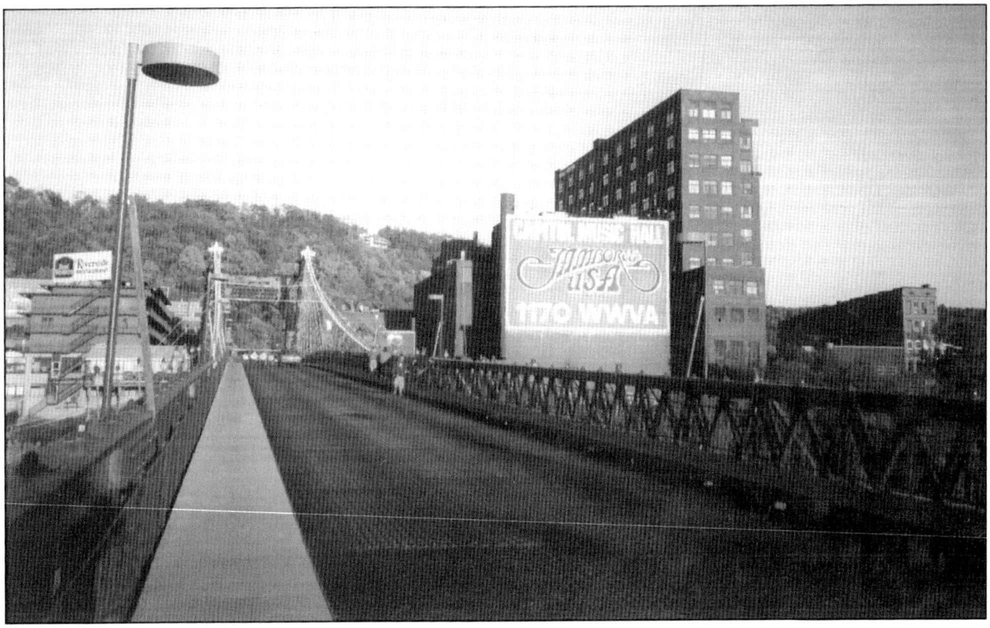

Suspension Bridge. Wheeling's most famous historic landmark is the Suspension Bridge, which was built in 1848. The bridge allowed US 40, along the path of the old National Road, to cross the Ohio River to Wheeling Island. The eastward view of downtown Wheeling shows the natural route for people to take to get to the college from the west in the 1950s.

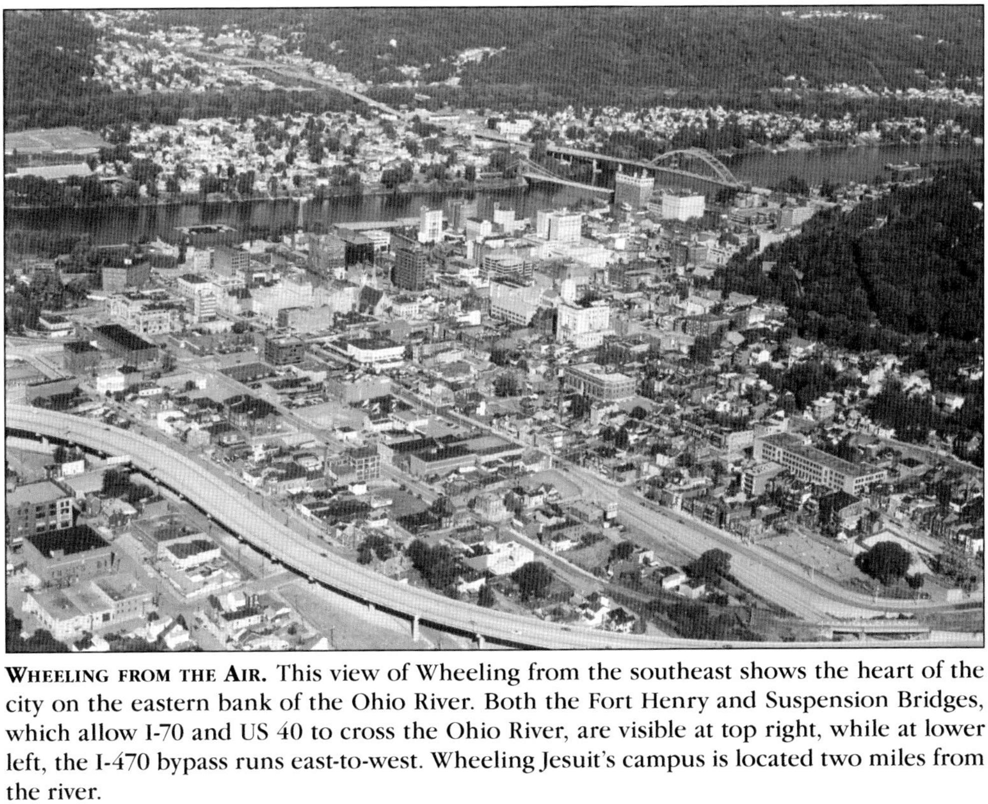

Wheeling from the Air. This view of Wheeling from the southeast shows the heart of the city on the eastern bank of the Ohio River. Both the Fort Henry and Suspension Bridges, which allow I-70 and US 40 to cross the Ohio River, are visible at top right, while at lower left, the I-470 bypass runs east-to-west. Wheeling Jesuit's campus is located two miles from the river.

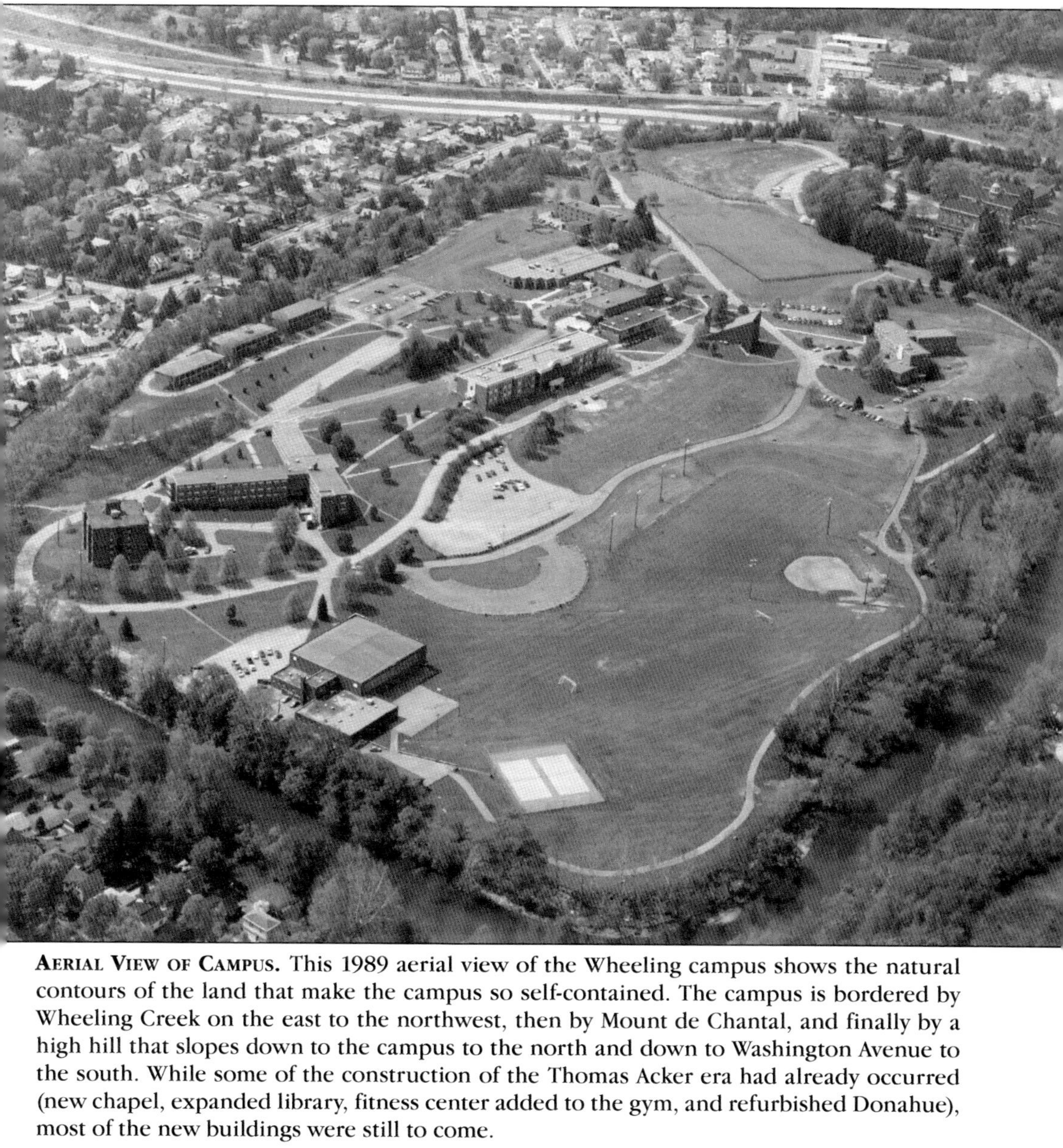

Aerial View of Campus. This 1989 aerial view of the Wheeling campus shows the natural contours of the land that make the campus so self-contained. The campus is bordered by Wheeling Creek on the east to the northwest, then by Mount de Chantal, and finally by a high hill that slopes down to the campus to the north and down to Washington Avenue to the south. While some of the construction of the Thomas Acker era had already occurred (new chapel, expanded library, fitness center added to the gym, and refurbished Donahue), most of the new buildings were still to come.

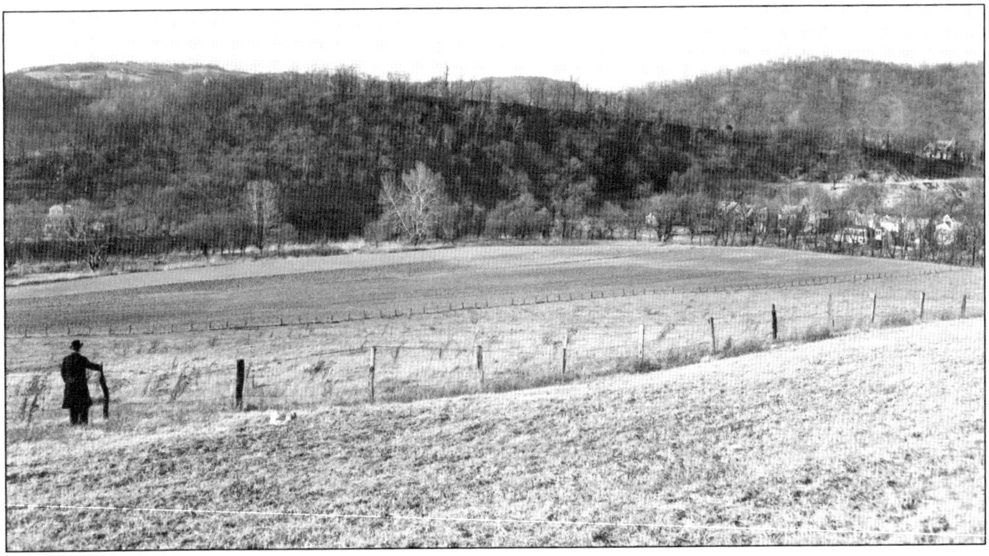

Father Lewis Views Location. Fr. Clifford Lewis, SJ, arrived in Wheeling in February 1953 as the educational representative of the Society of Jesus' Maryland Province to respond to Bishop John Swint's request that the Jesuits found a college in the city. Here, Lewis looks over the empty pasture that belonged to the adjacent Mount de Chantal; the bishop had already decided that this 61-acre tract was the best spot for the new college.

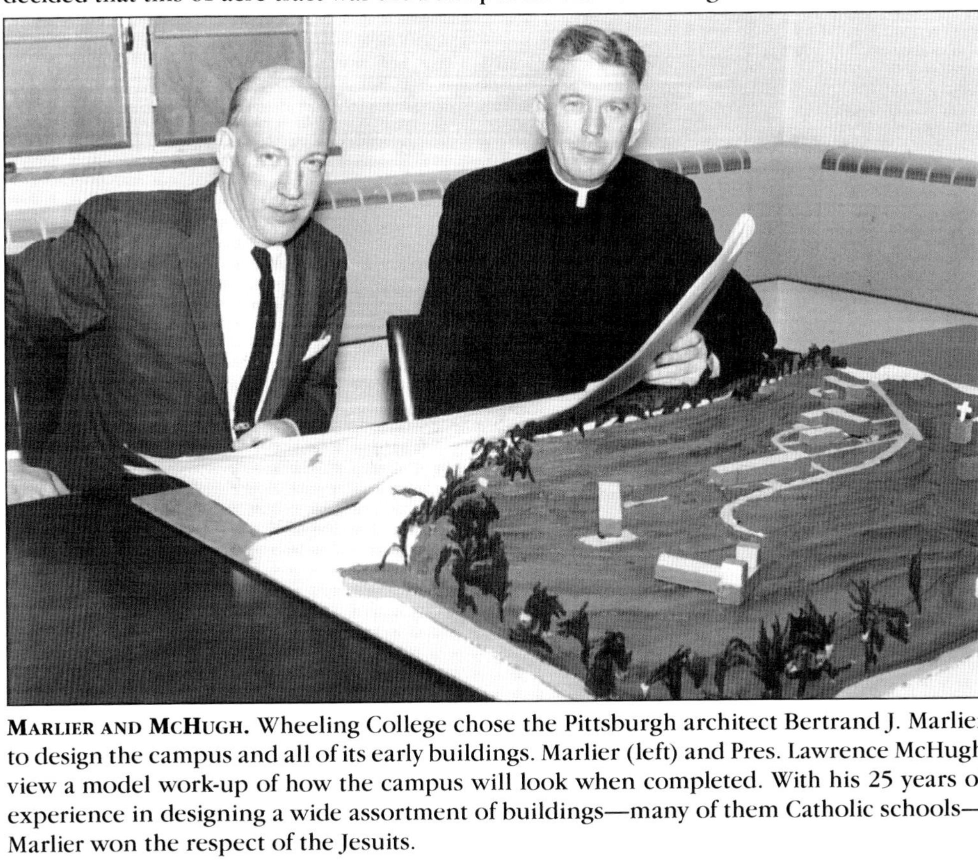

Marlier and McHugh. Wheeling College chose the Pittsburgh architect Bertrand J. Marlier to design the campus and all of its early buildings. Marlier (left) and Pres. Lawrence McHugh view a model work-up of how the campus will look when completed. With his 25 years of experience in designing a wide assortment of buildings—many of them Catholic schools—Marlier won the respect of the Jesuits.

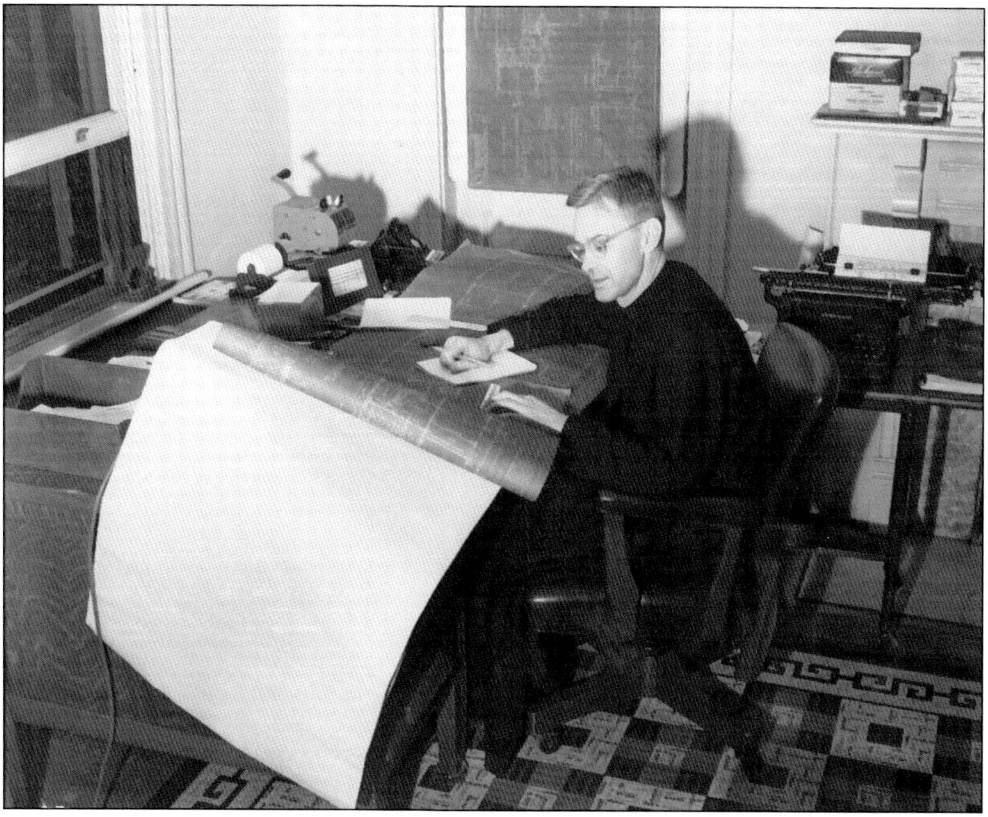

College Blueprints. Rev. Edward Powers, SJ, reviews the blueprints of one of the first buildings on campus. Powers was responsible for choosing and ordering equipment and furnishings. He was also responsible for accounting for all expenses in the creation of the college.

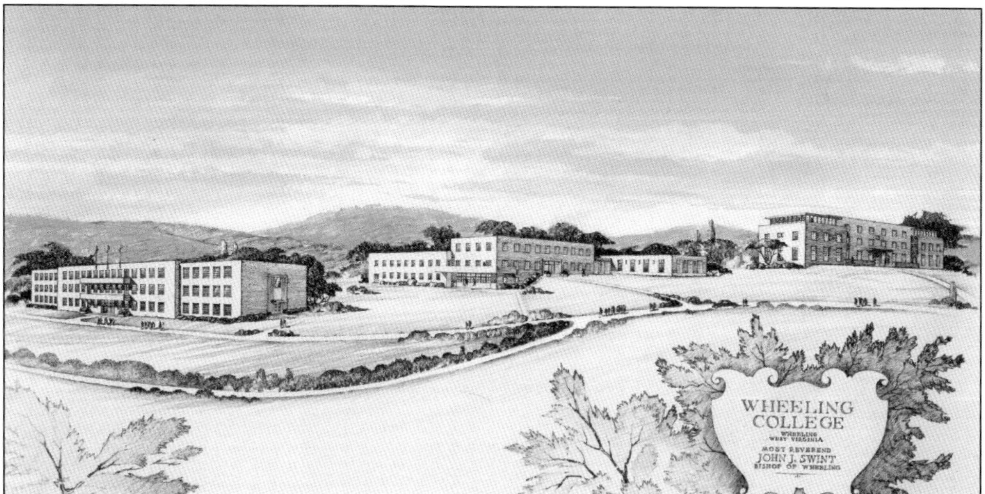

First Buildings. This sketch shows the first three buildings constructed on campus in the late 1950s. From left to right, they are Donahue (classrooms, labs, and offices), Swint (administrative offices, library, dining), and Whelan (Jesuit residence). The college used the sketch in its academic catalogues in the late 1950s and as a postcard to sell the institution.

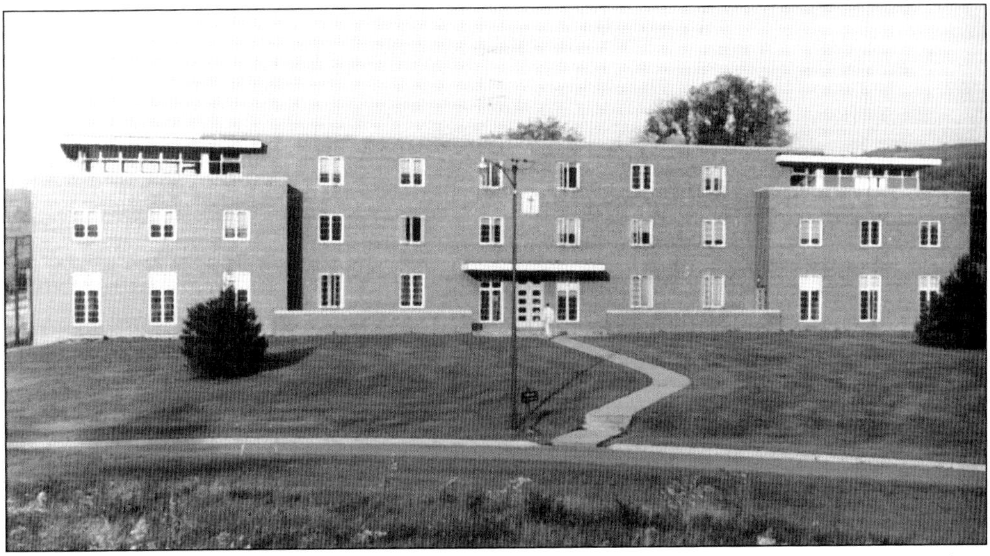

Whelan Hall, Built in 1954. Whelan was built as the home for the Jesuit community. When the college opened in 1955, the Jesuits were 18 in number and made up more than 75 percent of the faculty. While Whelan was mainly the Jesuit residence, lay faculty used parts of the building for offices and classrooms.

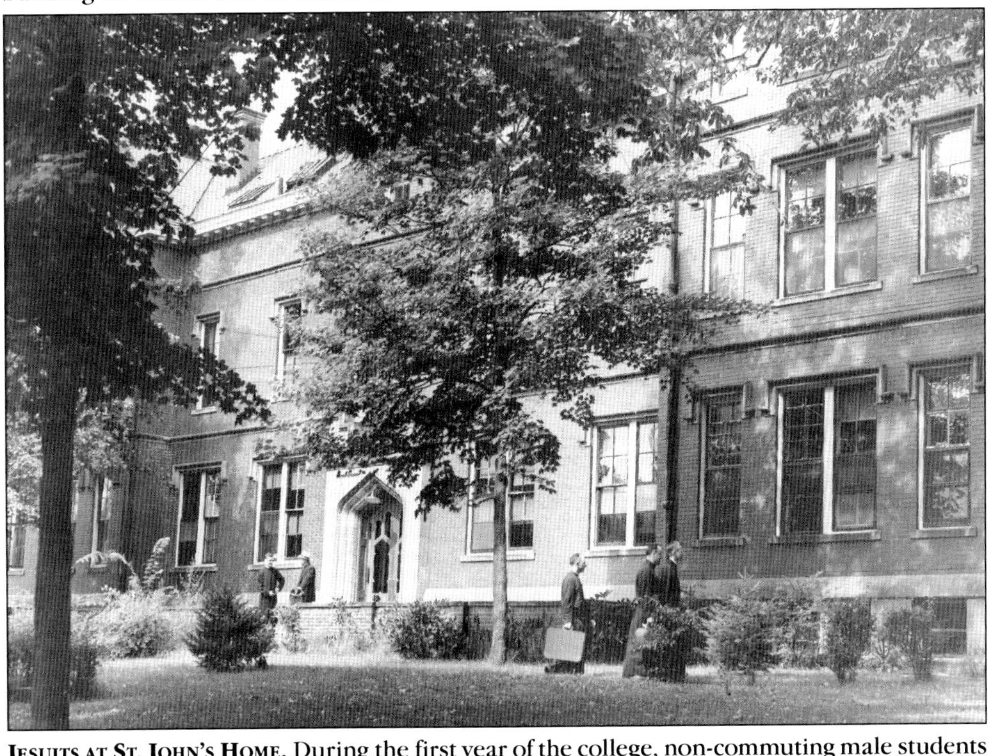

Jesuits at St. John's Home. During the first year of the college, non-commuting male students lived in empty dorm space at the Linsly Military Institute (across the creek from the campus) and in rooms rented in private homes in the neighborhood. When the student population grew in 1957 and the first men's dorm was still unfinished, the Jesuits moved out of Whelan to live in St. John's Home for Boys, located three miles east.

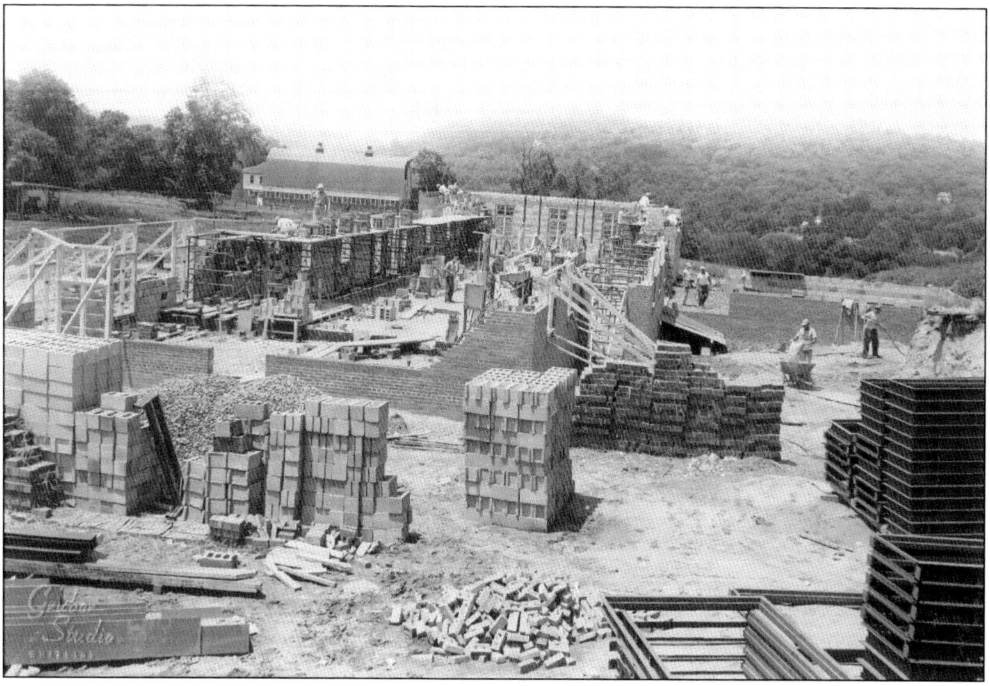

Constructing Swint. This is the construction of Swint Hall, which was to serve as home to administrative offices, the library, student activities, and dining facilities. Six additions have been made to the building since it was built in 1954. Just beyond the construction site is a barn that once belonged to Mount de Chantal. The Jesuits considered turning the barn into a dormitory for women, but the idea was abandoned; Sara Tracy Hall was built instead.

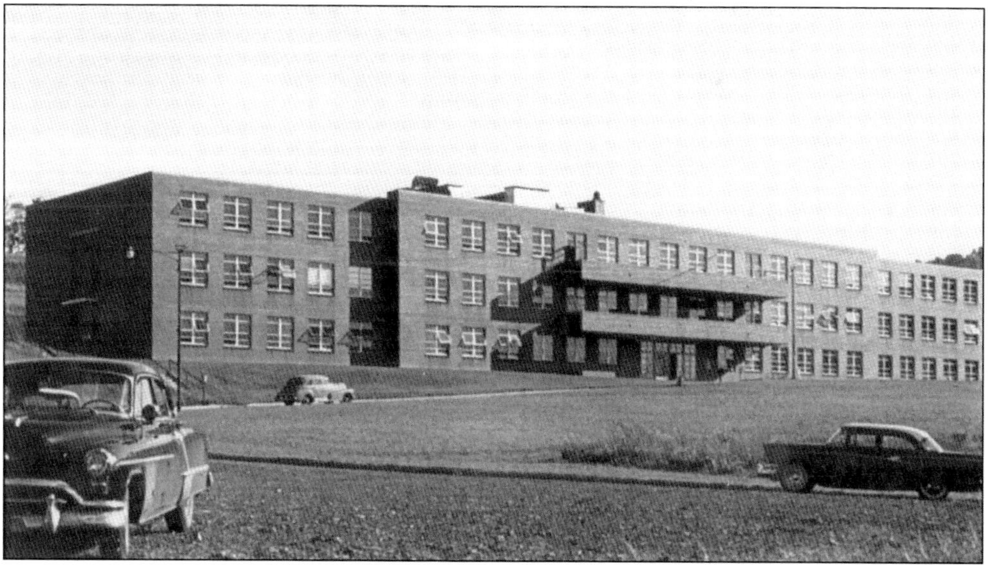

Donahue Hall. The college's main classroom building was named in honor of Rev. Patrick J. Donahue. The three-story structure contained most of the college's classrooms, laboratories, faculty offices, and a small chapel. Built in the modern style common to the 1950s, halls cut through the center of the building on each floor. On the ground floor, the hall was lined on both sides with student lockers.

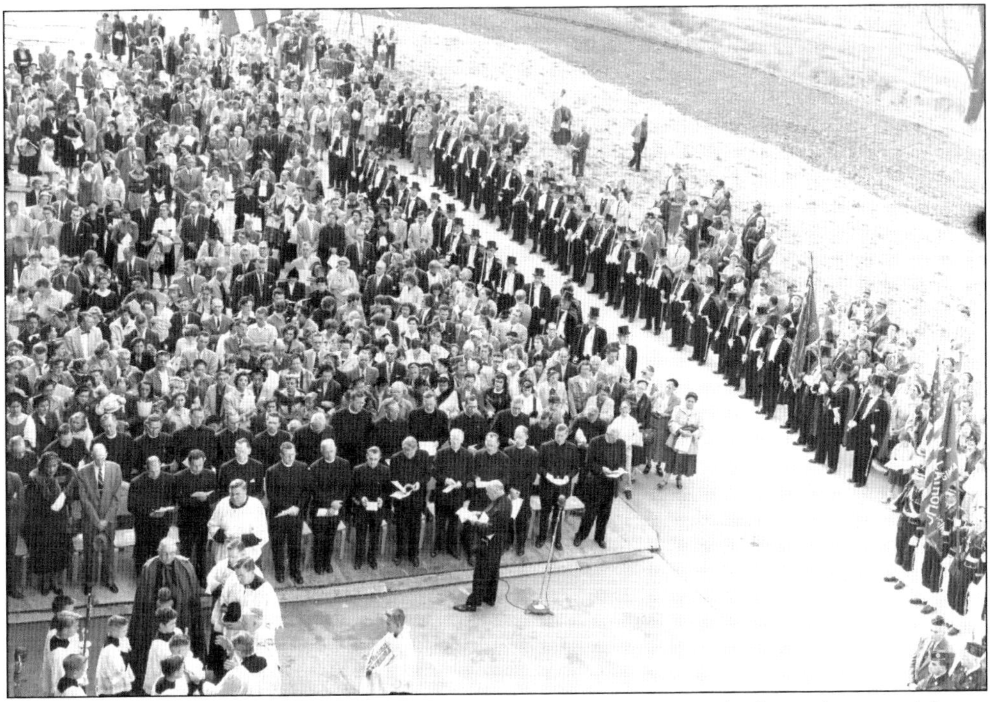

Dedication of Donahue Hall. A crowd of approximately 2,000 people showed up to celebrate the dedication of the main classroom building on October 23, 1955. The three main participants at the event were Archbishop John Swint, Bishop Thomas MacDonnell (the coadjutor of the diocese), and Pres. Lawrence McHugh. Many other notable citizens attended, including local politicians. After the cornerstone was blessed and speeches were given, the building was opened for public inspection.

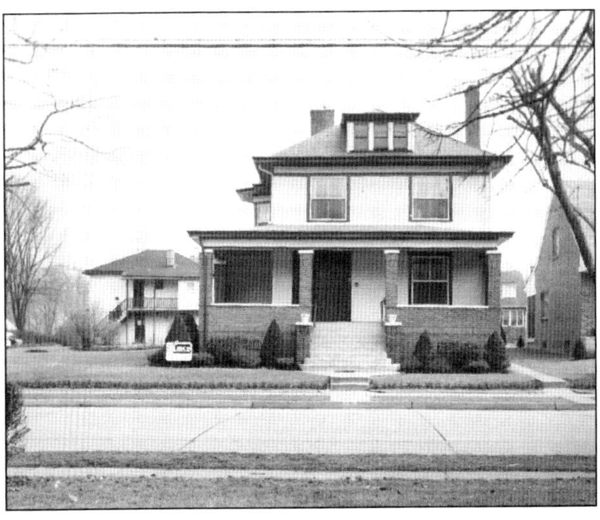

Avila and Avilita Halls. The college purchased several houses on Washington Avenue to serve as residences for women from 1957 through 1959, when Sara Tracy Hall was completed. Avila Hall was located at 221 Washington Avenue, and Avilita was the garage apartment behind the main house. Supposedly, 25 women could be housed in these two structures. Another residence was called Della Strada. The college later purchased or rented two more houses, called Marquette and Carroll, for female boarders.

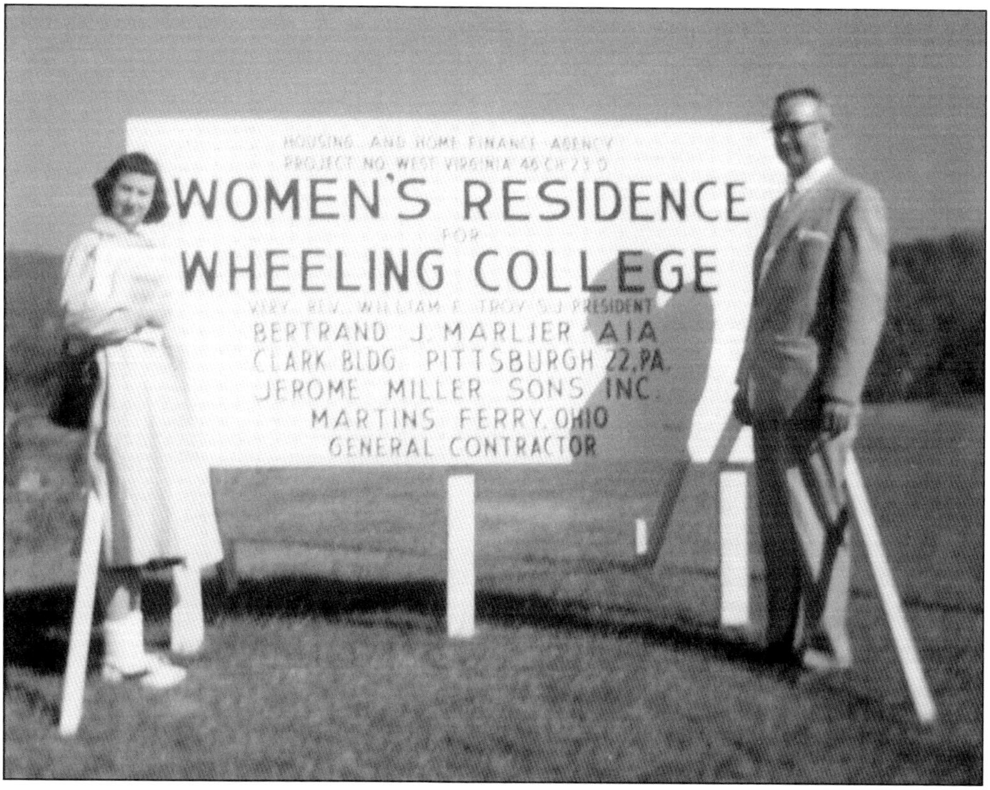

WAITING FOR A WOMEN'S DORM. Carol Cannon '59 and her father pose with the construction sign at the site of the future Sara Tracy Hall, the first women's dorm. The building was completed in 1959—in time for the 1959–1960 academic year. Carol probably never resided in the new dorm but spent her college years living first at Mount de Chantal and later at the Della Strada house on Washington Avenue. (Courtesy of Carol Cannon.)

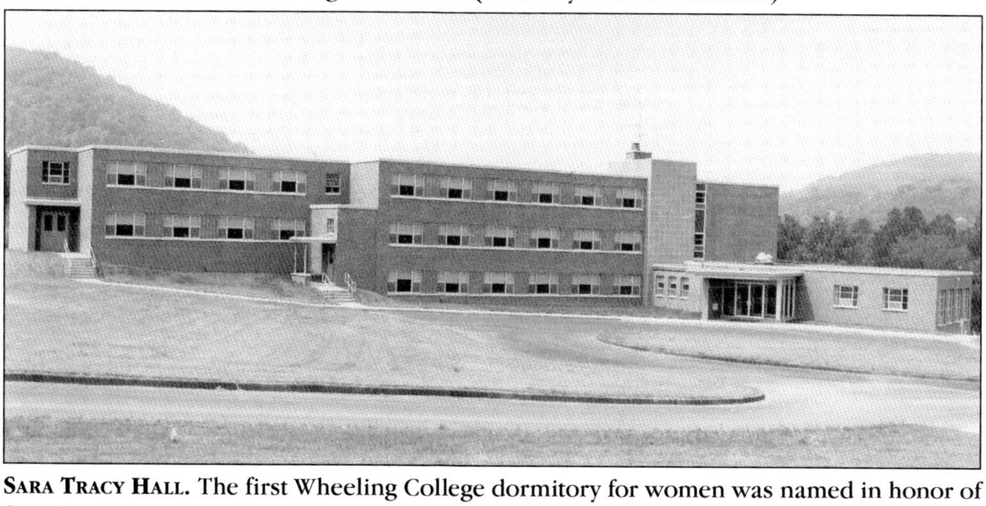

SARA TRACY HALL. The first Wheeling College dormitory for women was named in honor of Sara Tracy, a major benefactor of the diocese. Built and dedicated in 1959, the three-story dorm was to house 100 students and contained two large lounges and several small ones on each floor. In 1962, the building was enlarged by 25 percent, but the demand for more space soon led to the building of the Hill Apartments.

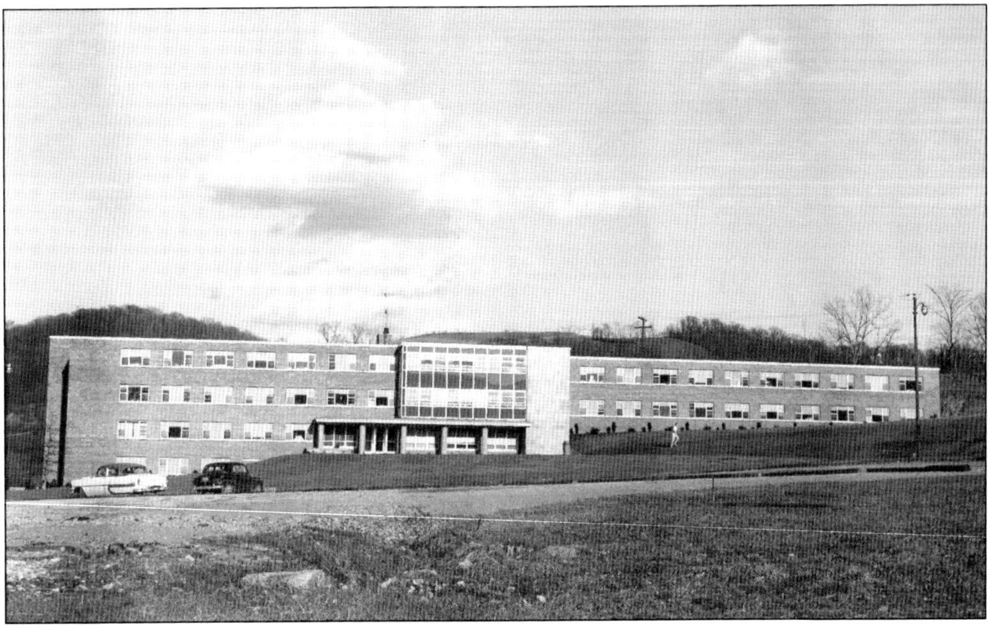

McHugh Hall. The first dormitory for men was named after the college's first president, Lawrence McHugh. The building was completed in 1958 and contained enough rooms for 150 residents. Four years later, an addition was made to increase dorm space for men. The new addition was called Campion to honor Edmund Campion, a 16th-century English Jesuit executed by Queen Elizabeth I for his efforts to spread Catholicism.

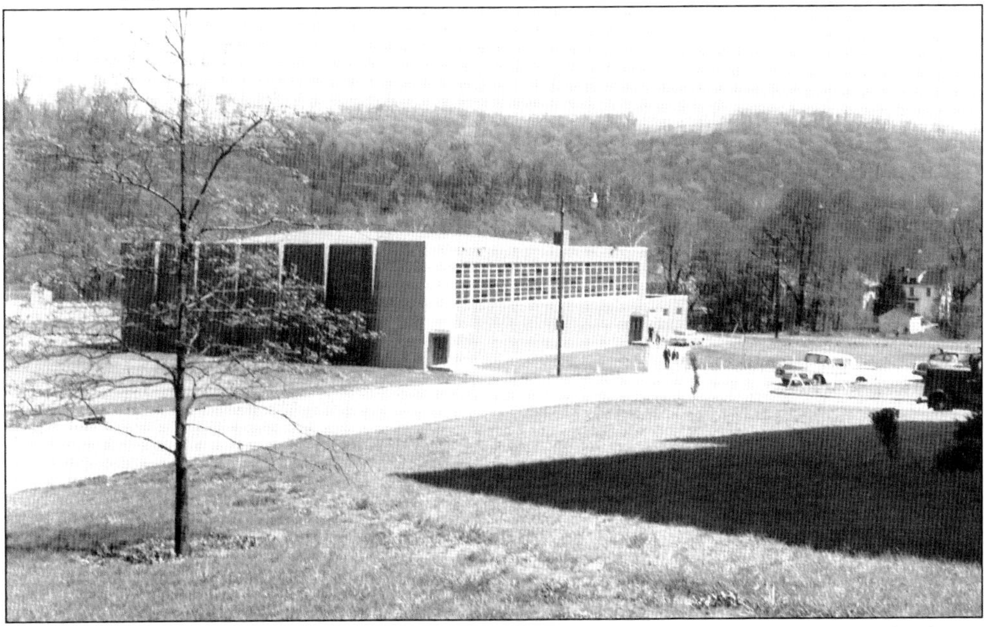

The Field House. One of Bishop John Swint's highest priorities while building Wheeling's campus was the construction of an athletic center that could also serve as an auditorium large enough to hold the entire campus community. Fortunately, construction of the gymnasium was completed in the fall of 1962, and the site was used for the fall 1962 honors convocation, at which Bishop Swint was the principal speaker; he died shortly afterward.

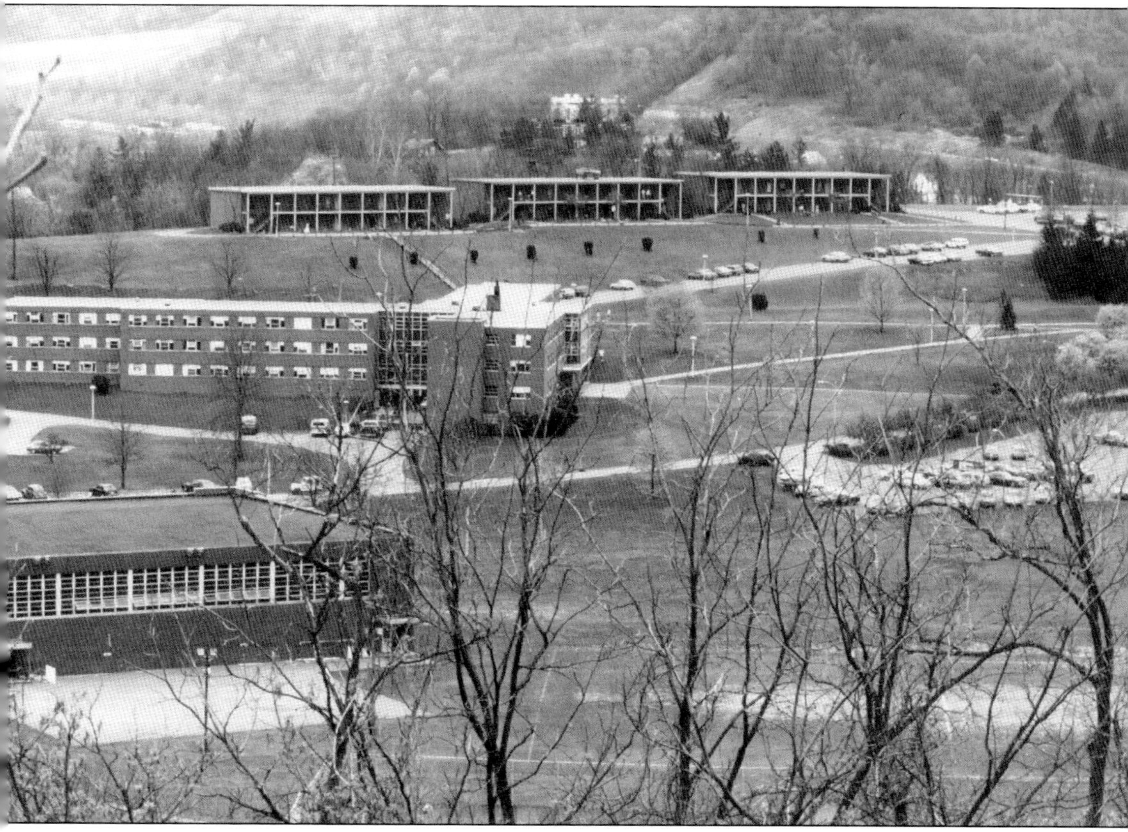

The Hill Apartments. In order to expand residential opportunities for students on campus, the college built three small dorms on the hill behind Donahue Hall. Known by the students as the Hill, or the R.S.T. apartments, they were officially named after famous Jesuits—Matteo Ricci, Robert Southwell, and Teihard de Chardin. Ricci and Southwell were each to house 48 men, while Teihard was to be home to 48 women. The buildings were divided into six apartments, each with four bedrooms, a lounge, and a large bathroom. In addition, a separate apartment existed for a dorm proctor. These living quarters were the most desired on campus and became the main centers for party life. The buildings were torn down in 1992 to make way for the seven-story coed dorm called Ignatius. The apartments are at the top of the picture, Campion-McHugh Hall is in the center, and the gymnasium is at the bottom.

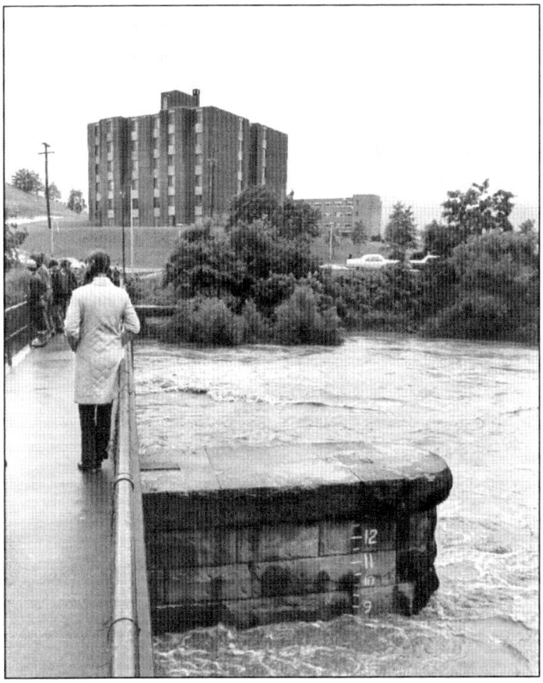

Thomas More Hall. This dorm opened in April 1968 for 20 students on an experimental basis. In the fall, there would be room for 150 students. The dorm had five floors, each with four sections. Each section held six to eight students. Here, the dorm is seen from the footbridge that crosses Wheeling Creek from the campus to the Woodsdale neighborhood.

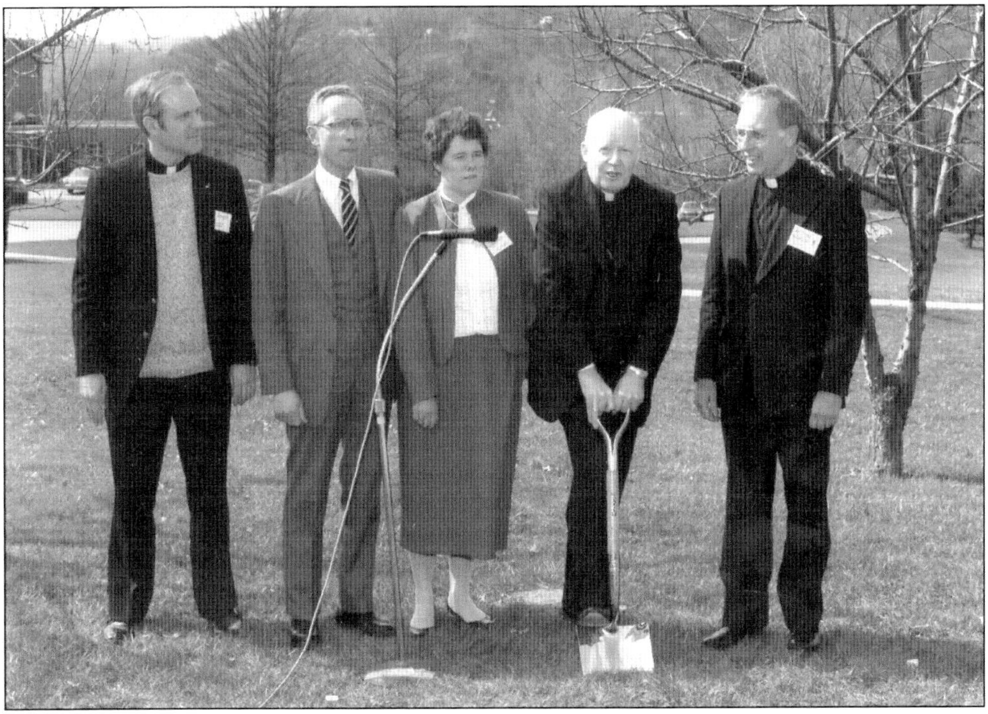

Chapel Ground Breaking. Pres. Thomas Acker, SJ, wanted a freestanding chapel to be the first building constructed during his presidency. Pictured here in 1984 are, from left to right, Joseph Hacala, SJ, rector of the Jesuit community; Dr. Donald Hofreuter, chairman of the board of directors; Courtney Cosgrove, president of student government; Bishop Joseph Hodges, the man with the shovel; and Acker.

CHAPEL OF MARY AND JOSEPH. People gather for a reception on the plaza between Swint Hall and the Chapel of Mary and Joseph. Most of the surface of the building is covered with brick, so it fits in with the older campus buildings, but the architecture is more daring and exciting than that of the older structures. The chapel's central location and its bell tower clearly identify the spiritual dimension of the college.

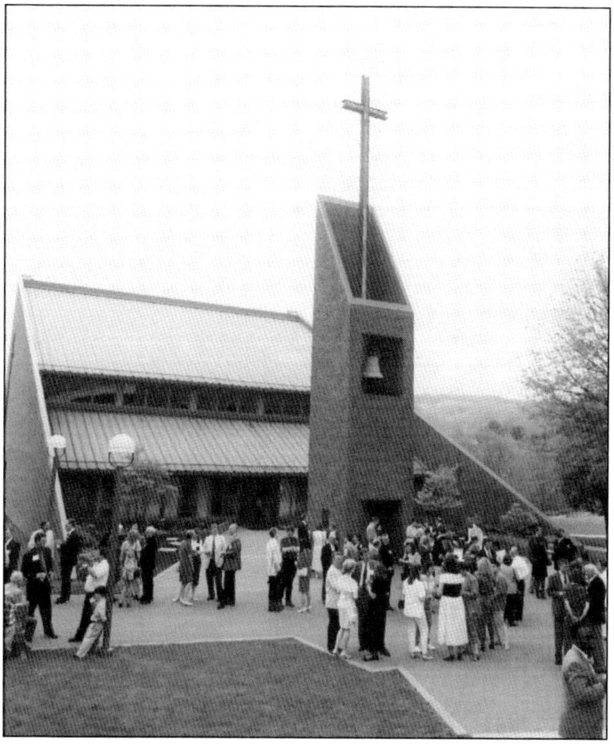

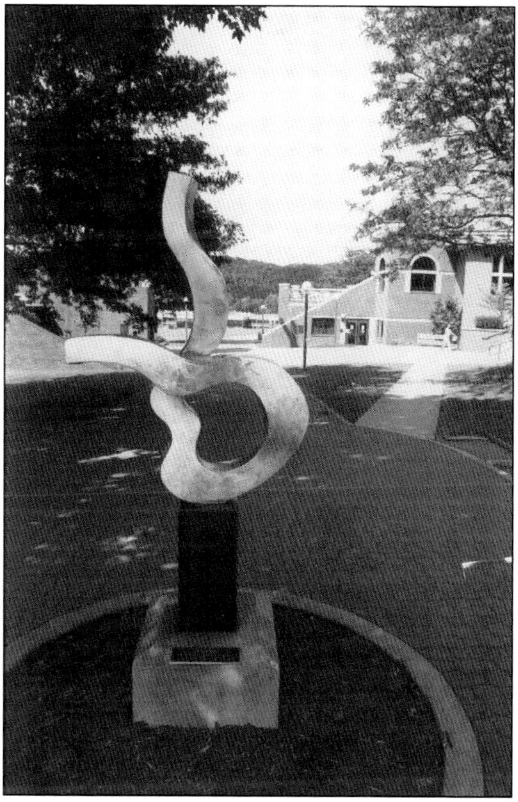

CRESCENDO. The noted Dutch sculptor Hans Van de Bovencamp created this stainless steel sculpture at the request of the university. Dedicated in June 1987, it stands in the center of McShain Plaza, between Swint Hall and the chapel.

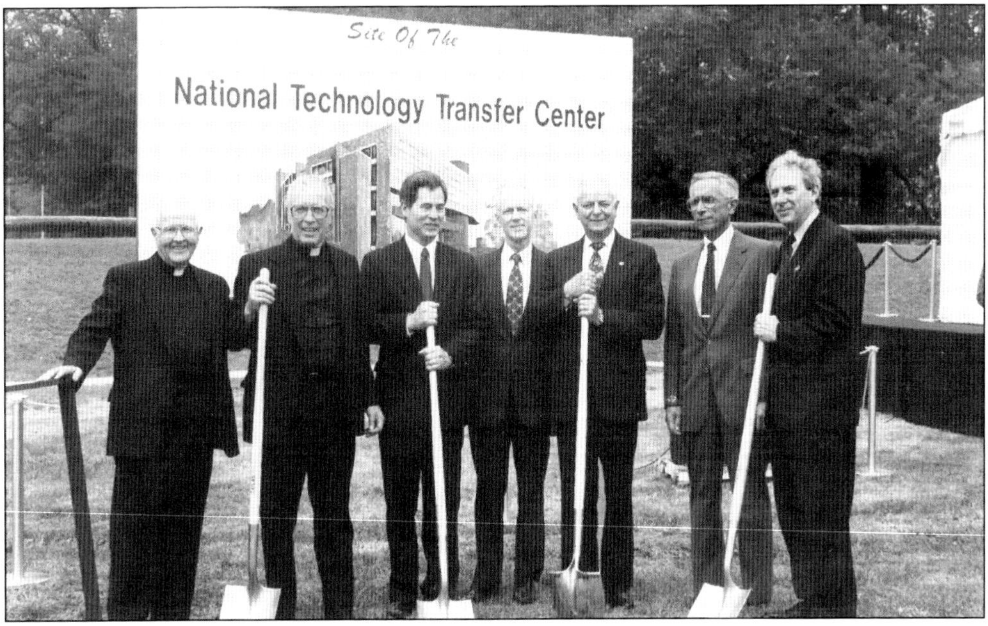

NTTC Ground Breaking. The ground breaking for both government buildings—the National Technology Transfer Center and the Center for Educational Technologies—took place on September 3, 1994. Pictured are, from left to right, Joseph Burke, SJ; Pres. Thomas Acker SJ; Rep. Alan Mollohan; Lee Rivers; Sen. Robert Byrd; Donald Hofreuter; and Daniel Goldin, the chief administrator of NASA. Approximately 1,500 people attended.

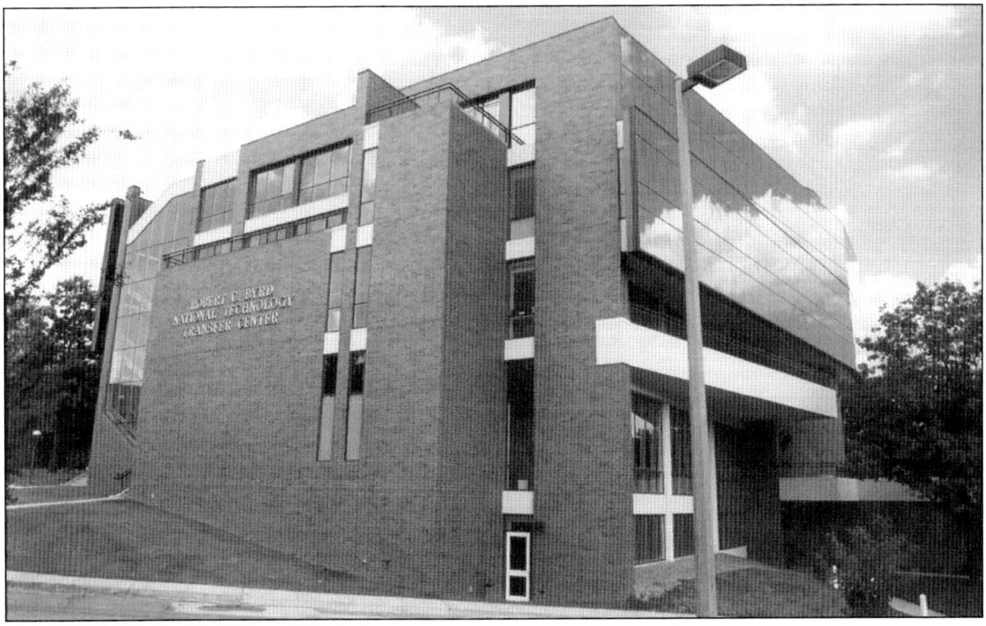

NTTC Building. The Robert C. Byrd National Technology Transfer Center (NTTC) was named in honor of West Virginia's senior US senator, who secured the funds to finance the building and initial operations. The mission of the NTTC is to transfer research and technologies produced by federal monies to private firms. The building currently houses the federal program, the business department, and admissions and registrar offices.

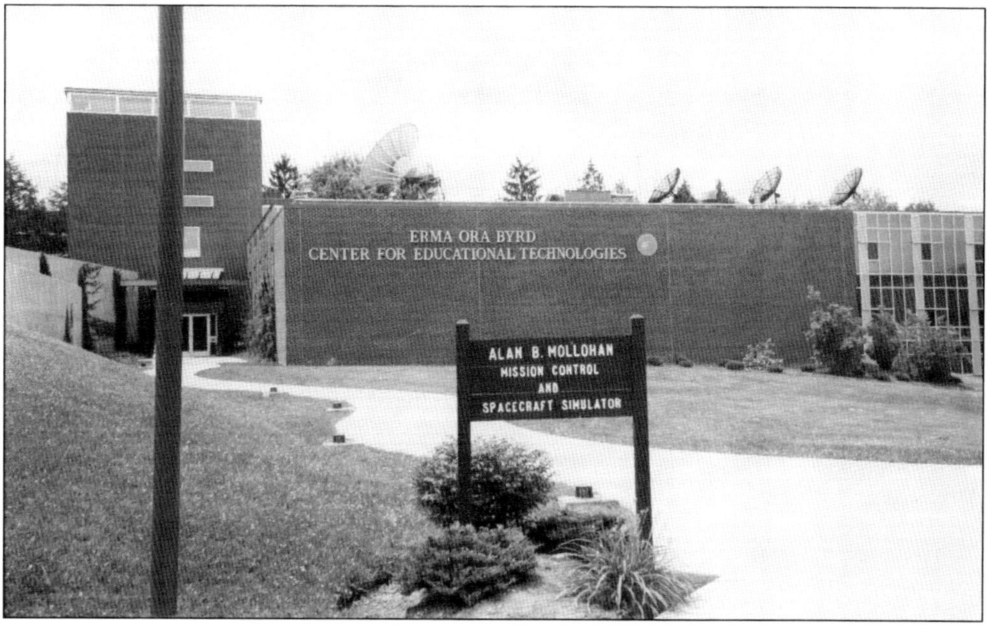

THE CET BUILDING. Seen here from McShain Plaza, the Erma Ora Byrd Center For Educational Technologies (CET) houses two federal programs and the offices for the president, advancement, public relations, and alumni. One federal program produces materials for use by elementary and secondary school teachers and students; the second is the Challenger Learning Center.

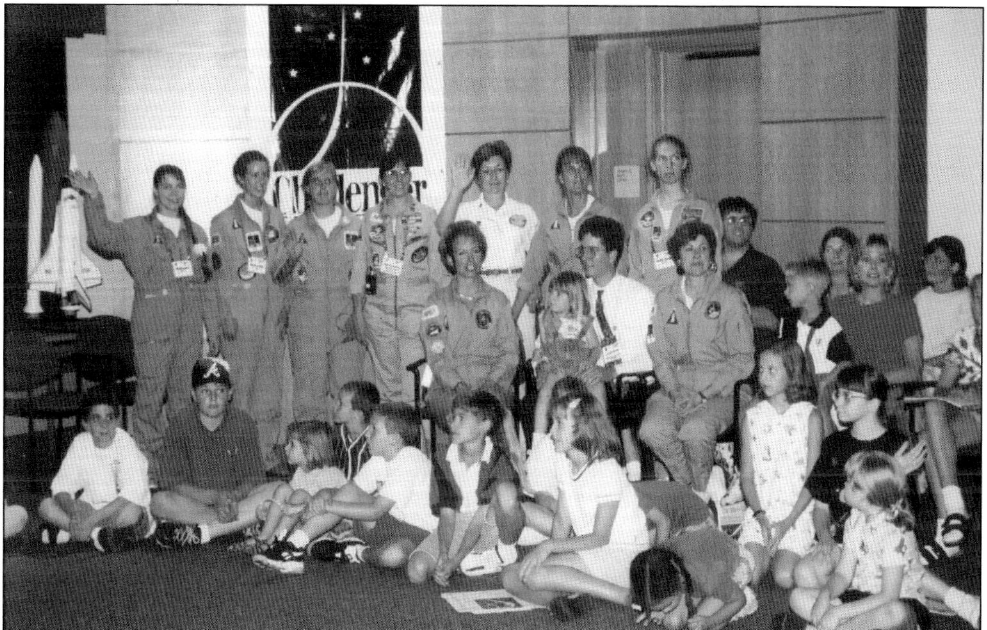

CHALLENGER LEARNING CENTER. Located in the CET building, this program has two core components—Mission Control and the Spacecraft Simulator. The program was shepherded through Congress by Rep. Alan B. Mollohan, from West Virginia's First Congressional District. The Mollohan Challenger Learning Center is named in his honor. The center's staff, pictured here, work to improve the teaching and learning of math, science, and technology.

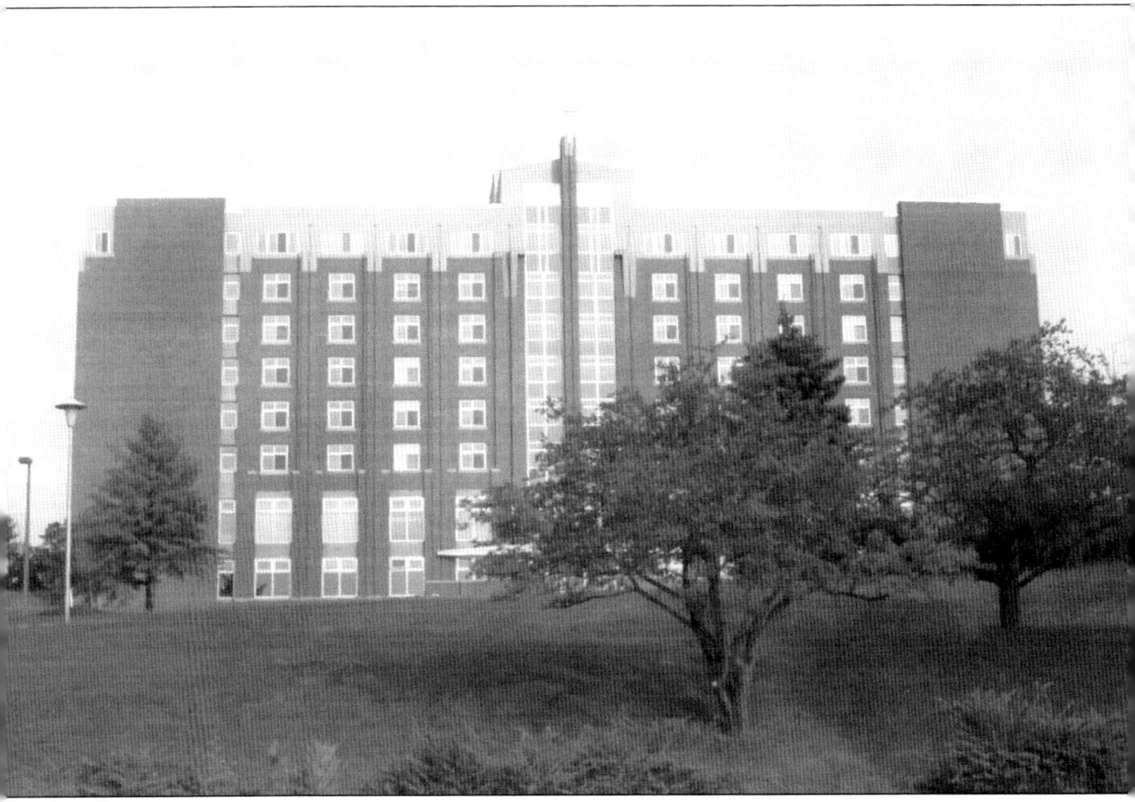

IGNATIUS HALL. Wheeling Jesuit built an eight-story coed dorm to replace the R.S.T. apartments. With rooms for 275 students, the dorm remained unnamed in the hope that a wealthy donor would contribute. When no such donor materialized, the university named the building after Ignatius Loyola, the founder of the Society of Jesus.

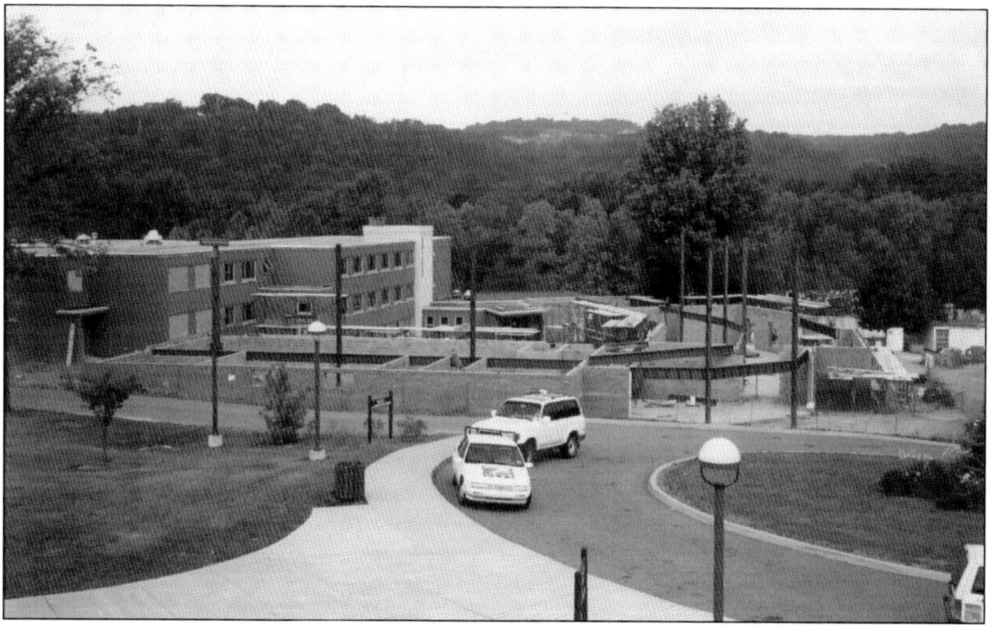

Kirby Addition to Sara Tracy. A substantial addition made to Sara Tracy Hall in 1999–2000 completely changed the appearance of the building. The addition, named after Philip and Evelyn Kirby, has the nicest rooms on campus, which are much sought by senior women. Philip Kirby was on the Wheeling Jesuit Board of Directors for 18 years, including seven as chairman.

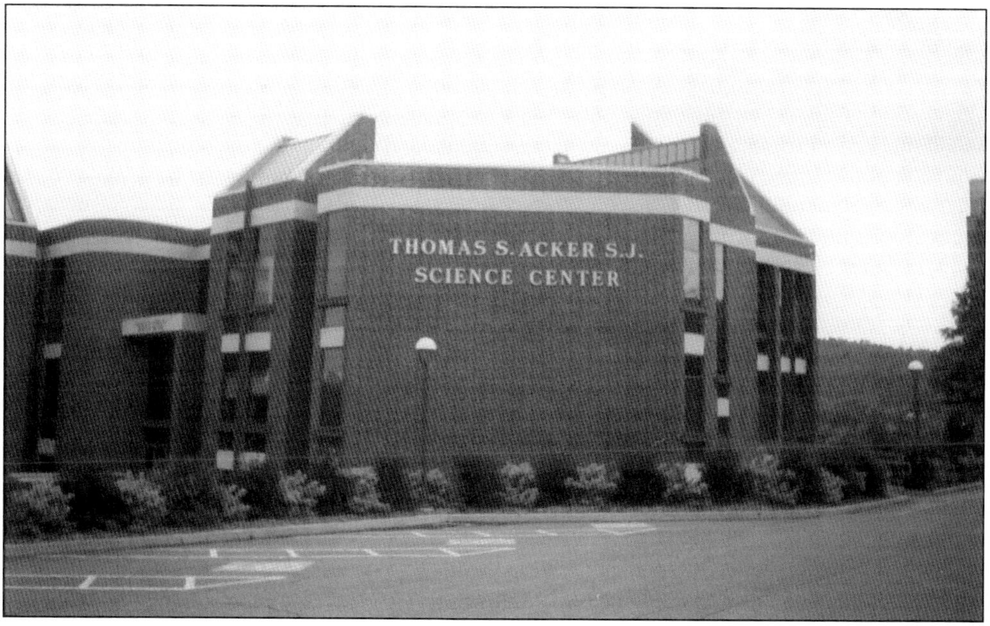

Acker Science Center. The university's new science center was constructed with federal monies secured through the efforts of Sen. Robert Byrd. It is connected to Donohue Hall by an enclosed bridge that contains various offices. The science center houses natural and computer science labs, as well as classrooms and offices used by the academic dean and the English and Modern Language departments.

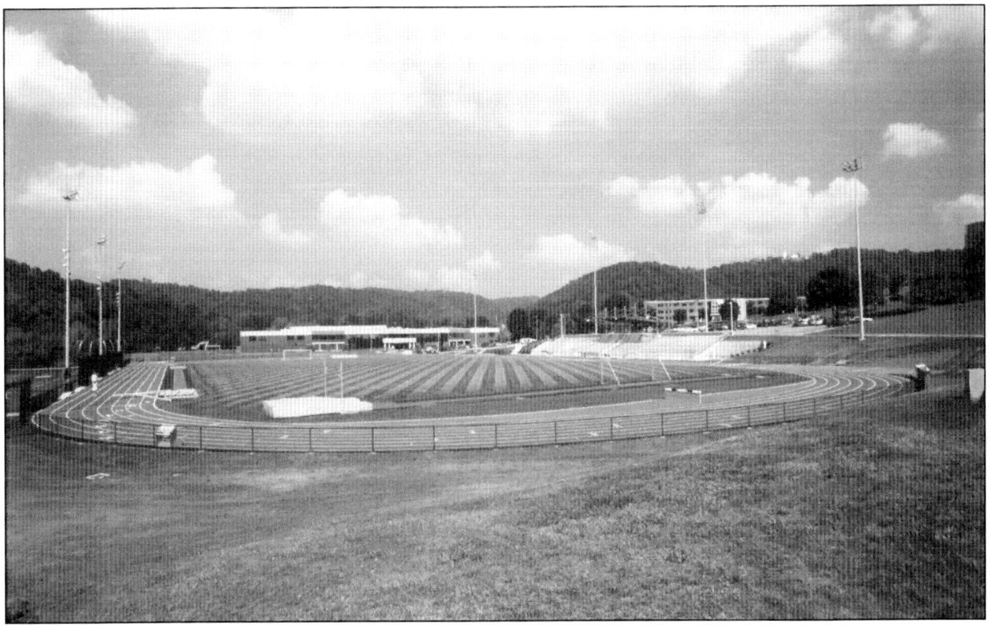

Athletic Field. The main athletic field on campus was named in honor of James LaRosa, a Clarksburg, West Virginia, businessman who operated coal mines, restaurants, and other businesses. Most soccer and lacrosse, and all track-and-field events take place at this facility. Concrete stands line the southeast side of the track. The field was dedicated on March 17, 1986. The softball field and tennis courts are now located to the southwest of the main field.

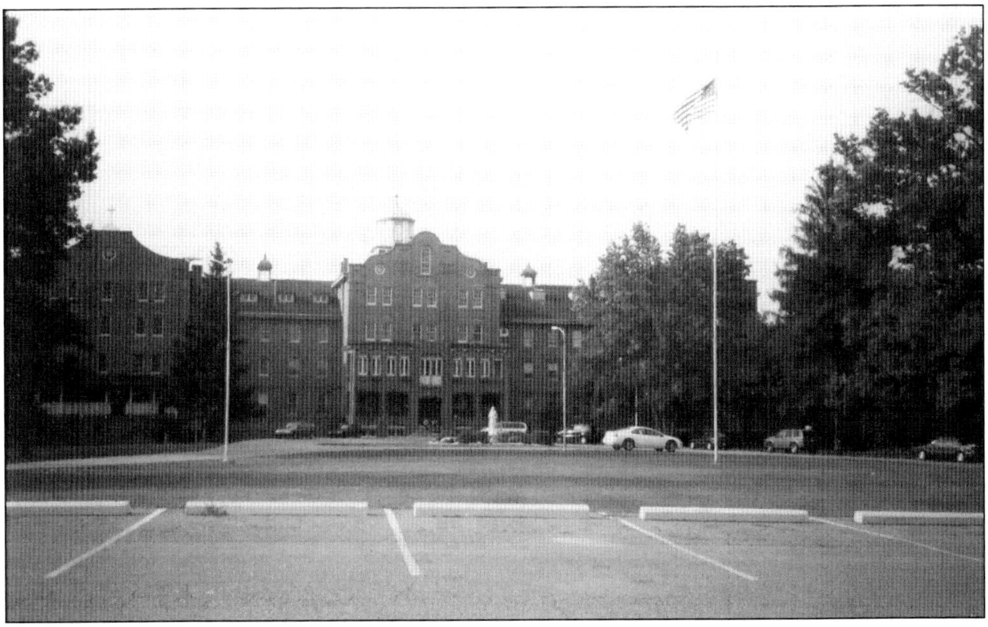

Mount de Chantal. The Mount de Chantal Visitation Academy was originally located in downtown Wheeling, but the Visitation Order purchased the Steenrod farm in the late 1850s and moved into this newly constructed, magnificent building in 1865. The structure was refurbished and expanded on numerous occasions over the next 140 years. Wheeling Hospital purchased the property when Mount de Chantal closed in 2008.

Three

THE ACADEMIC PROGRAM

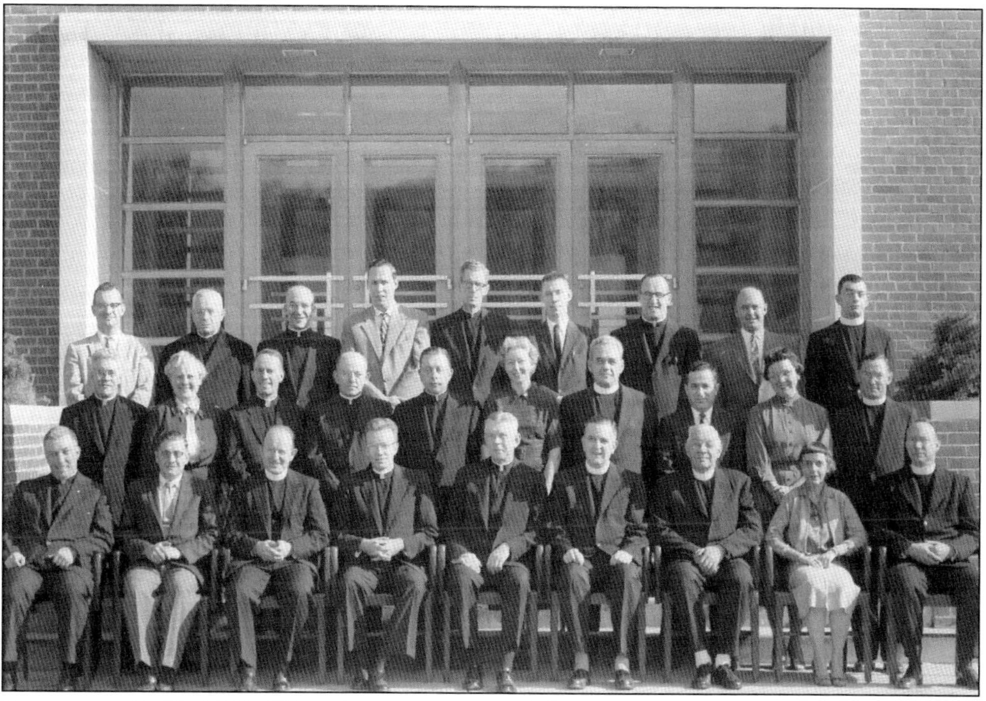

FACULTY OF 1957–1958. This administration and faculty group picture shows 18 Jesuits, 6 laymen, and 4 women making up the faculty in the college's second year of operation. Eight of the people pictured are administrators, and 20 are full-time teachers. The heavy Jesuit presence shows the commitment that the religious order made to the college in its first years.

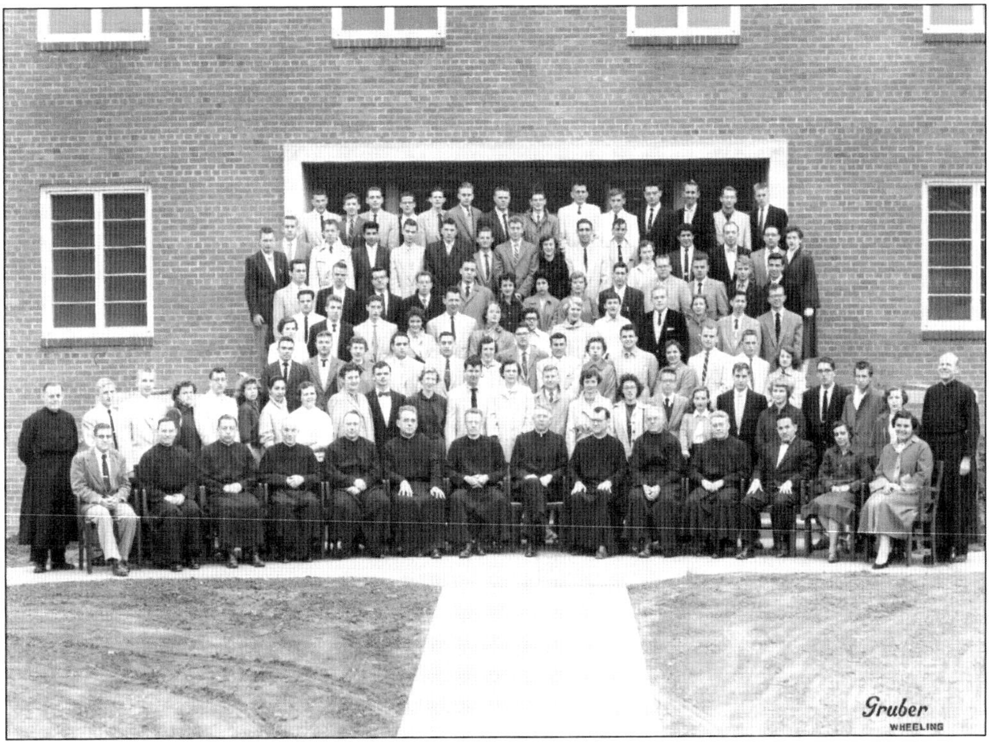

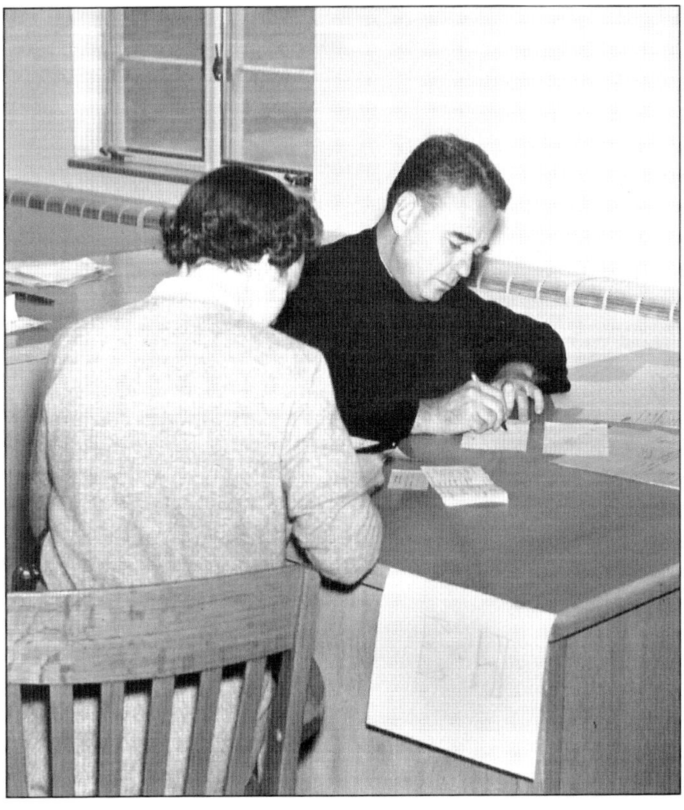

First Faculty, Staff, and Students. This fall 1955 picture of the first Wheeling College class, along with faculty and staff, shows that there are 12 Jesuits, 2 laymen, and 5 women on the faculty and staff, and that of the 90 freshmen, 21 are women.

First Registration. In this 1955 image, Rev. Gerald Kernan, SJ, registers student Eleanor Ewing for the first class; she graduated in 1960. Today, WJU students register online.

KITTY MCCREADY AND PRES. THOMAS ACKER. Kitty began working at Wheeling College—in the registrar's office—in 1958, became registrar in 1972, and held that position until her retirement in 1996. She received an honorary degree from Wheeling College in 1974, the Clifford M. Lewis, SJ Award from the alumni association for extraordinary service and dedication, and was inducted into the WJU Athletic Hall of Fame for her strong support of women's sports at the university.

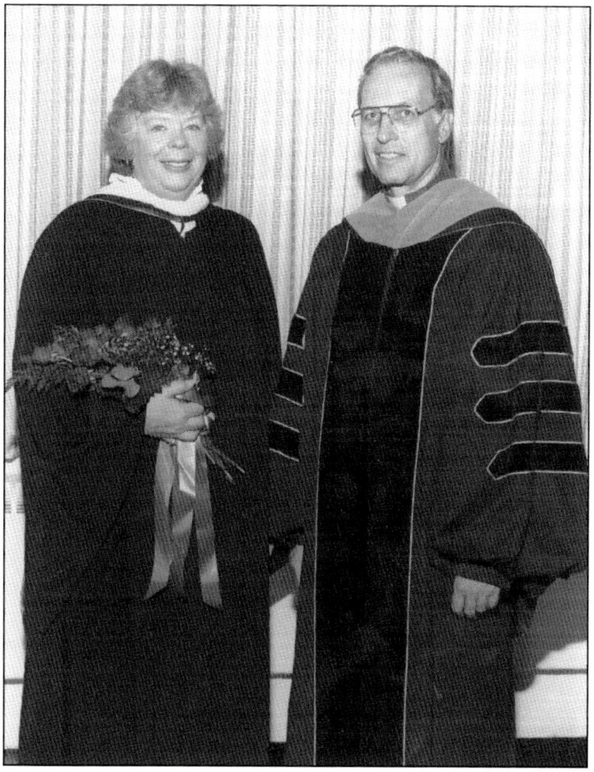

FRESHMEN TESTS. In this picture from the late 1950s, freshmen take aptitude tests after entering Wheeling College. It seems like this included a considerable amount of looking at other people's answers and even good-humored conversations.

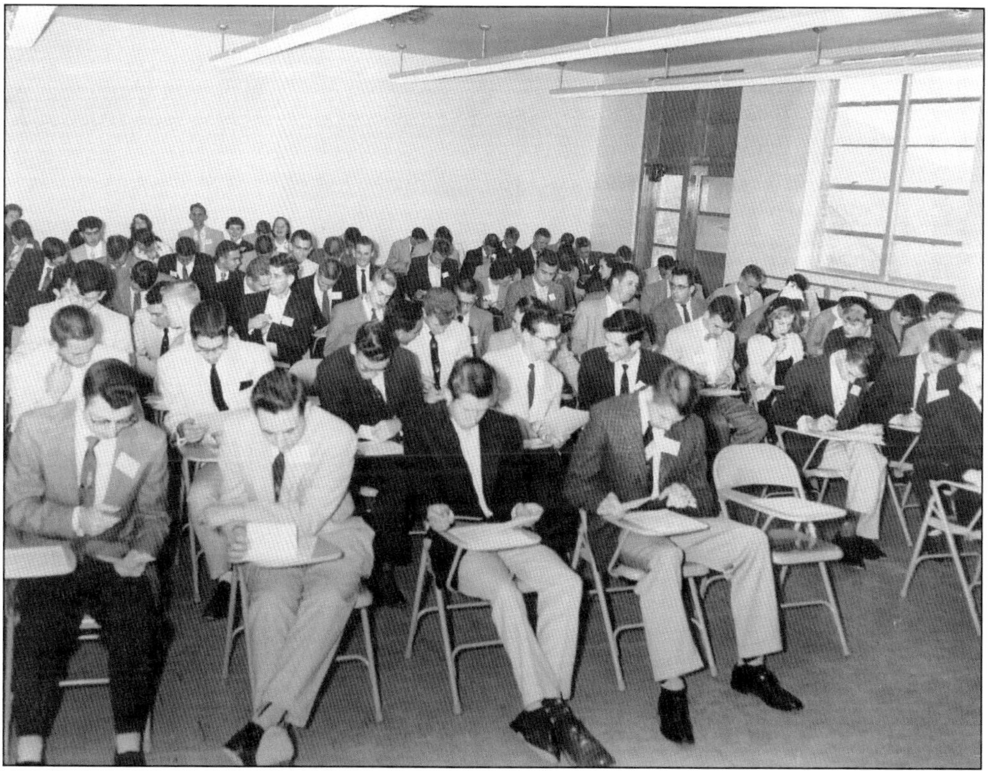

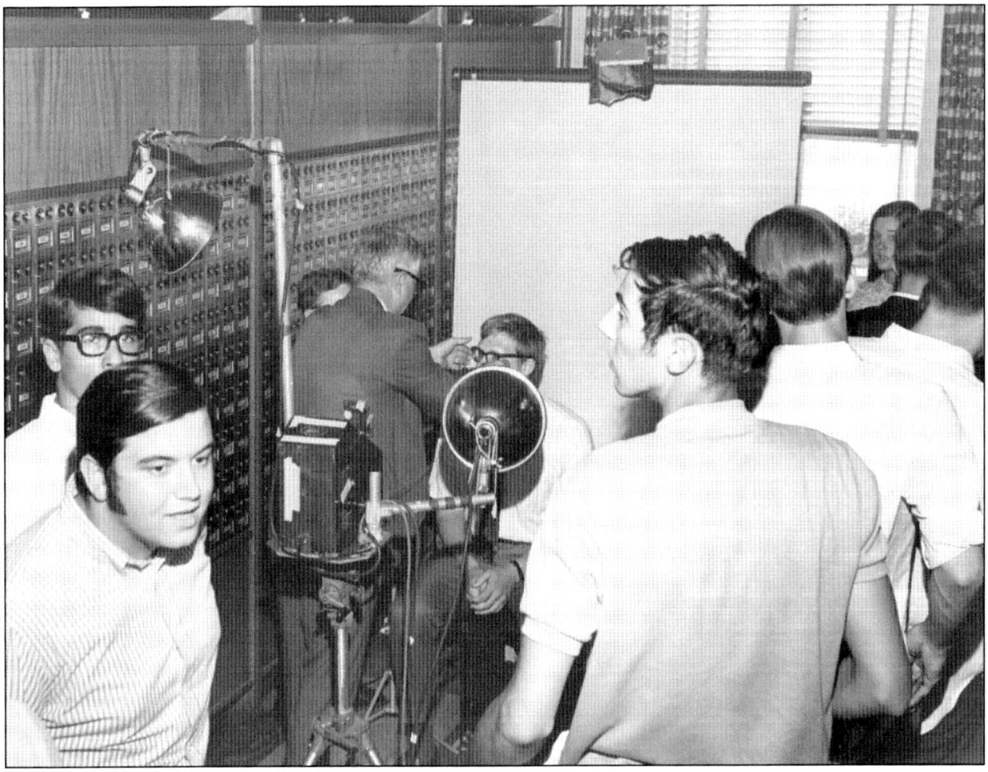

PHOTOGRAPHIC IDENTIFICATION. One experience that all freshmen have upon coming to the college is getting a photo identification card. Here, Sal Scafidi (far left), Ernie Trakus (second from left), and other students line up in the snack bar for their photographs. Behind the camera are the old student mailboxes on the first floor of Swint; today, student mailboxes are located on the ground level of the same building, across from the security office.

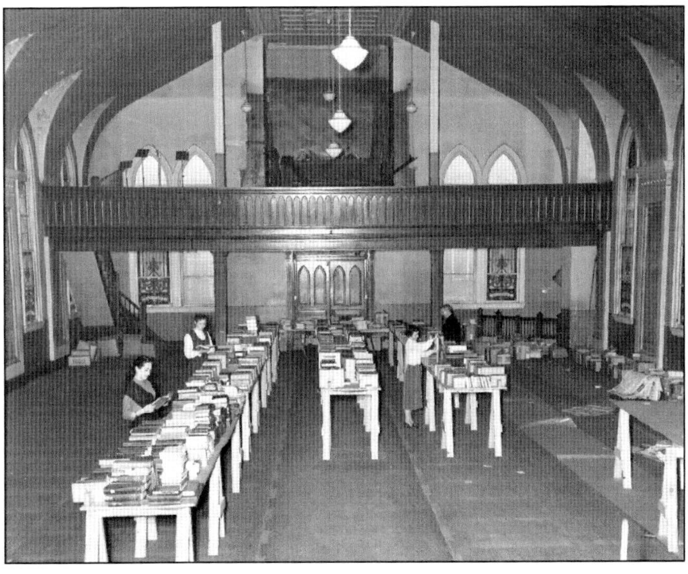

CREATING THE LIBRARY. The library of Wheeling College was first assembled in old St. Michael's Church on Edgington Lane, about one half-mile from campus. The early collection consisted of many books donated by other Jesuit colleges that had duplicate copies. By the late 1980s, the collection included more than 100,000 volumes. Currently, with online databases, the library's resources are much larger.

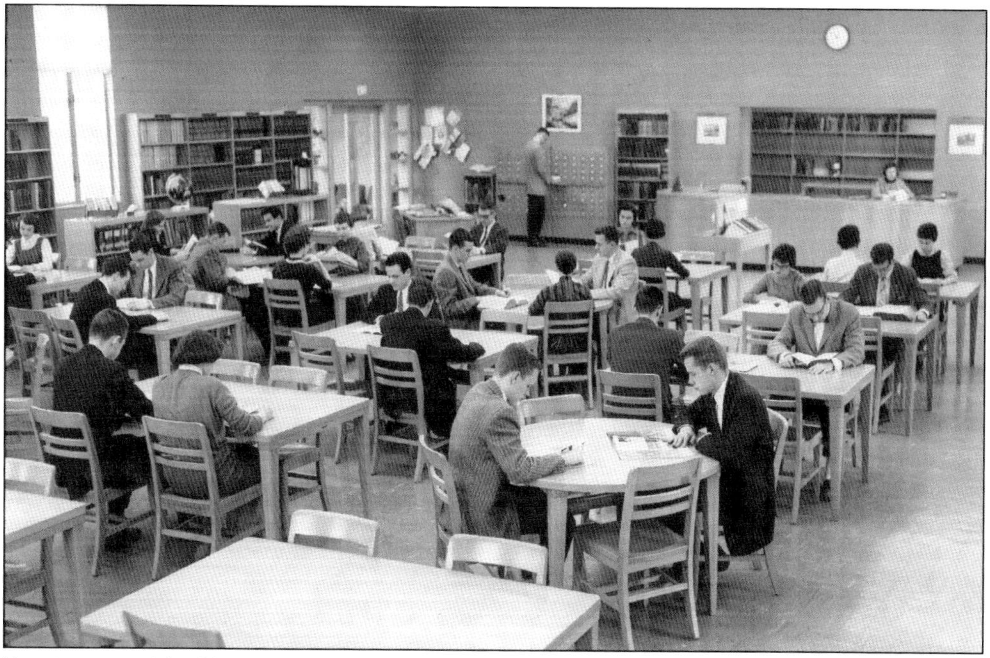

The Library. The library seems busy and the students studious in this 1950s photograph. The card catalog near the front entrance appears rather small. The floor is linoleum, not the carpeted surface of today, so it was likely noisy when people moved chairs or got up, even if they tried to do so quietly.

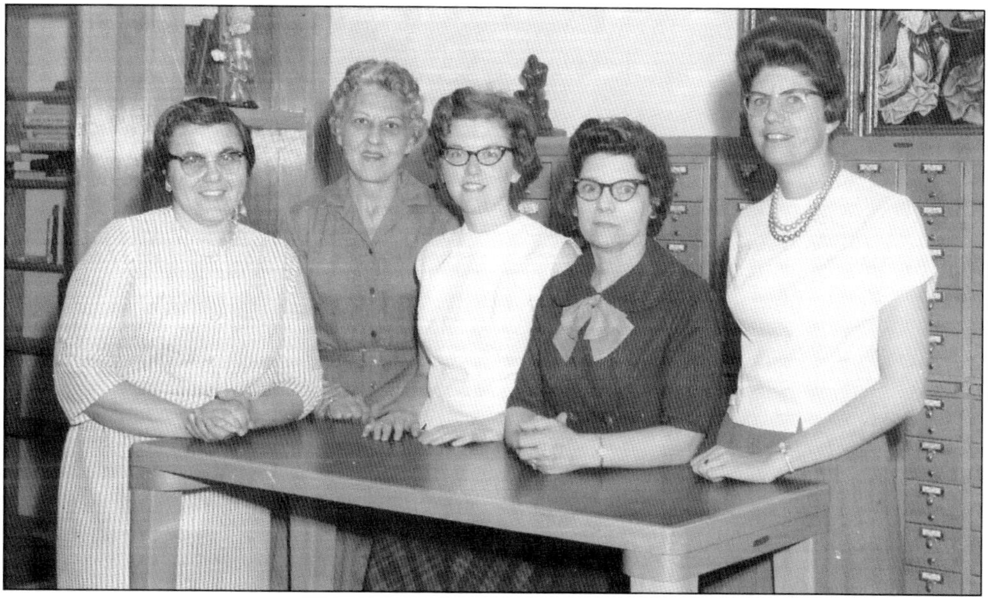

Library Staff. Eileen Carpino, head librarian from 1963 to 2001, is shown here with her staff. Carpino started working under Josephine Savaro in 1955 and recalled in the spring 1994 *Wheeling Jesuit Chronicle* that "when the library opened the doors weren't even done. The carpenters nailed plywood in the doorways at night to keep people out." Pictured, from left to right, are Eileen Carpino, Loretta Conroy, Mary Dougherty, Regina Pettit, and Barbara Miller, the assistant librarian.

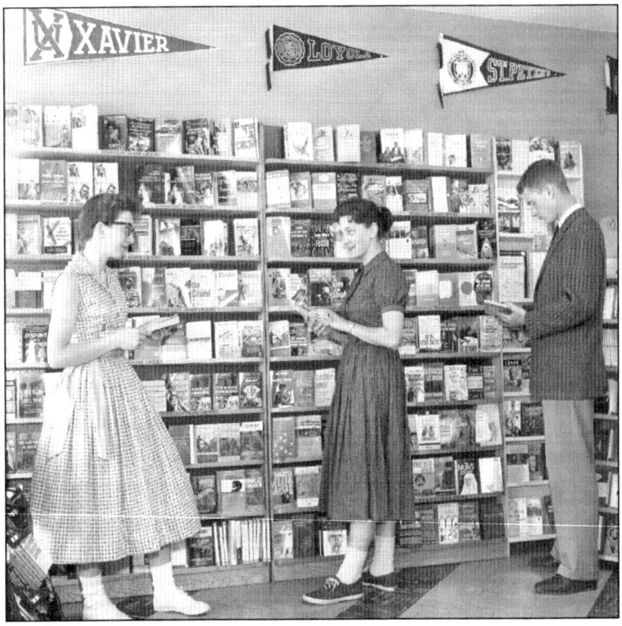

Bookstore. This 1959 photograph of three students in the Wheeling College bookstore shows the typical attire of students during the first decade of the college's existence. The flags above the books represent three of the 28 Jesuit colleges and universities established in the United States. The students are Virginia Fragale (left), Barbara Creamer (center), and Peter May.

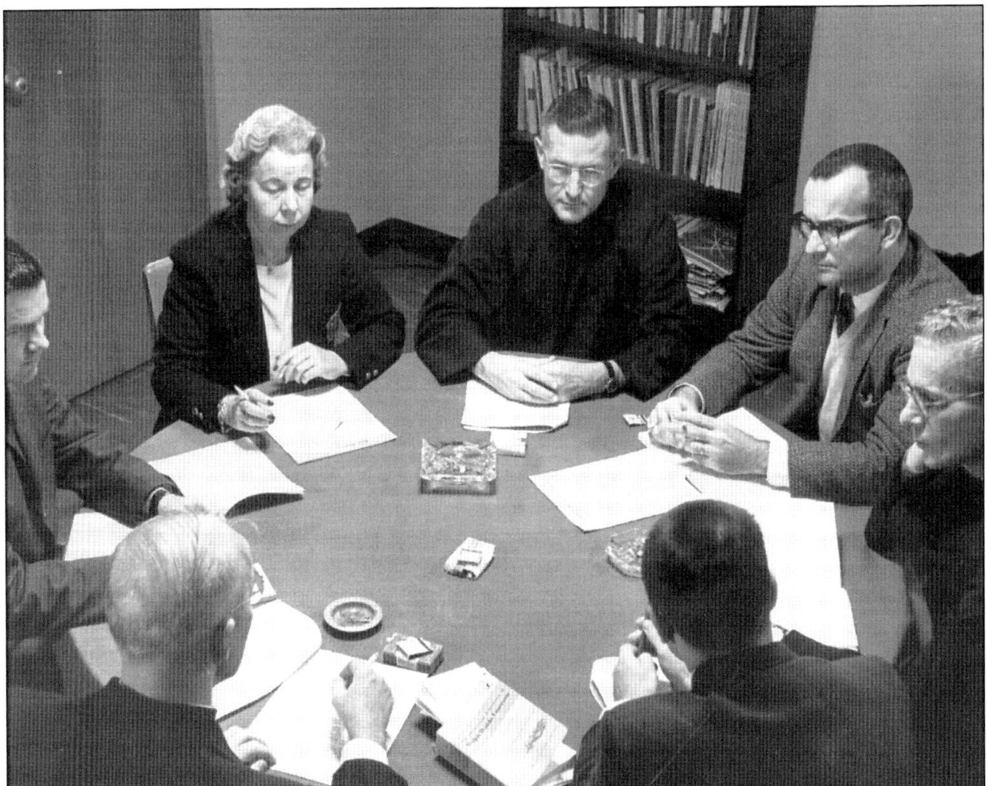

Faculty Committee. At this early 1960s conference, Anne Barry, dean of women, meets with a number of faculty members. Note that at least two and possibly more of the seven people are smoking. Smoking was widely practiced on campus until the 1990s, but it is now restricted to just a half-dozen outside areas.

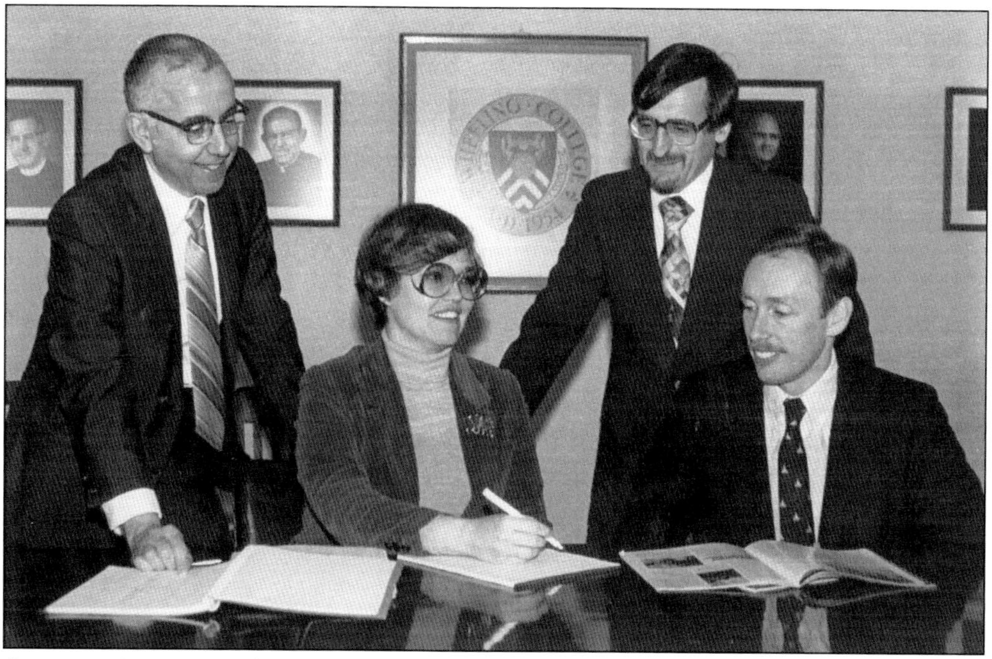

Graduate Council. In the early 1980s, Wheeling College created a graduate council after the creation of master's degree programs. Pictured here are, from left to right, Thomas Knorr (science and mathematics), Dr. Jeanne Neff (academic vice president), Dr. Normand Paulhus (theology and religious studies), and Dr. Robert Rush (business).

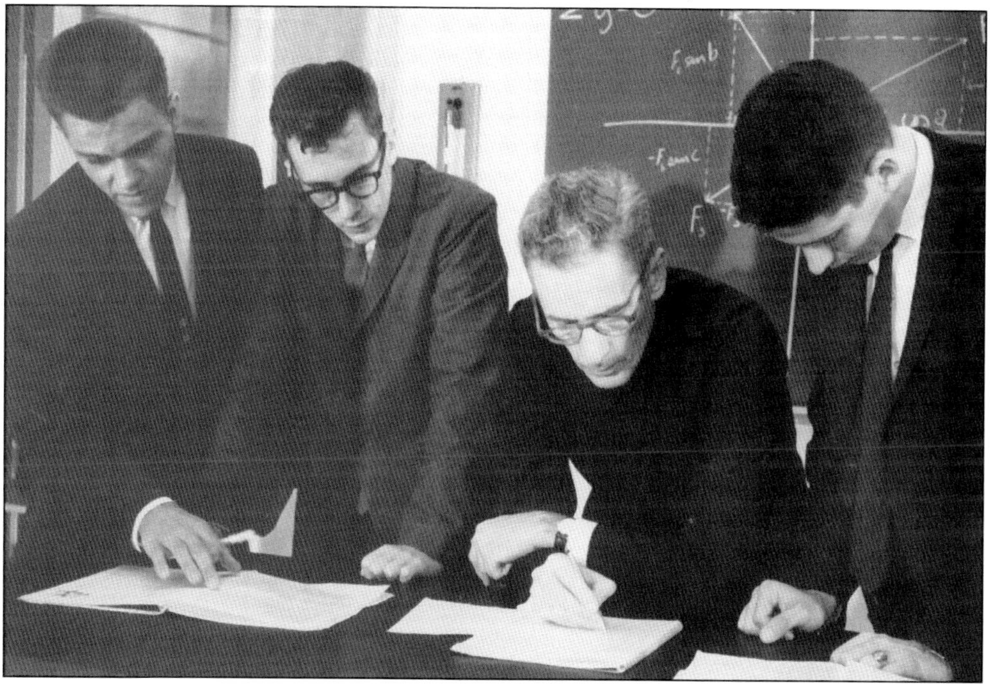

Math with Winslow. From left to right, Ron Teufel, Pat O'Brien, Fr. Regis Winslow, SJ, and an unidentified student work math problems in 1969. With small classes, students received a lot of personal attention.

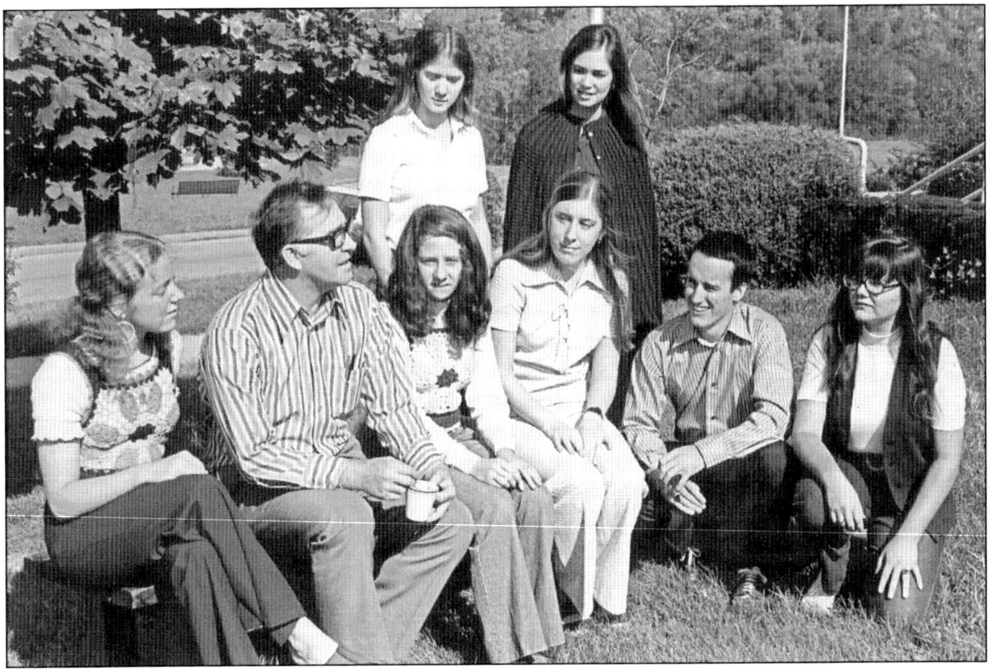

CONVERSING WITH DOC SUTHERLAND. One of the most colorful professors at Wheeling College was Dr. Henry Sutherland, of the modern languages department. Sutherland was often found holding either a cigarette or a cup of coffee when in meetings or engaging in idle chitchat. He mainly taught Spanish and Russian. He was the school's most avid basketball fan and frequently traveled to games with the men's team.

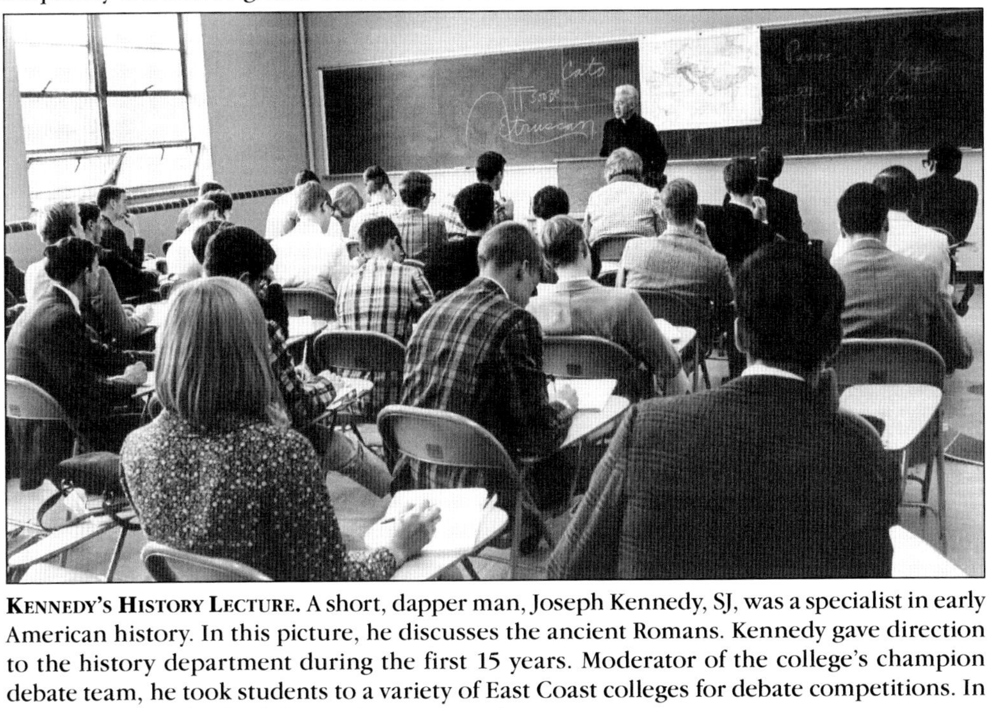

KENNEDY'S HISTORY LECTURE. A short, dapper man, Joseph Kennedy, SJ, was a specialist in early American history. In this picture, he discusses the ancient Romans. Kennedy gave direction to the history department during the first 15 years. Moderator of the college's champion debate team, he took students to a variety of East Coast colleges for debate competitions. In the early 1960s, Dr. Paul Orr took over as moderator.

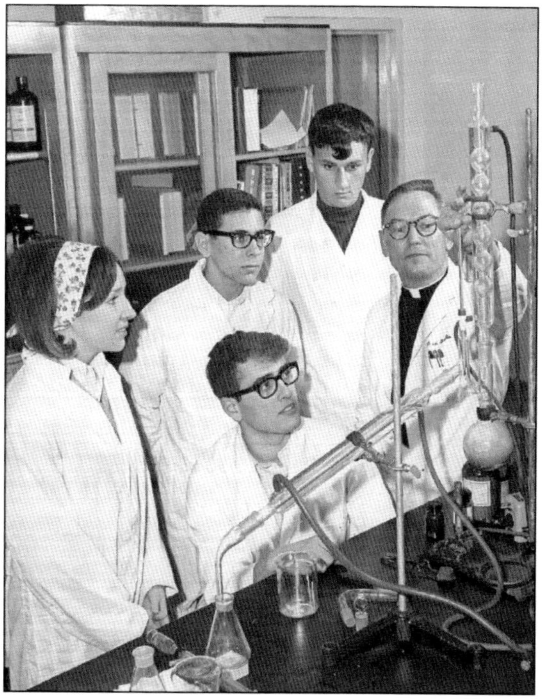

FATHER DUKE'S CHEMISTRY LAB. Students pay close attention while Fr. Joseph Duke, SJ, adjusts tubes in the chemistry lab. Father Duke spent almost 10 years at the college, establishing the chemistry program.

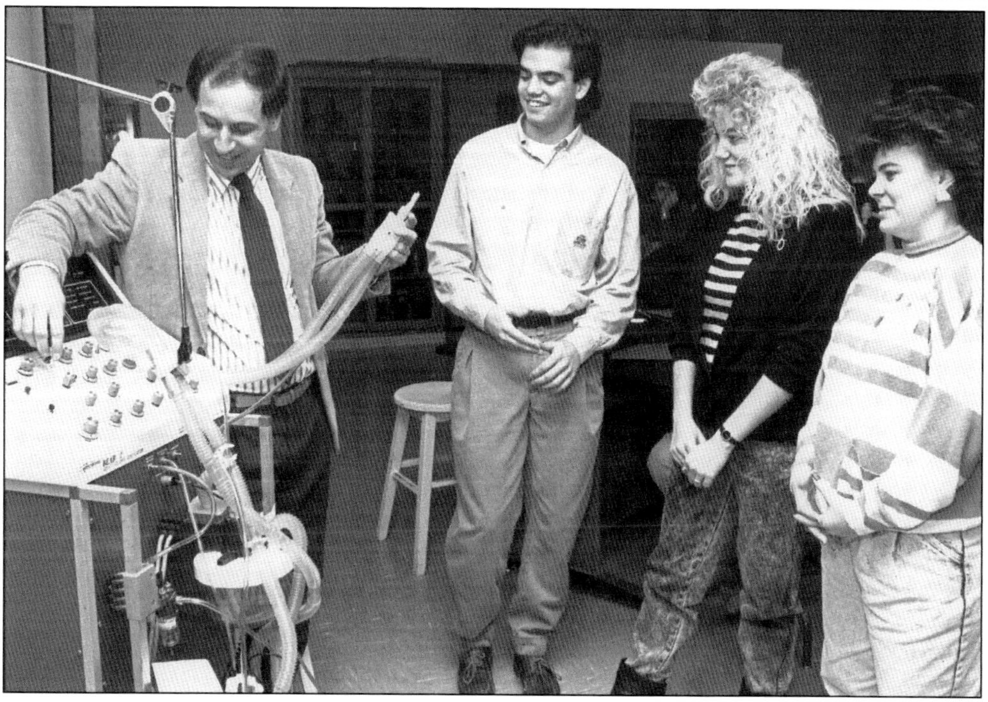

MARANGONI AND NEW EQUIPMENT. Alan Marangoni shows off new equipment for students of a new major: respiratory therapy. The major was one of three created in the late 1970s, when the college received federal grants to expand into the health sciences. The other two programs were nuclear medicine and nursing. Wheeling Jesuit has since added more health science programs, like physical therapy and athletic training.

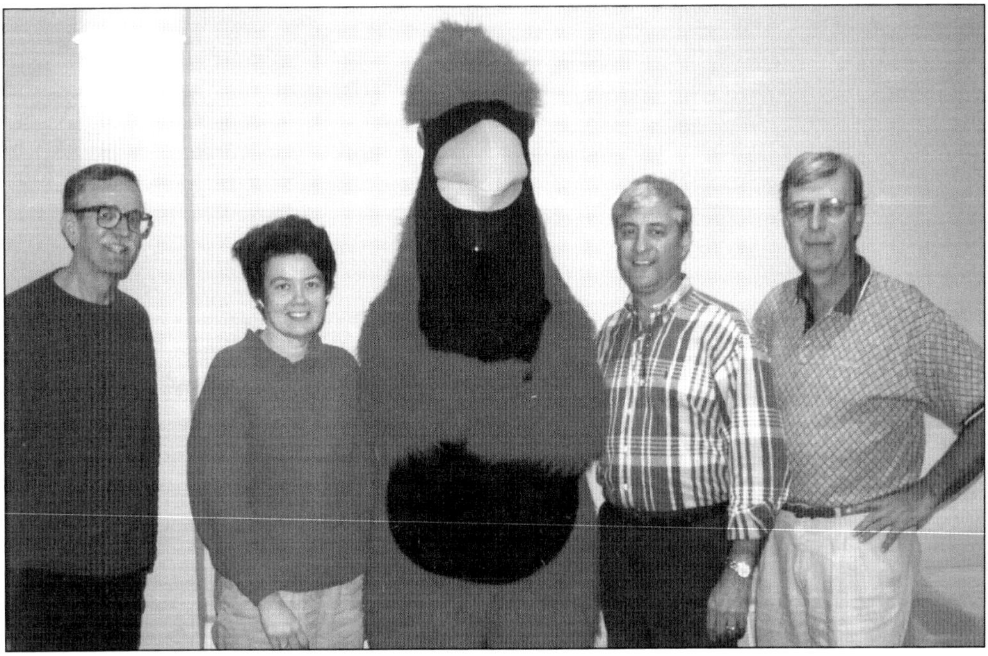

Psych Department and the Cardinal. Almost every year, students working on the yearbook, ***The Manifest***, take group pictures of different academic departments. The psychology department took this playful picture with the college's mascot, the Cardinal. Pictured here are, from left to right, Fr. Joseph Hayden, SJ, Dr. Deborah Hull, the Cardinal, Dennis Maceiko, and Dr. James Goodwin.

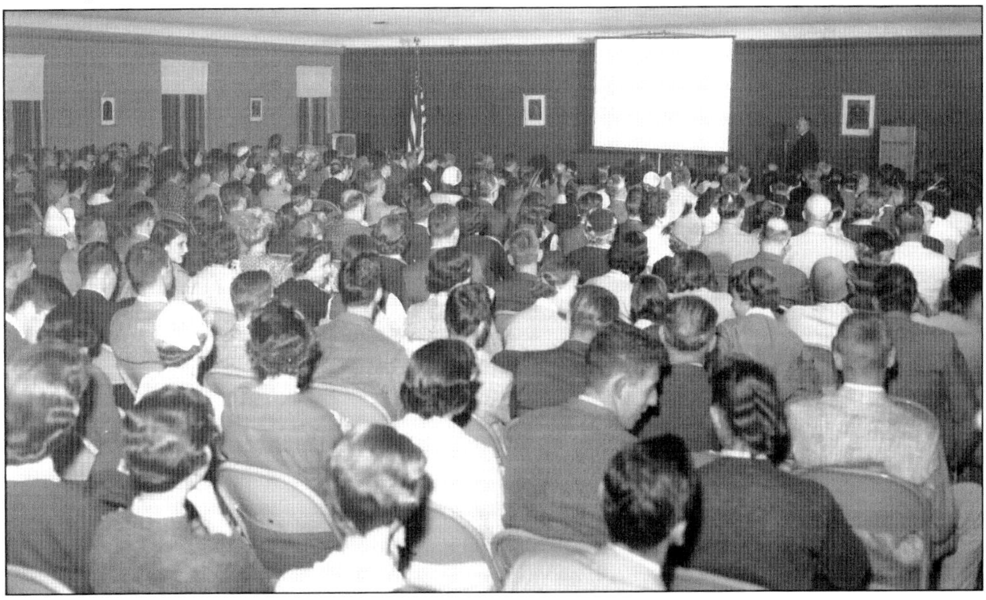

Daedalian Space Society. Organized in October 1957, the society invited Fr. Francis Heyden, SJ, the director of the astronomical observatory at Georgetown University, to speak here concerning the United States' satellite program. The talk was given after the USSR had successfully launched its first satellite into space, and many feared that the Americans had fallen behind the Soviets in the space race.

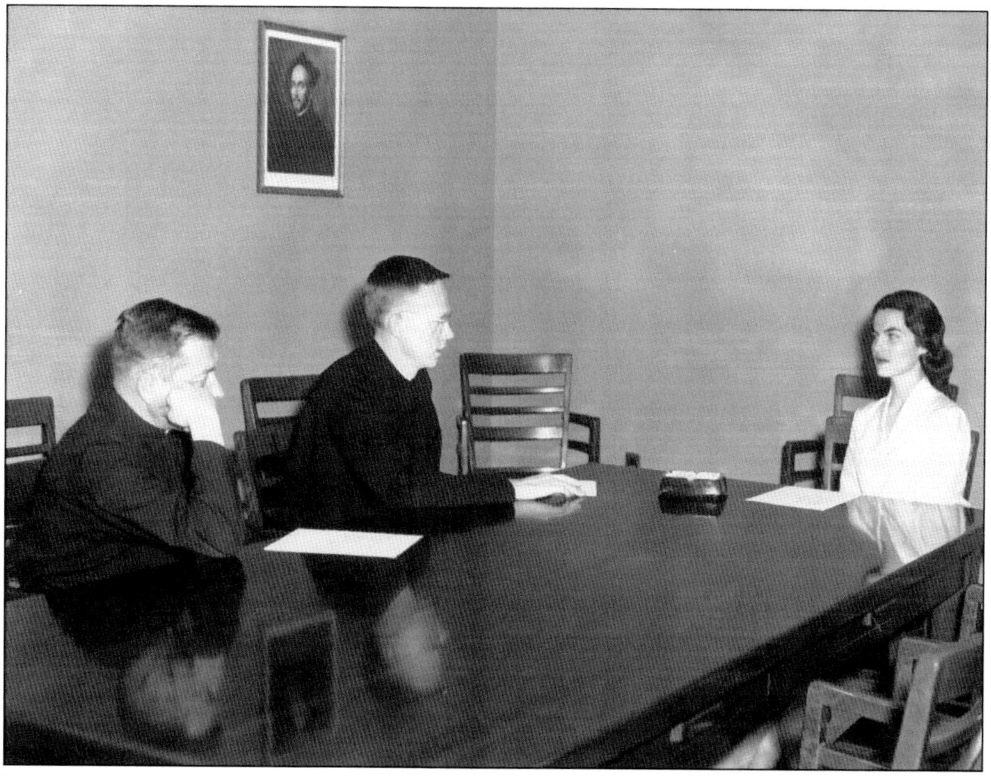

PHILOSOPHY ORALS. One of the more stressful events that all students have to undergo is taking philosophy orals. Here, Frs. John Coll, SJ (center), and Ed Gannon, SJ, quiz an unidentified female student. The questioning usually lasted about 20 minutes, and the exam was held in the spring, after students finished the first two philosophy courses.

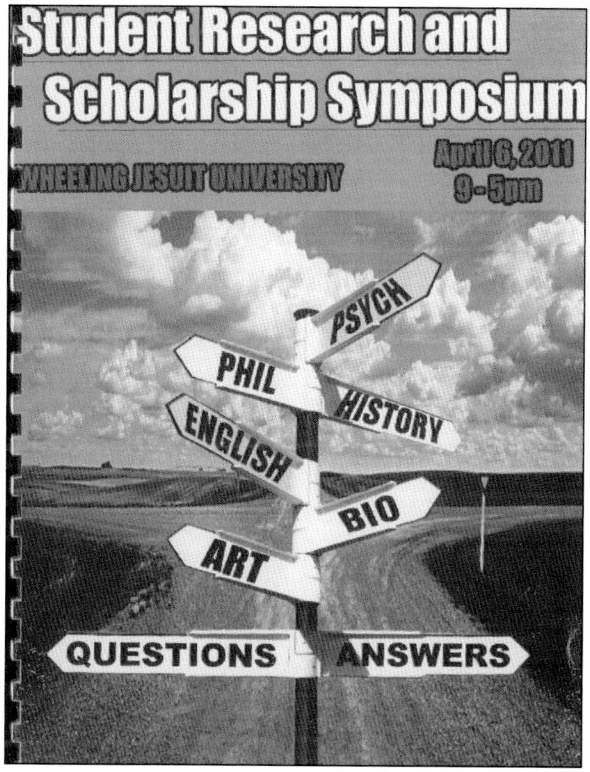

RESEARCH DAY. In the spring semester of 2000, the university held the first of its annual Research and Scholarship Symposiums. Students present a research project from that academic year to faculty, visitors, and fellow students. Faculty judges select the best presentations and award prizes. At the first symposium, 60 students presented work via lecture, PowerPoint demonstrations, and poster boards.

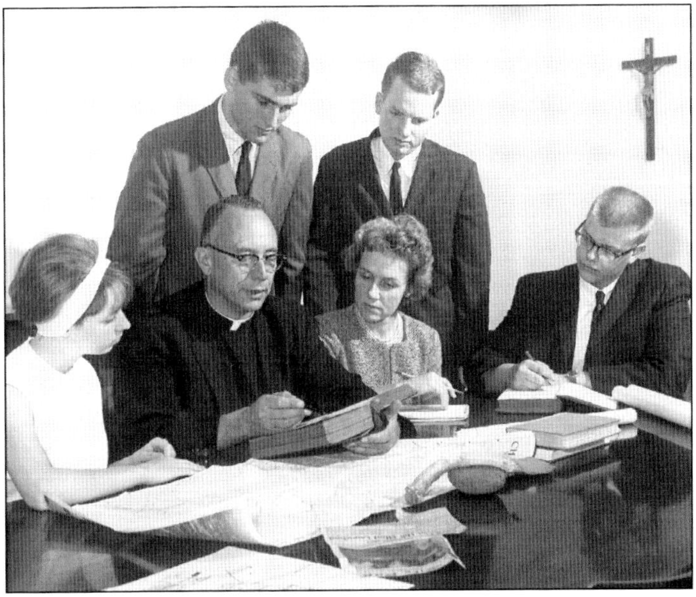

Redevelopment Study. In the fall of 1964, Wheeling College was awarded an Area Redevelopment Project to study how the state of West Virginia might improve its economy. Under the direction of Fr. Clifford Lewis, eight students each spent about 200 hours studying how tourism might impact unemployment, traffic patterns, and so forth. The project was part of Pres. Lyndon Johnson's Great Society initiative.

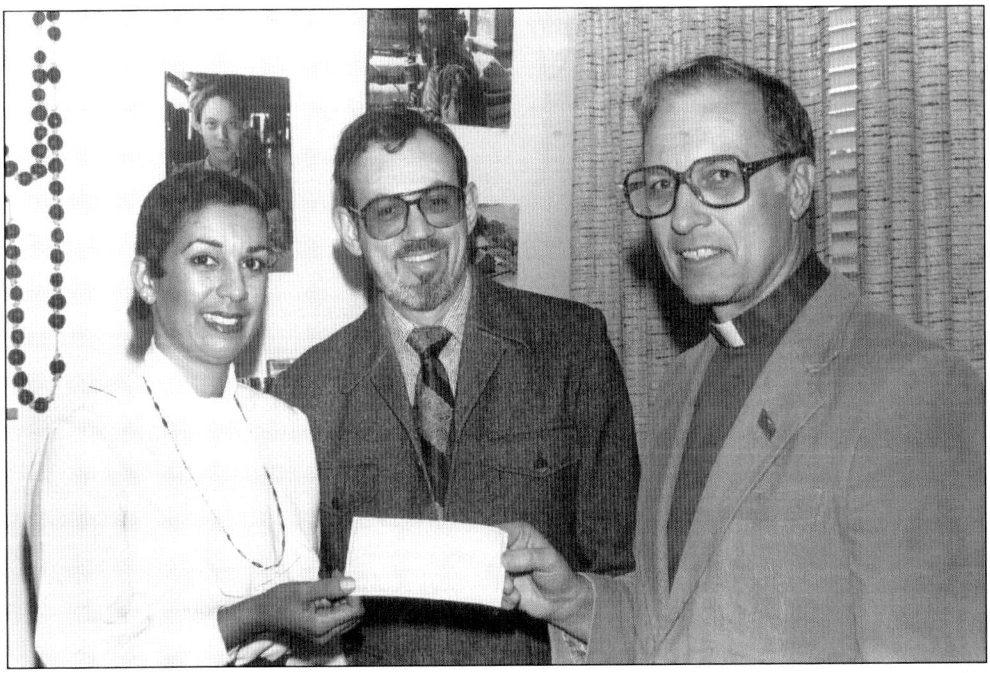

Holocaust Symposium. In 1988, Dr. Walter Renn, of the history department, organized a three-day symposium on the Holocaust. The colloquium was supported by a number of donors. Here, Fr. Thomas Acker (right) receives a check from Betty Pickett, an executive of the National Conference of Christians and Jews. Dr. Renn is in the center. The symposium sparked student interest in the Holocaust and led to the creation of a course about it.

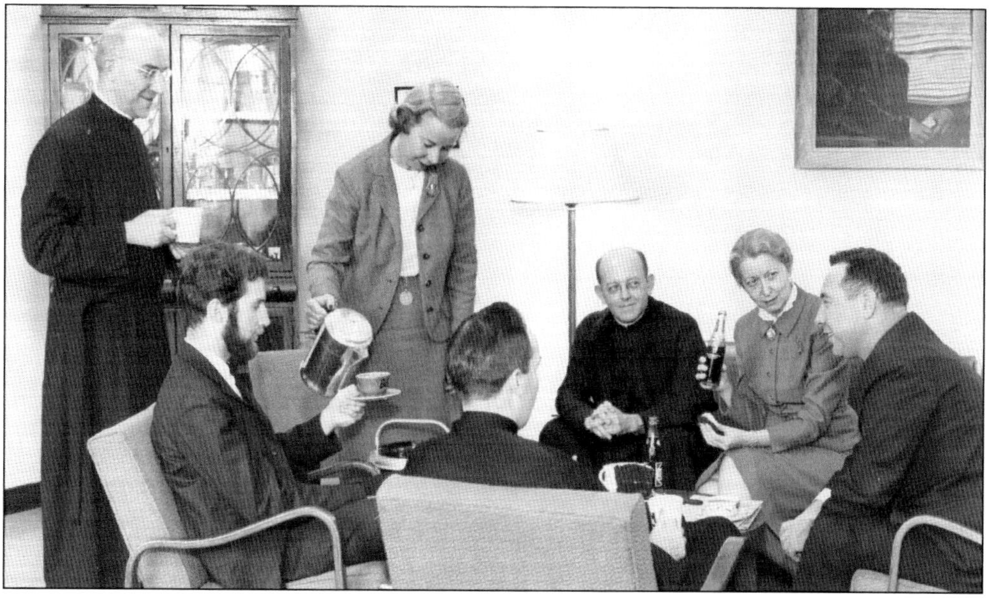

Kaffeeklatsch. From the beginning, faculty have not only worked but also socialized with each other. This is an early Kaffeeklatsch (coffee club). By the late 1960s, the academic dean, Thomas Wack, had started to sponsor TGIF parties for the faculty—usually after faculty meetings, but often on other Fridays as well.

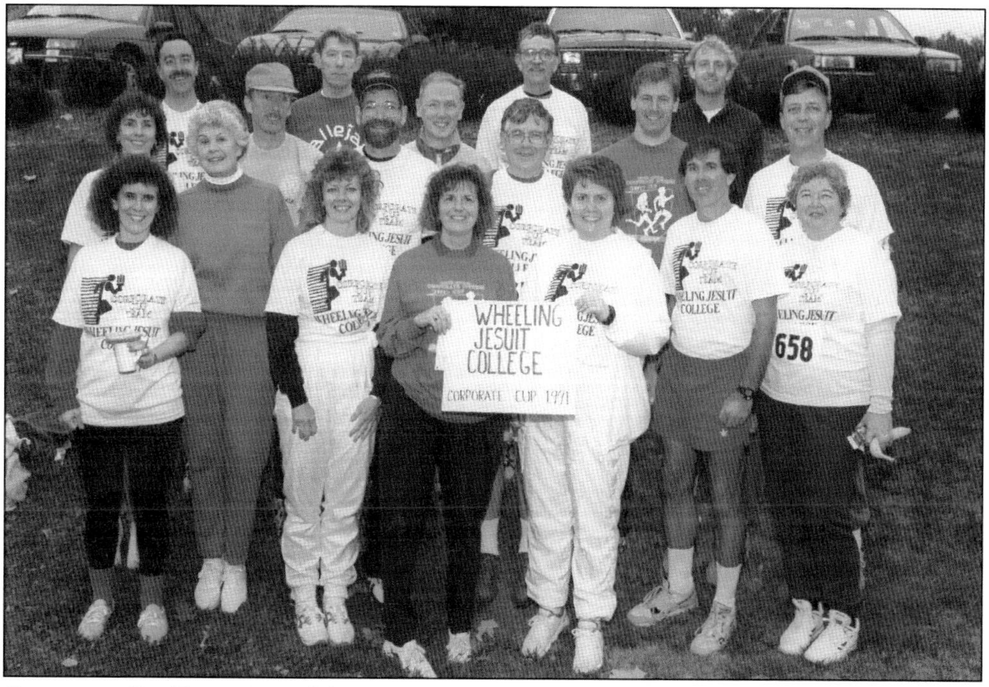

Corporate Cup Team. One of the important ways that faculty and administrators developed a sense of community was through team participation in events. One of the most popular was the annual Corporate Cup competition between teams from various companies and organizations in the Wheeling area. Although the university had individual standouts, it rarely won a trophy.

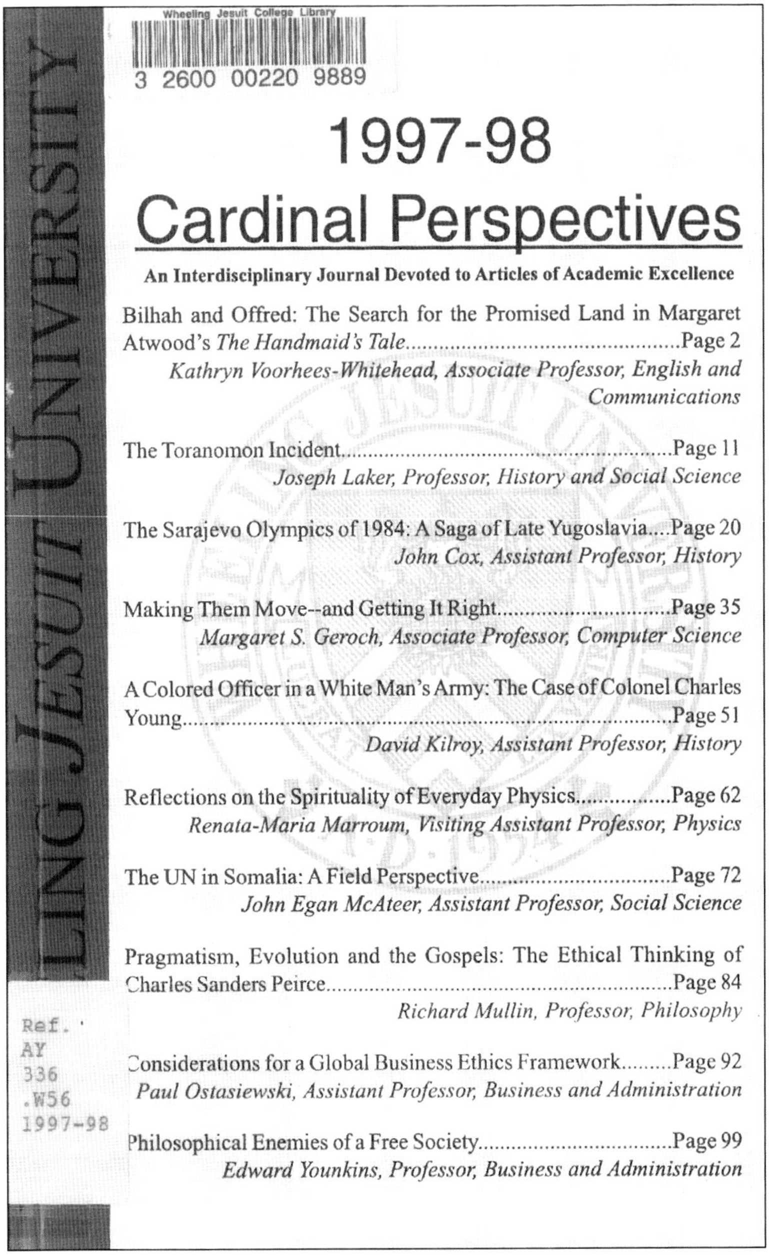

LING JESUIT UNIVERSITY

1997-98

Cardinal Perspectives

An Interdisciplinary Journal Devoted to Articles of Academic Excellence

FACULTY RESEARCH JOURNAL. In October 1966, Wheeling faculty launched an in-house journal called *Avalanche*; 10 faculty members contributed essays, poems, and translations, but the effort died after one issue. They tried again in 1979 with the *Wheeling Annual*, and between 1979 and 2008, the publication was produced nearly every year (there were three years without a journal). The name changed to *Cardinal Perspectives* in 1993. During this 30-year period, some 231 articles and reviews were printed in the journal. Some articles were revised and got into peer-reviewed journals and books. Awards were given each year for the three best articles. At first, the awards were $100, $75, and $50; but by 1999, they had grown to $500, $300, and $200. The journal made faculty aware of what their colleagues were working on and created a sense that Wheeling was a community of scholars.

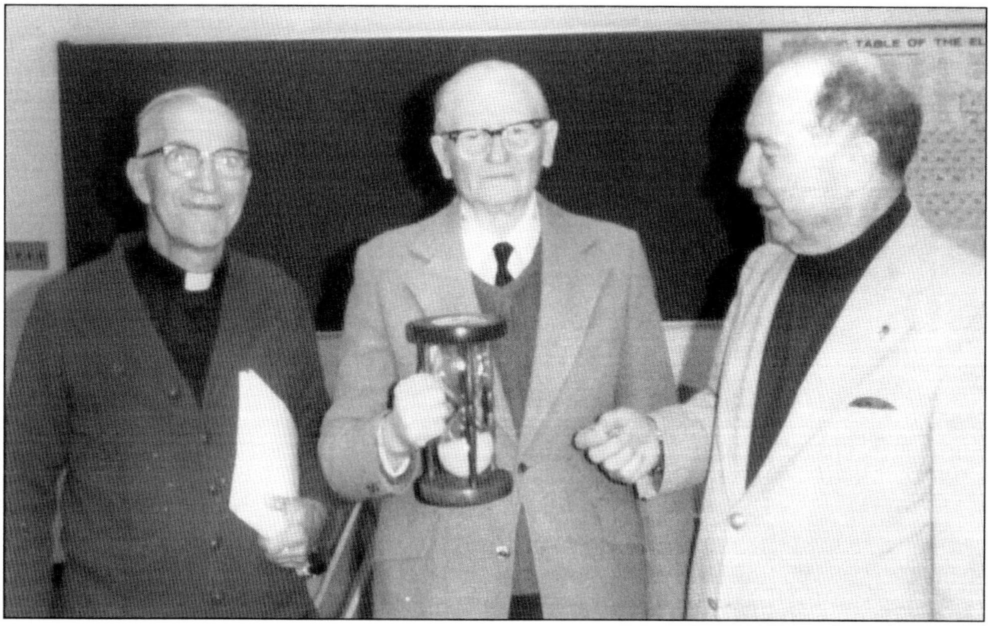

Professor Alexander Retires. Dr. George Alexander holds the gift that he received upon his official retirement from teaching. Dr. Alexander, who was known as Alexander Novak for most of his career at Wheeling Jesuit, taught German. Flanking Dr. Alexander are Fr. Joseph Hanzley, SJ (left), a professor of biology who came to the college in 1956, and Dr. Bruno Hartung, professor of economics.

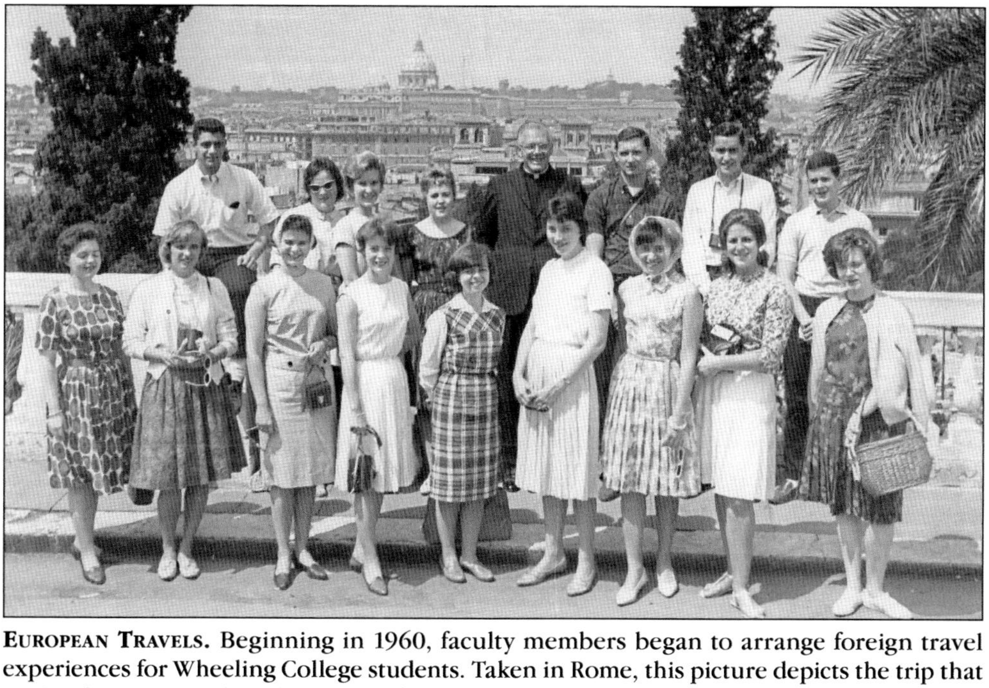

European Travels. Beginning in 1960, faculty members began to arrange foreign travel experiences for Wheeling College students. Taken in Rome, this picture depicts the trip that Fr. Stephen Laut took with students from May 24 to July 8, 1963. Students traveled by ship from New York to Amsterdam, and then visited the Swiss Alps, Rome, Paris, and London before returning to New York by steamer. The cost was around $1,200.

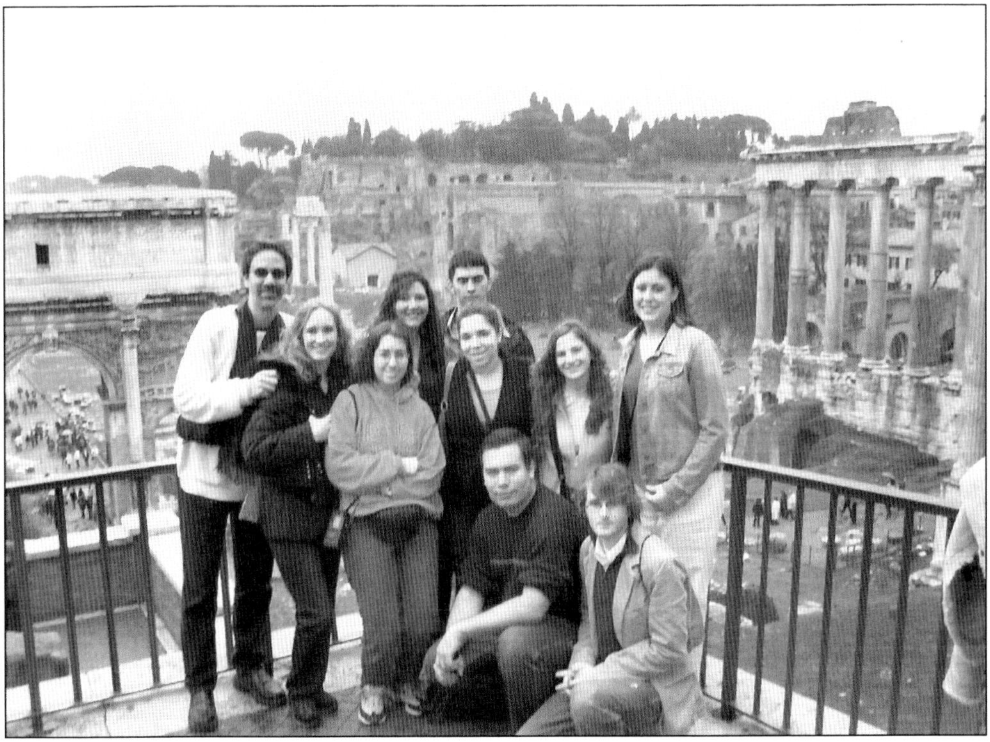

Laut Scholars Tour Italy. In the spring of 2011, associate professor John Whitehead, director of the Laut Scholars program, took students to Italy for one week. Here, they pose in Rome.

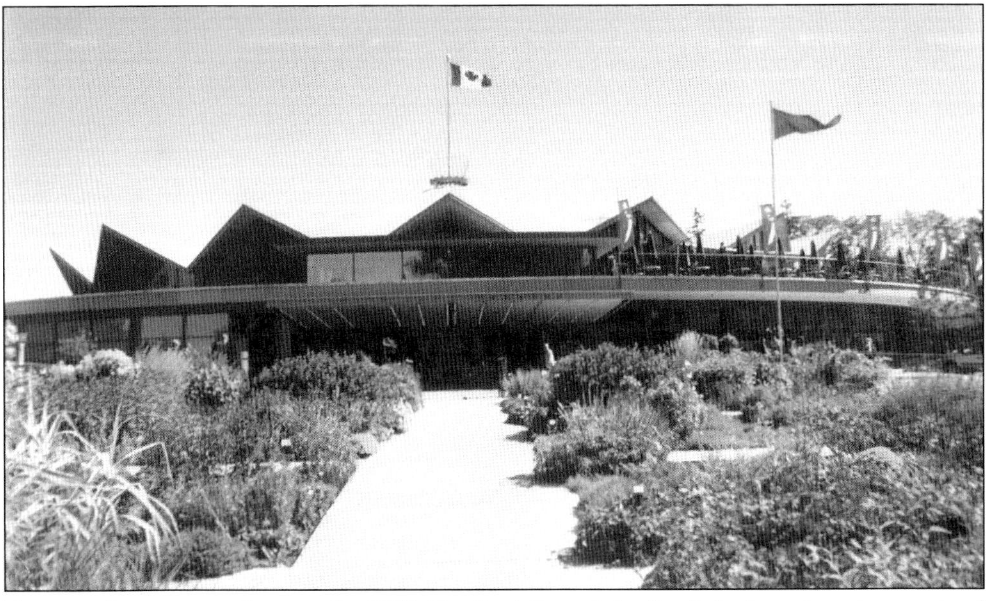

Trips to Stratford, Canada. In 1969, Dr. Paul Orr of the English department organized an annual trip to Stratford, Ontario, for students and faculty to see first-class dramatic performances, especially of Shakespeare's plays. One Wheeling Jesuit student who attended, Dathan Williams, became a professional actor and later appeared at the Festival Theatre, which is pictured here. The trips continue today.

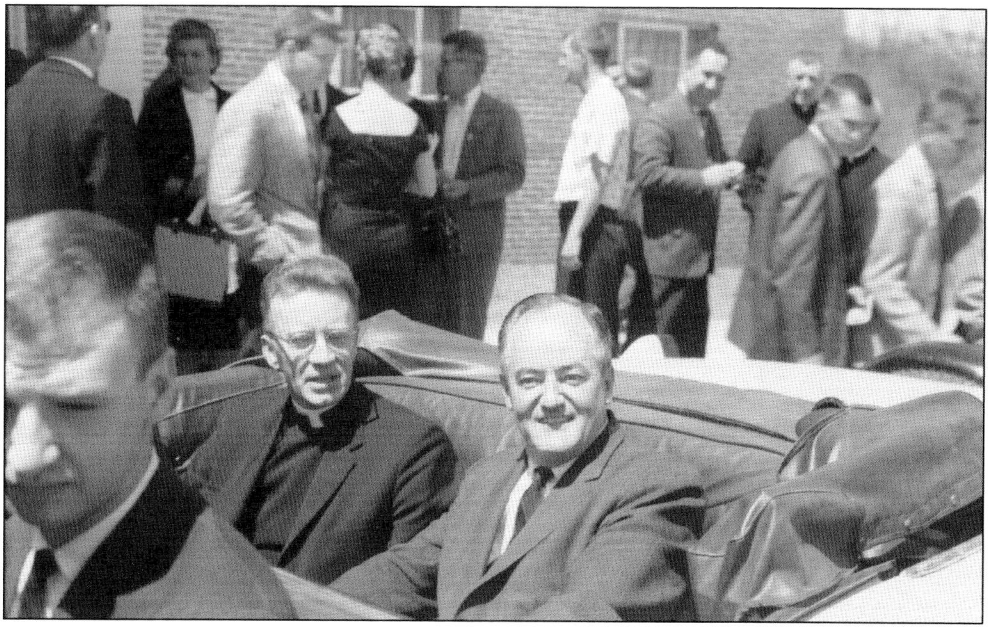

PRIMARY ELECTION. Sen. Hubert Humphrey visited Wheeling College as part of his campaign to win the Democratic nomination for president in 1960. His main rival in West Virginia's primary was Sen. John Kennedy, a Catholic who avoided Wheeling College and instead spoke at nearby West Liberty State. Here, Humphrey (right) is accompanied by Fr. William Troy, the college's president. Humphrey was well received but dropped out of the race when Kennedy took 61 percent of the vote.

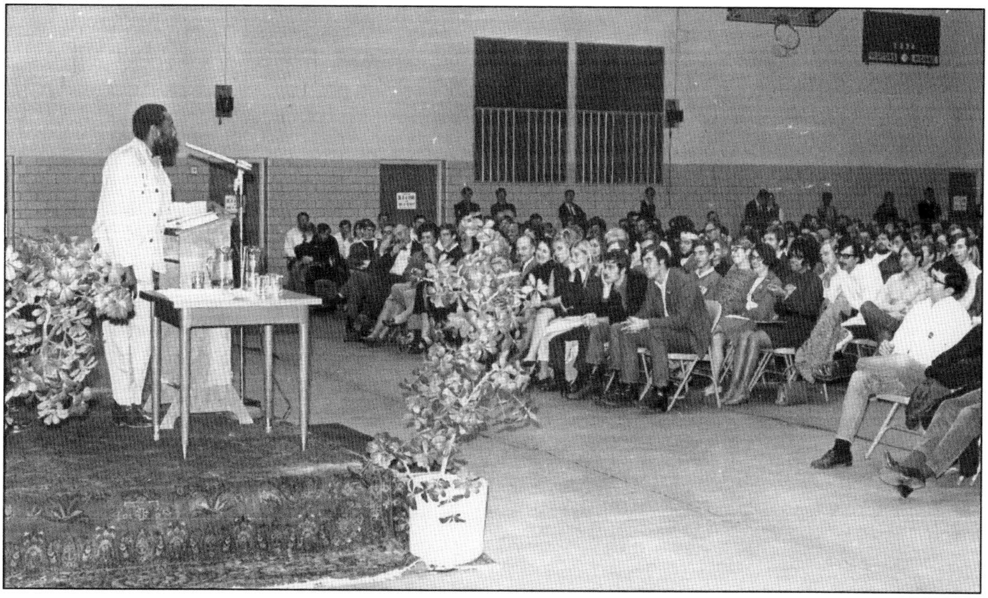

DICK GREGORY. Comedian and political activist Dick Gregory speaks to a large crowd of Wheeling College students on October 16, 1968. The presidential candidate of the Peace and Freedom Party, Gregory claimed that the country suffered from moral pollution and a corrupt establishment and called for fair treatment of all minorities. It cost $2,000 to get him to campus.

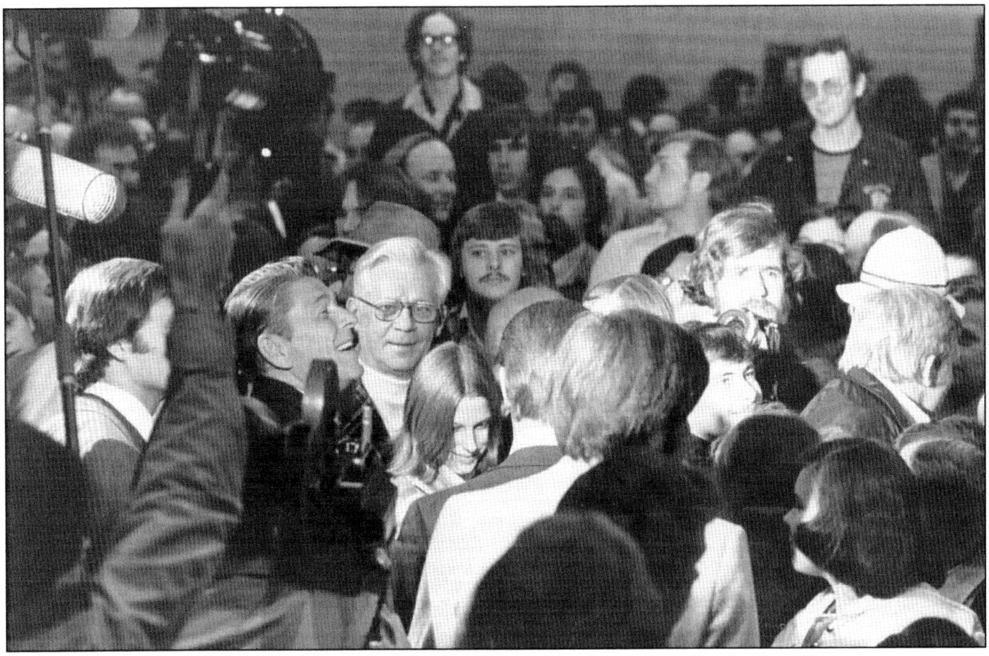

Ronald Reagan's Visit in 1976. Reagan appeared at Wheeling College on May 4, 1976, when he was running against Gerald Ford in the Republican presidential primary. Ford won the primary and the nomination but lost the presidency to Jimmy Carter. Students, faculty, and staff were among the more than 1,200 people who jammed the field house.

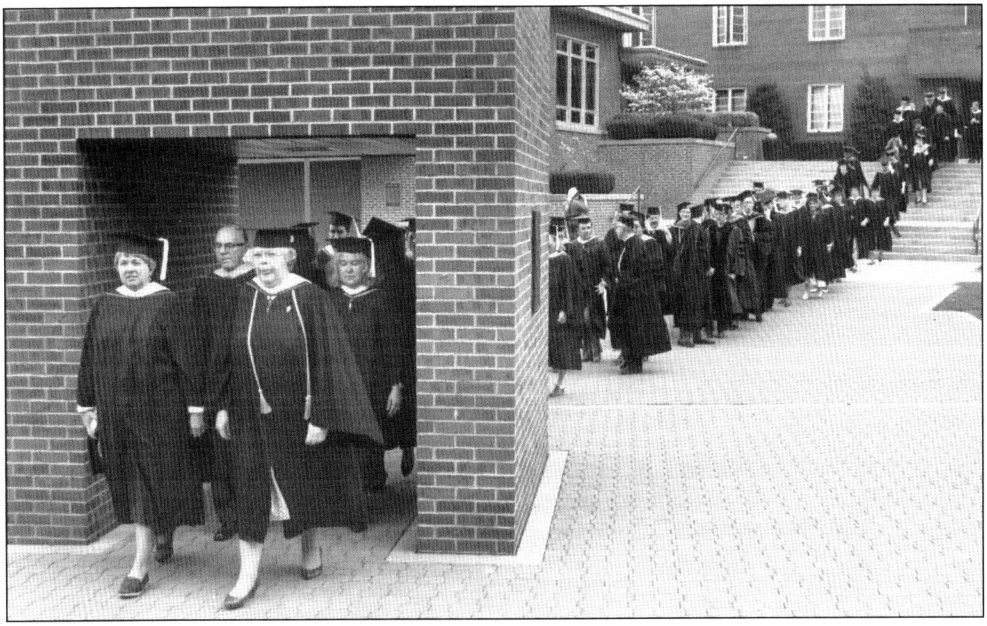

Spring Honors Convocation. Most years, faculty don their academic caps and gowns on only five occasions: opening convocation at the beginning of the semester, fall and spring honors assemblies, baccalaureate Mass, and graduation. Here, Margaret Geroch (left), chair of faculty council, and registrar Kitty McCready lead the faculty and administrators from the library to the chapel in the spring of 1988.

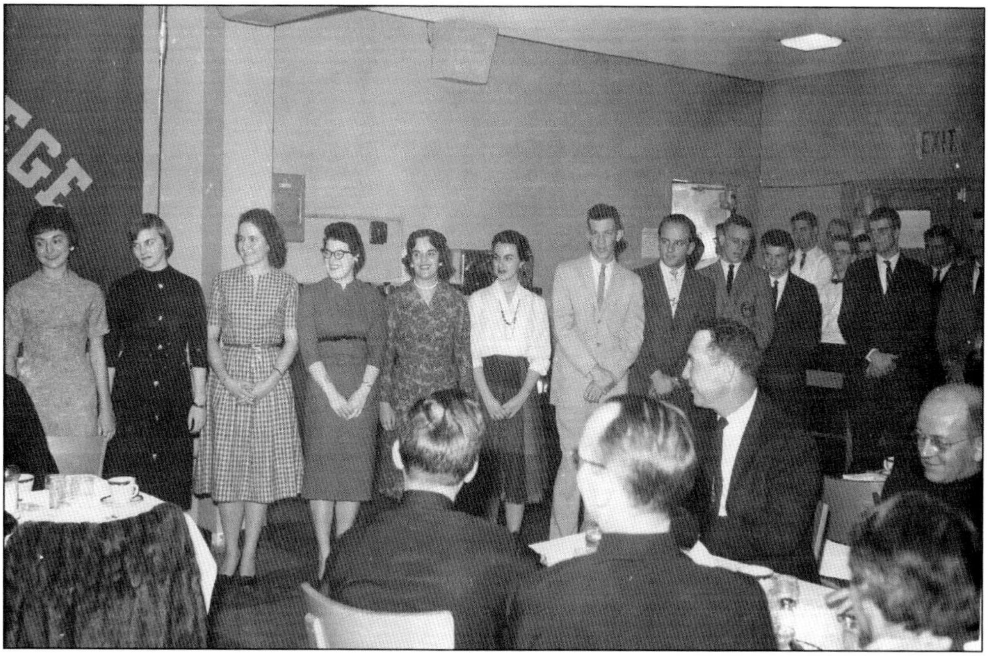

ALPHA SIGMA NU. Induction into the Jesuit Honors Society—Alpha Sigma Nu—is a prestigious event at Wheeling. The society, founded at Marquette in 1915, was once limited to men. In 1924, Gamma Pi Epsilon, a companion society for women, was created. The two societies merged in 1973. In 1960, Wheeling inducted six men and six women into their respective societies.

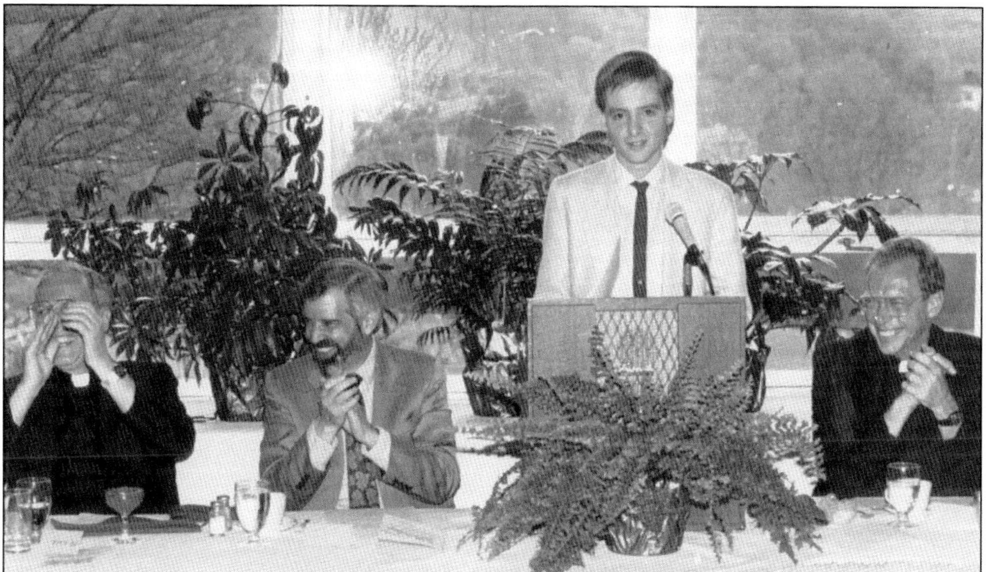

SENIOR AWARDS DINNER. The most important academic event celebrating student excellence is the senior awards banquet that occurs two days before graduation. Various departments and administrative units give numerous awards. In 1988, the senior speaker, chosen by the class more for popularity than academic excellence, was Joseph Conway II. He obviously has President Acker, SJ (far left), and others at the main table in stitches.

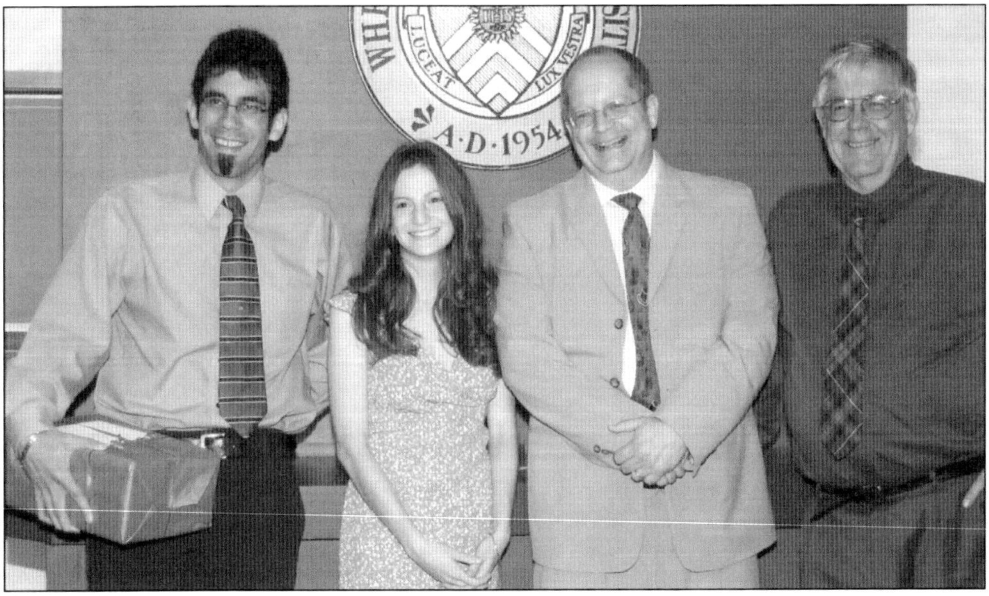

History Award. Pictured here are, from left to right, Hal Gorby, Jessica Blissit, Dr. John Cox (chairman of the History Department), and Dr. Joseph Laker (teacher of the senior seminar). In 2007, the winners of the two history prizes were Gorby (John Wack Prize) and Blissit (Joseph Kennedy Award). Almost every department gives one or two prizes to its outstanding students at a dinner held the Thursday before graduation.

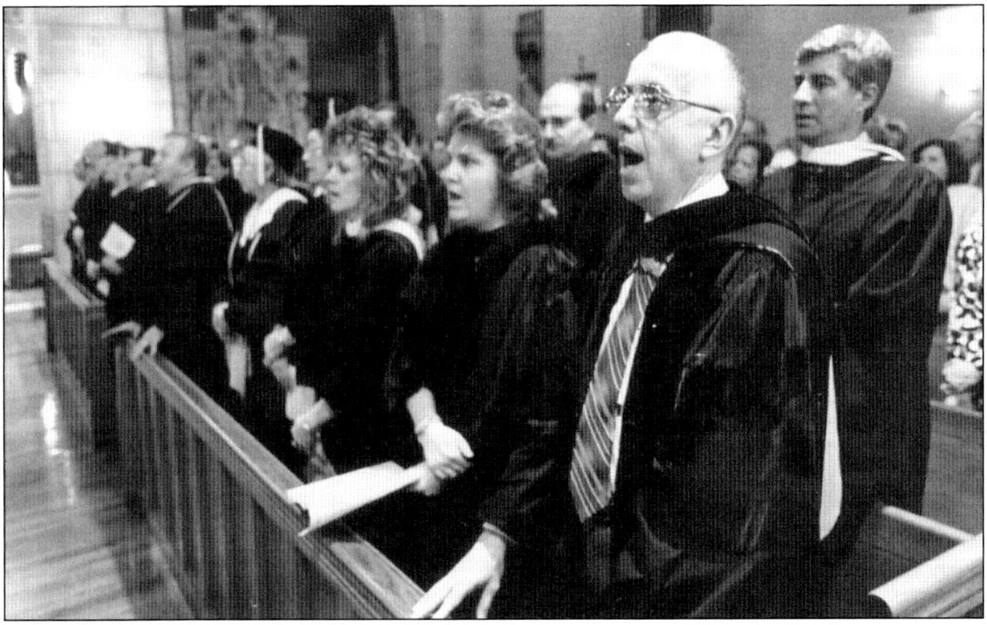

Faculty at Baccalaureate. The celebratory Mass held on the eve of graduation is the most ceremonial event that most students experience during their college years. Some faculty attending this 1988 baccalaureate in St. Michael's Church are, from left to right, (first row) Thomas Wack (English), Betty Thacker (biology), Margie Bowman (nursing), Rose Kutlenios (nursing), Tom Knorr (physics); (second row) Rick Pomazal (business), and Dennis Maceiko (psychology).

Baccalaureate Mass. Priests, followed by faculty, administrators, and then students, leave St. Joseph's Cathedral in downtown Wheeling after the 1965 baccalaureate Mass. Following the Mass, the crowd returned to campus for the most elaborate party of the year.

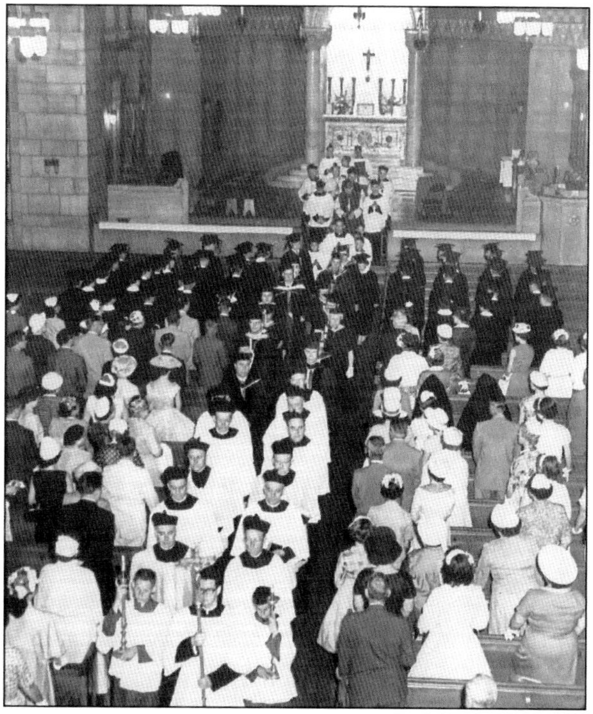

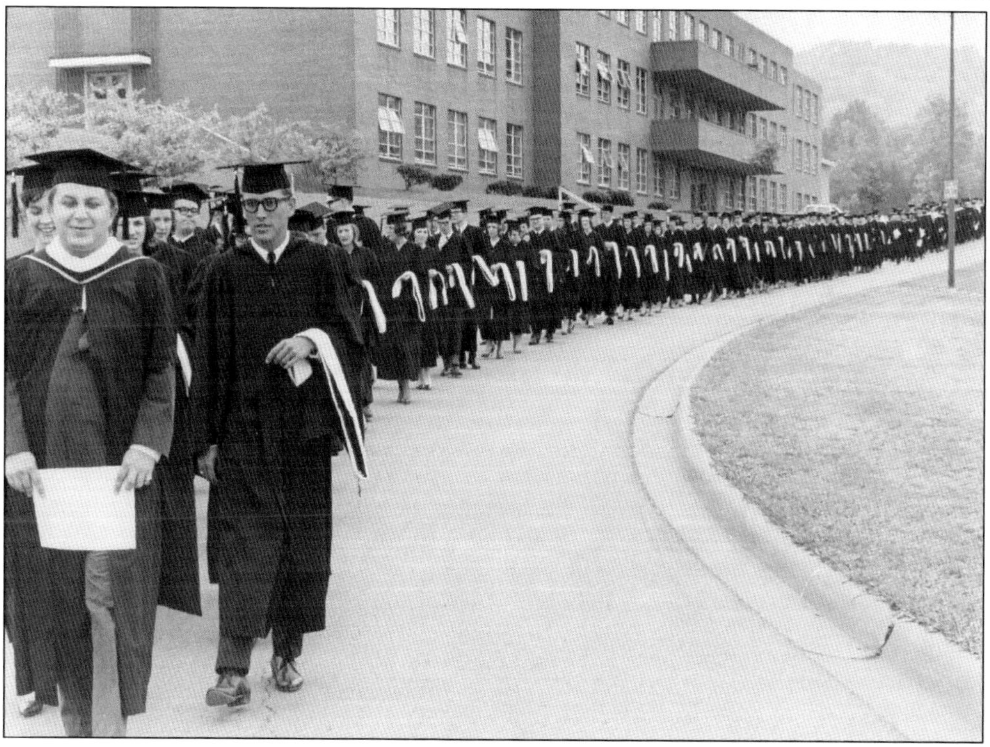

Graduation Procession. John Wack, associate professor of history, leads the students, followed by the faculty and administration, in the 1965 graduation procession from Swint Hall to the gymnasium. Students carry their hoods; faculty and administrators wear theirs.

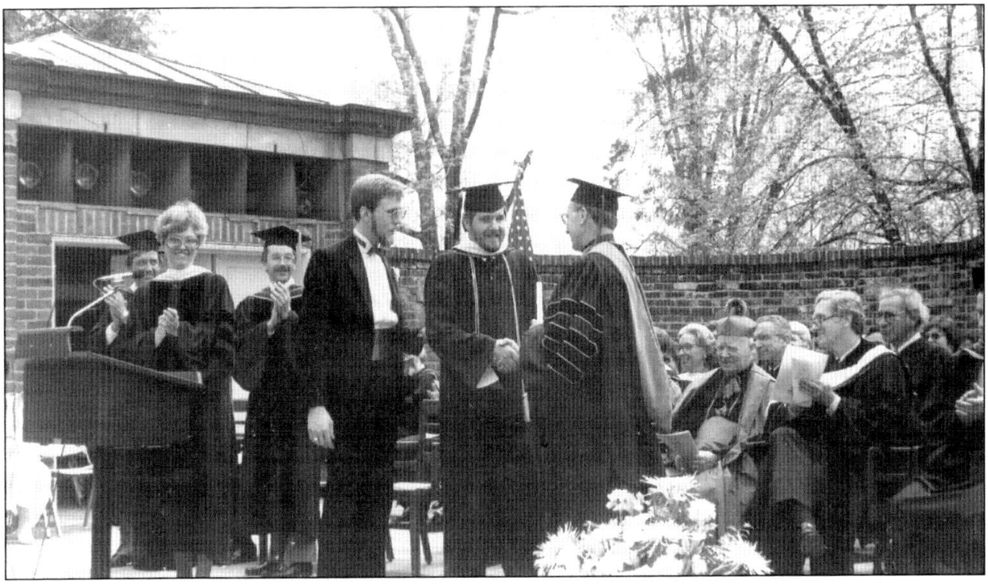

Valedictorian. In this May 1983 photograph, Robert L. Hicks III receives his diploma from Pres. Thomas Acker in Oglebay Park. Hicks, who was blind, was the valedictorian of his class, graduating summa cum laude and receiving the Henry F. Paul Medal for having the highest four-year GPA. (Courtesy of the Wheeling-Charleston Diocese Archives.)

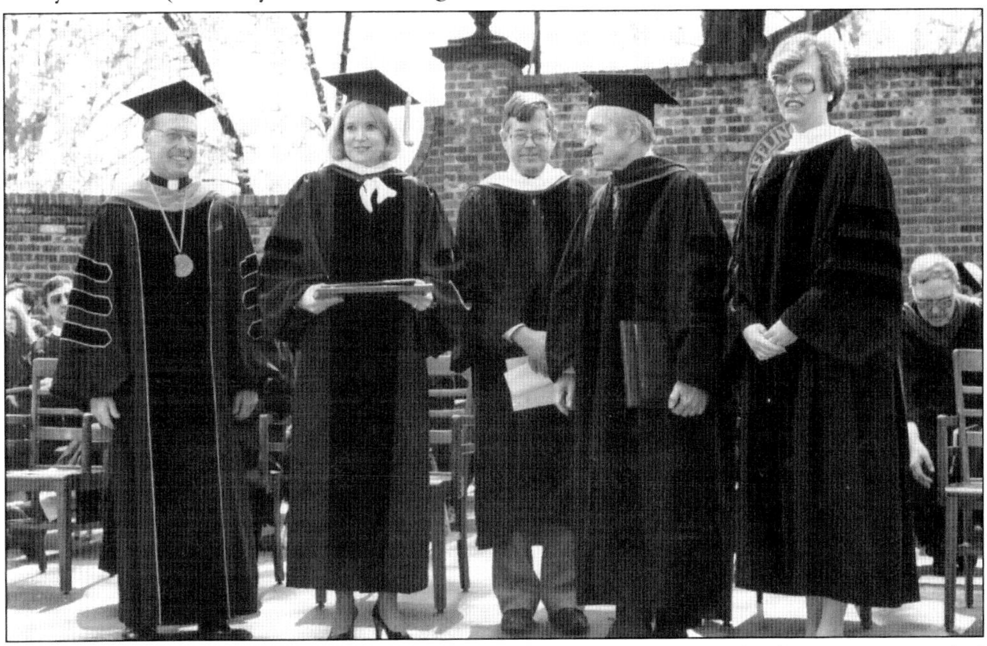

Honorary Degrees. At the May 1984 graduation in Oglebay Park, Wheeling Jesuit awarded honorary doctorates in law and the humanities to Charles Percy, chairman of the Senate Foreign Relations Committee, and Sharon Percy Rockefeller, chair of the board of public broadcasting and the wife of then governor of West Virginia Jay Rockefeller. Sharon Rockefeller gave the main commencement address. From left to right are Pres. Acker, SJ; Sharon Rockefeller; Dr. Joseph Laker; Charles Percy; and Dr. Jeanne Kammer, academic vice president (Courtesy of the Wheeling-Charleston Diocese Archives.)

Four

Student Life on Campus

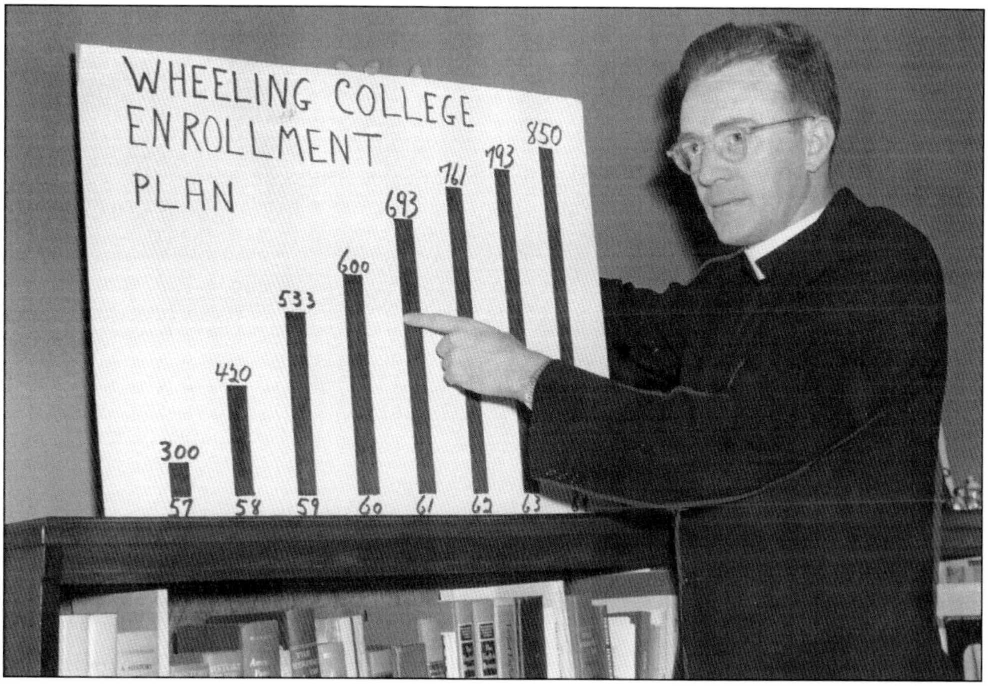

College Enrollment Hopes. In this 1960 photograph, Pres. William Troy illustrates the optimism of the founders of the college in depicting how rapidly enrollment is expected to rise. The dream was largely achieved by 1964, but then internal divisions within the college, financial difficulties, and stresses connected to the Vietnam War led to a decade of slow growth.

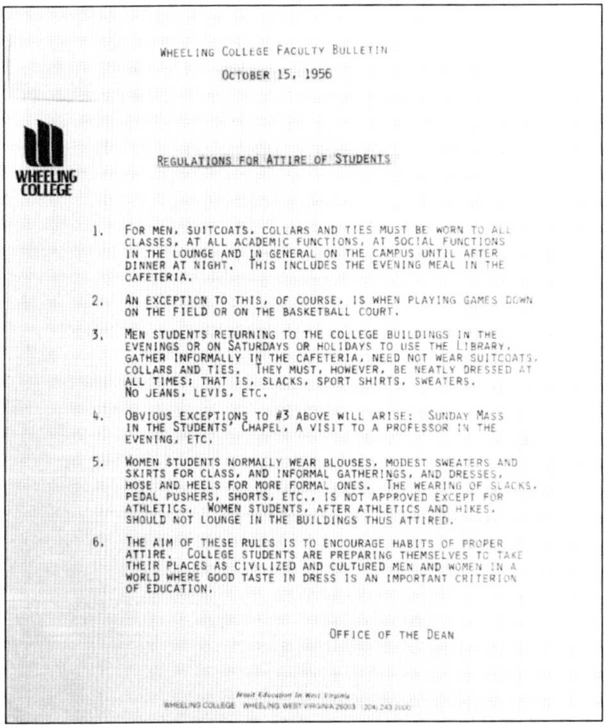

WHEELING COLLEGE FACULTY BULLETIN

OCTOBER 15, 1956

WHEELING COLLEGE

REGULATIONS FOR ATTIRE OF STUDENTS

1. FOR MEN, SUITCOATS, COLLARS AND TIES MUST BE WORN TO ALL CLASSES, AT ALL ACADEMIC FUNCTIONS, AT SOCIAL FUNCTIONS IN THE LOUNGE AND IN GENERAL ON THE CAMPUS UNTIL AFTER DINNER AT NIGHT. THIS INCLUDES THE EVENING MEAL IN THE CAFETERIA.

2. AN EXCEPTION TO THIS, OF COURSE, IS WHEN PLAYING GAMES DOWN ON THE FIELD OR ON THE BASKETBALL COURT.

3. MEN STUDENTS RETURNING TO THE COLLEGE BUILDINGS IN THE EVENINGS OR ON SATURDAYS OR HOLIDAYS TO USE THE LIBRARY, GATHER INFORMALLY IN THE CAFETERIA, NEED NOT WEAR SUITCOATS, COLLARS AND TIES. THEY MUST, HOWEVER, BE NEATLY DRESSED AT ALL TIMES; THAT IS, SLACKS, SPORT SHIRTS, SWEATERS. NO JEANS, LEVIS, ETC.

4. OBVIOUS EXCEPTIONS TO #3 ABOVE WILL ARISE: SUNDAY MASS IN THE STUDENTS' CHAPEL, A VISIT TO A PROFESSOR IN THE EVENING, ETC.

5. WOMEN STUDENTS NORMALLY WEAR BLOUSES, MODEST SWEATERS AND SKIRTS FOR CLASS, AND INFORMAL GATHERINGS, AND DRESSES, HOSE AND HEELS FOR MORE FORMAL ONES. THE WEARING OF SLACKS, PEDAL PUSHERS, SHORTS, ETC., IS NOT APPROVED EXCEPT FOR ATHLETICS. WOMEN STUDENTS, AFTER ATHLETICS AND HIKES, SHOULD NOT LOUNGE IN THE BUILDINGS THUS ATTIRED.

6. THE AIM OF THESE RULES IS TO ENCOURAGE HABITS OF PROPER ATTIRE. COLLEGE STUDENTS ARE PREPARING THEMSELVES TO TAKE THEIR PLACES AS CIVILIZED AND CULTURED MEN AND WOMEN IN A WORLD WHERE GOOD TASTE IN DRESS IS AN IMPORTANT CRITERION OF EDUCATION.

OFFICE OF THE DEAN

Jesuit Education in West Virginia
WHEELING COLLEGE WHEELING WEST VIRGINIA 26003 (304) 243-2000

ATTIRE REGULATIONS. The dress code outlined in this document expresses both the high expectations that the Jesuits have for students and the social values of American society in the 1950s. During the late 1960s and early 1970s, the college's ability and desire to control student behavior and dress dramatically declined.

STUDENT ELECTION. Bernice Eichenlaub '63 looks over some of the posters taped on the windows of Swint Hall during the 1962 student government election. The Jesuits encouraged students to create a student government so that they would not only have a stake in the school, but also a voice to make their concerns known to the administration.

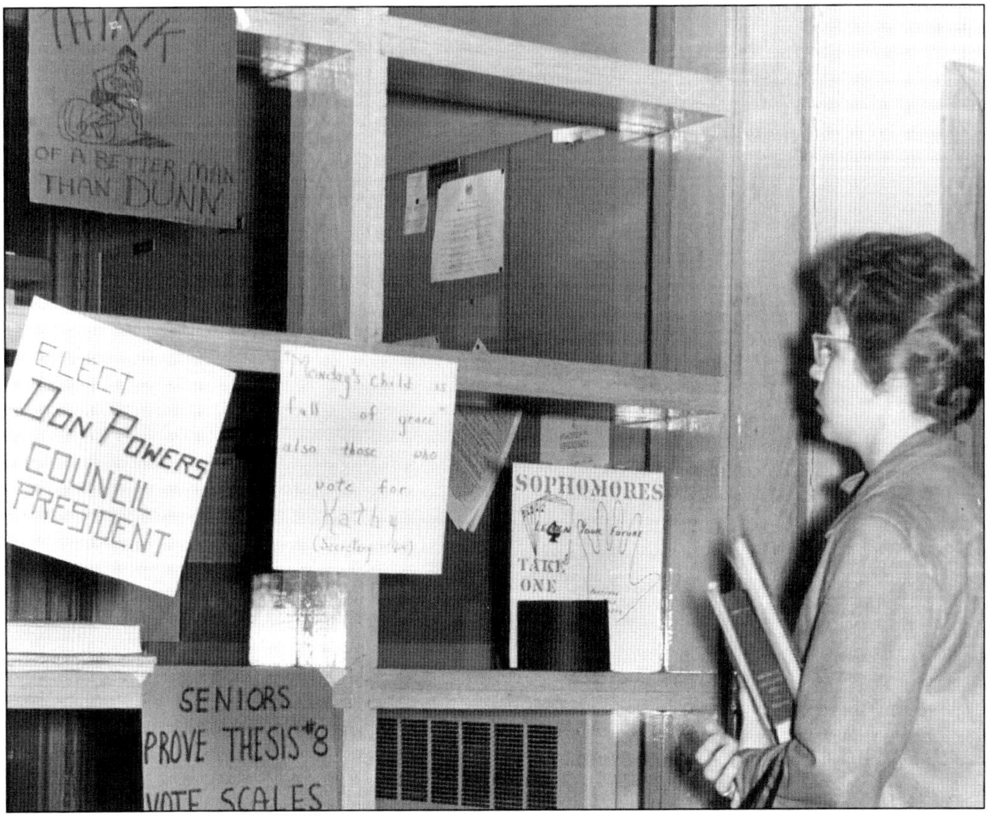

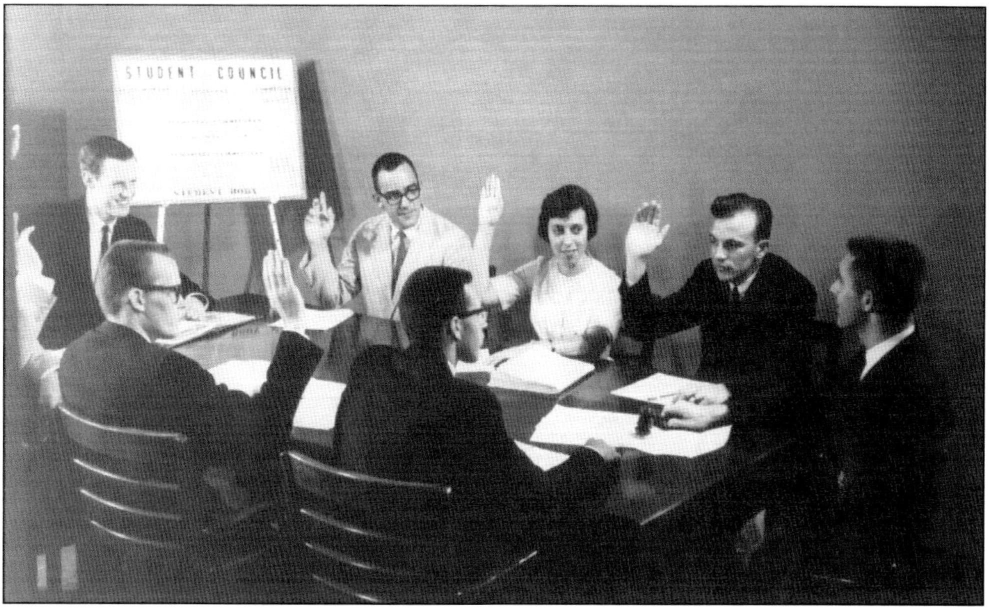

Student Executive Meeting. A 1963 meeting of the Executive Board of Student Government sees a vote on some question being approved with amusement on the part of most of the participants. The poster shows the structure of the student council at the end of the first year of the college's existence.

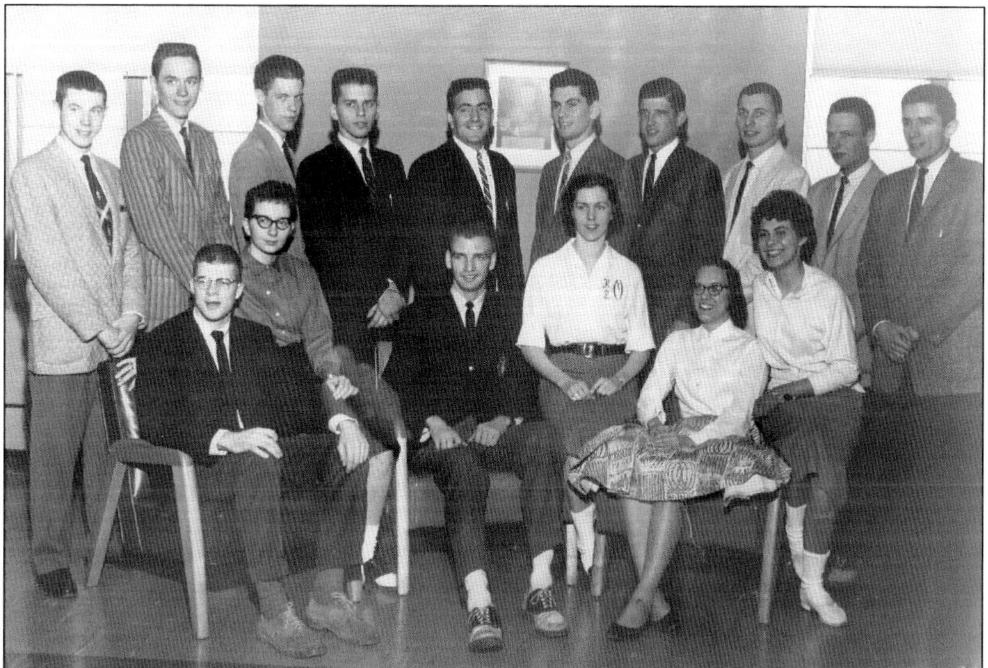

Student Government. The student council elected in May 1959 is composed of seven seniors, five juniors, and four sophomores (no freshmen, because they entered the college the following fall). The president, secretary, and treasurer are seniors, and the vice president is a junior. Over time, the number of students in campus government has only slightly increased.

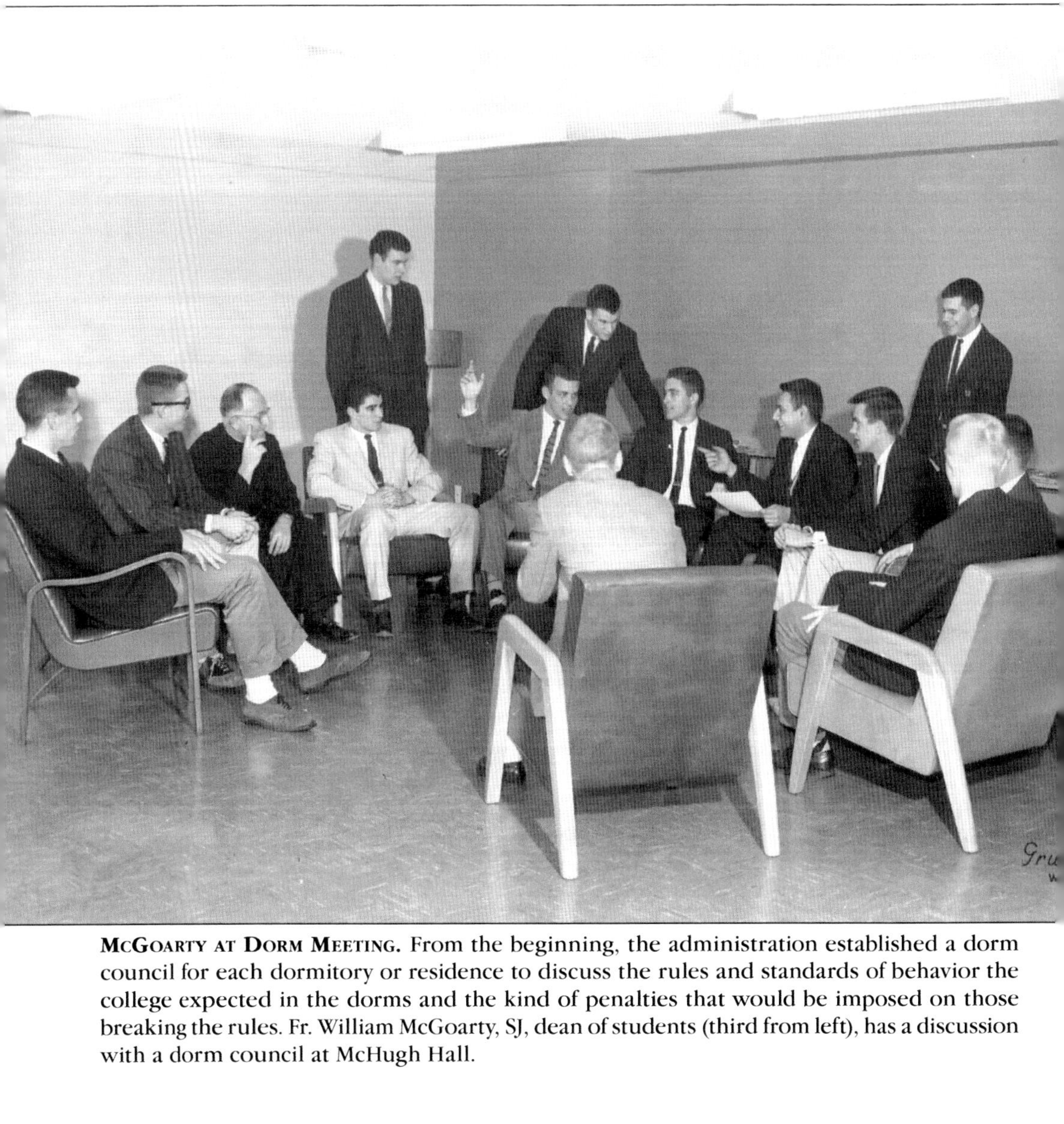

McGoarty at Dorm Meeting. From the beginning, the administration established a dorm council for each dormitory or residence to discuss the rules and standards of behavior the college expected in the dorms and the kind of penalties that would be imposed on those breaking the rules. Fr. William McGoarty, SJ, dean of students (third from left), has a discussion with a dorm council at McHugh Hall.

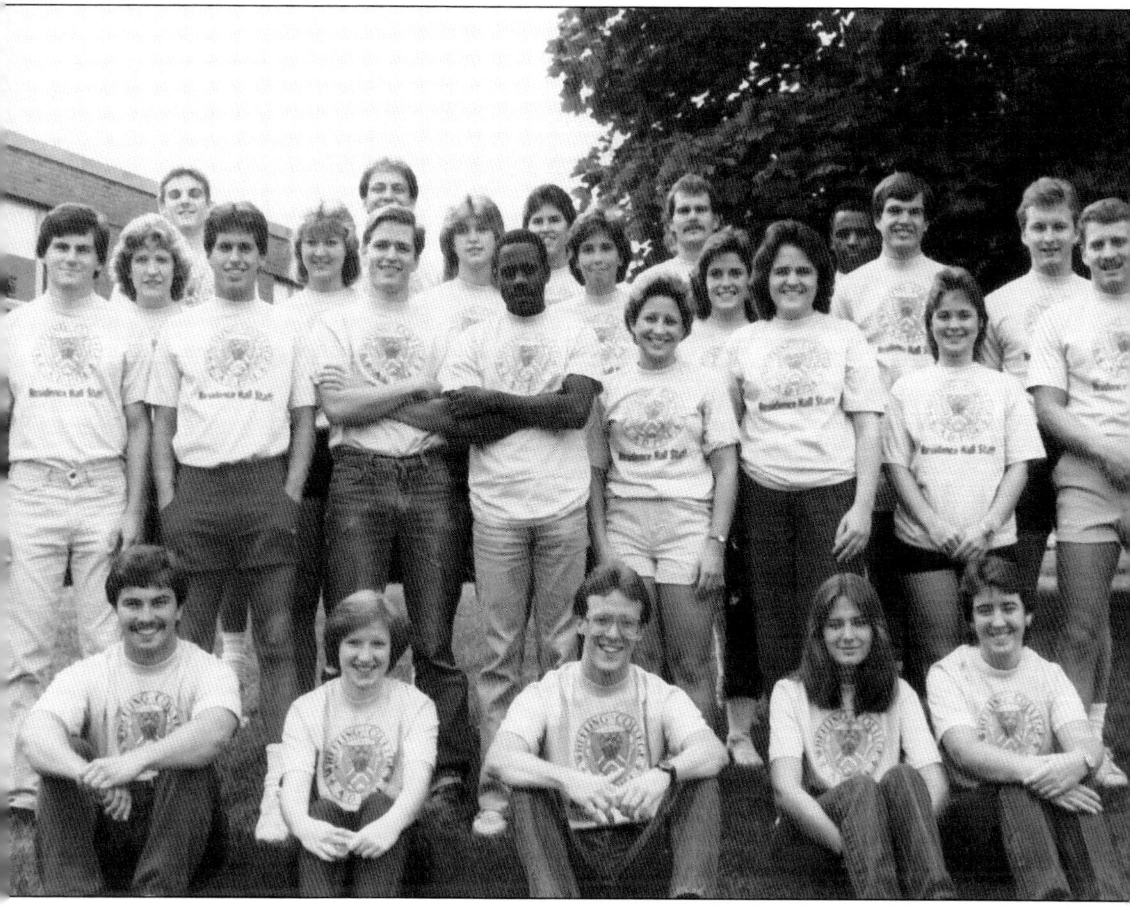

Resident Assistants. This group picture of the resident assistants of the late 1980s depicts individuals selected by student development to maintain order in the dormitories and ensure that the rules of behavior were followed. Student resident assistants are key liaisons between students and the college.

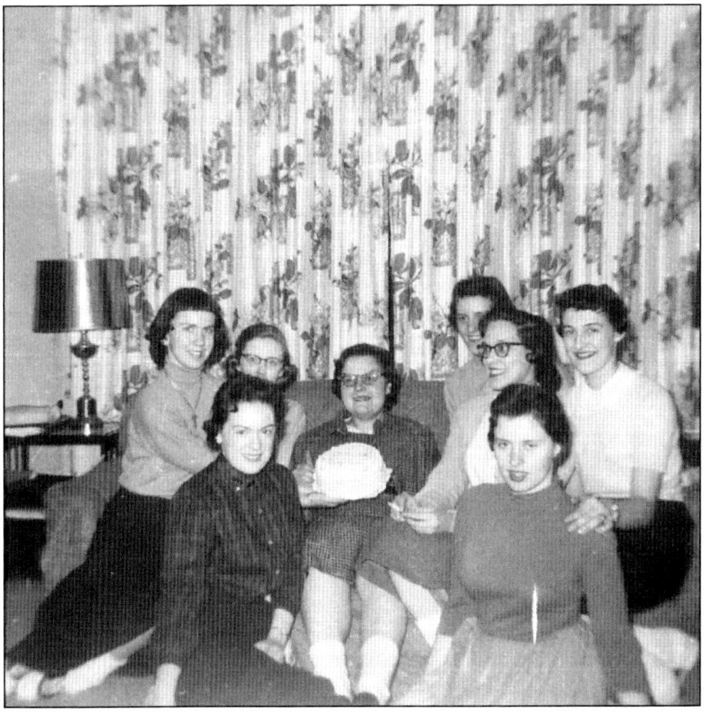

GIRLS OF DELLA STRADA. Since there was no women's dorm on campus until 1959, women from outside of the local area lived in houses purchased by the college, such as Avila, Marquette, and Della Strada. The eight girls pictured here lived at Della Strada, which was located near campus at 305 Washington Avenue. One of them was assigned the role of proctor and was responsible for keeping an account of when the girls came and went in the evenings.

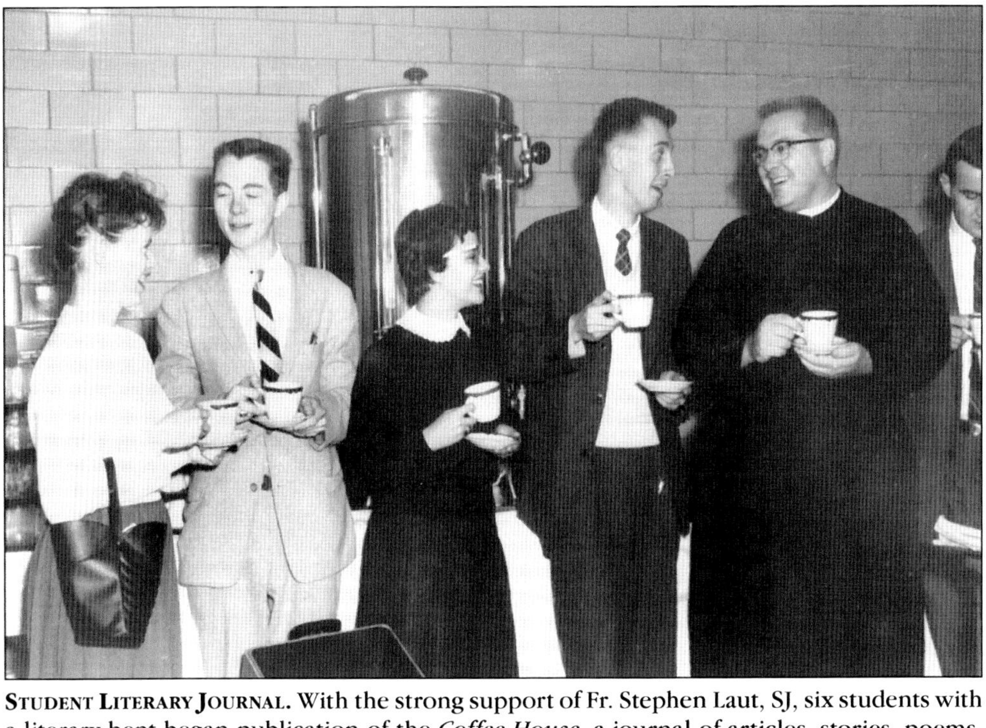

STUDENT LITERARY JOURNAL. With the strong support of Fr. Stephen Laut, SJ, six students with a literary bent began publication of the *Coffee House*, a journal of articles, stories, poems, translations, and book and movie reviews. The students claimed the journal would come out three times per academic year, but it rarely did. In 1980, a new literary journal, *Jewelweed*, made its appearance and has been regularly published each year in late spring.

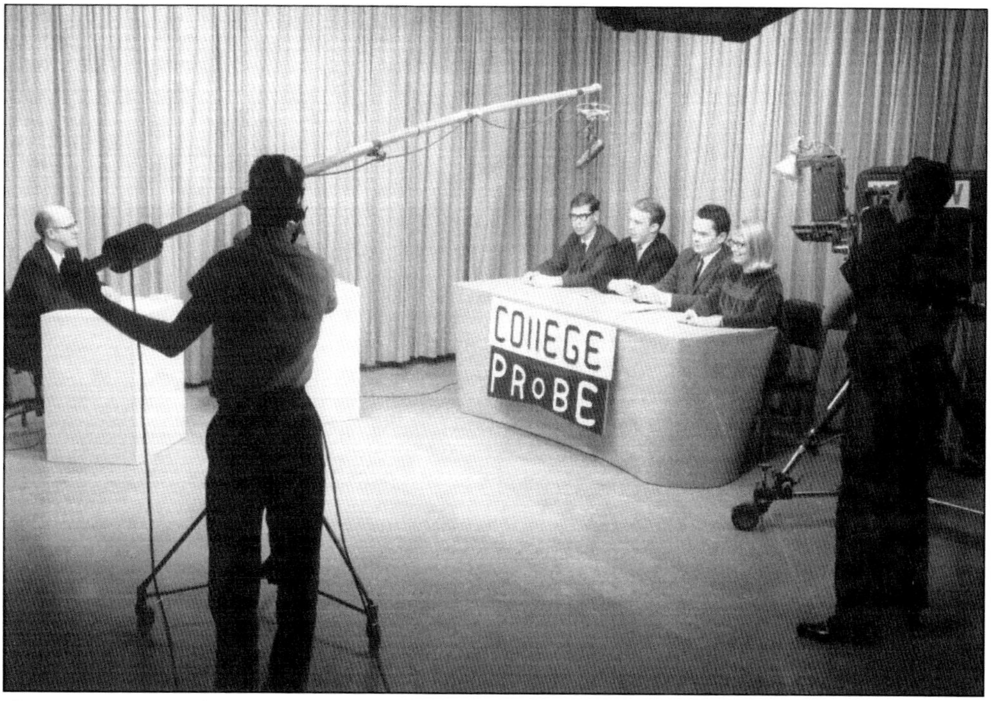

College Probe. The WTRF television station briefly carried a half-hour program called *College Probe* on Sundays at 2:30 p.m. The show featured two students from Wheeling and two students from Bethany College serving as a panel that interviewed local scholars on topics such as the United Nations, the Test Ban Treaty of 1963, and so on.

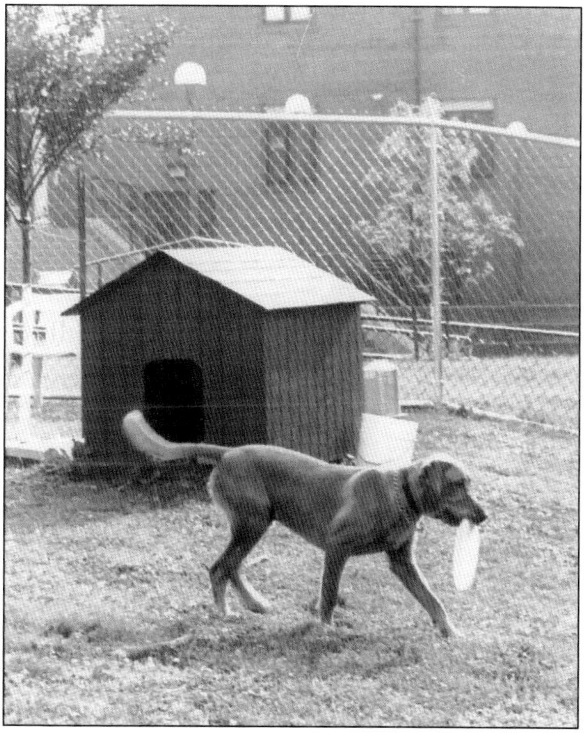

Ignatius, School Mascot? Pres. Thomas Acker, SJ, tried to boost school spirit and a sense of community by urging the adoption of a live mascot. He first suggested a llama, but turned to a dog when students rejected the llama. The dog, named Ignatius, was kept in a fenced enclosure between Donahue and Swint Halls. However, students remained loyal to the Cardinal and rejected the administration-imposed mascot. After some months, Ignatius was sent to a new, off-campus home.

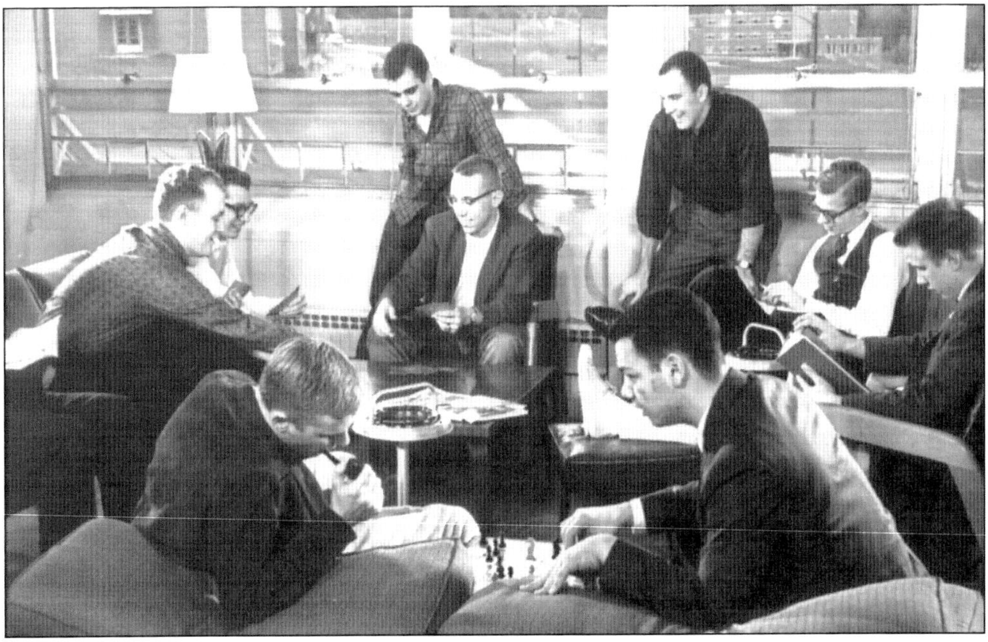

Relaxation Time. Male students are reading, playing cards and chess, or just watching the action in the second floor lounge of McHugh Hall in the this early-1960s picture. Through the window, Donahue Hall is on the left and Sara Tracy dorm is on the right. (Courtesy of Fr. Joseph Sanders, SJ.)

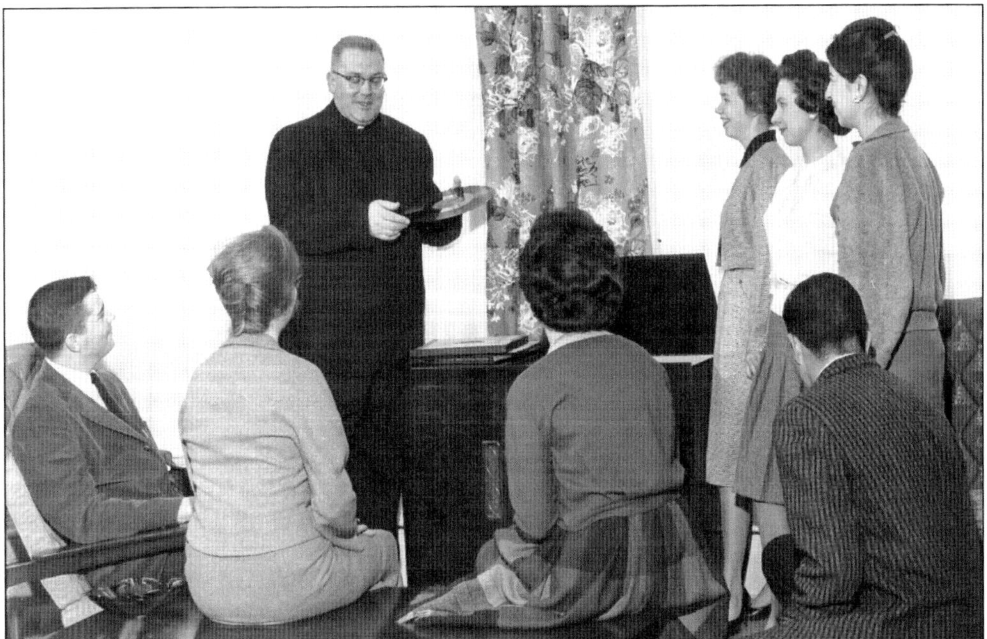

Music Appreciation. Although Wheeling College had no formal course in music in its early years, Fr. Stephen Laut, SJ, head of the English department, helped students learn to appreciate good music by playing records in Sara Tracy lounge on Sunday afternoons. In this photograph from February 12, 1961, he is playing Giacomo Puccini's opera *La Bohème*.

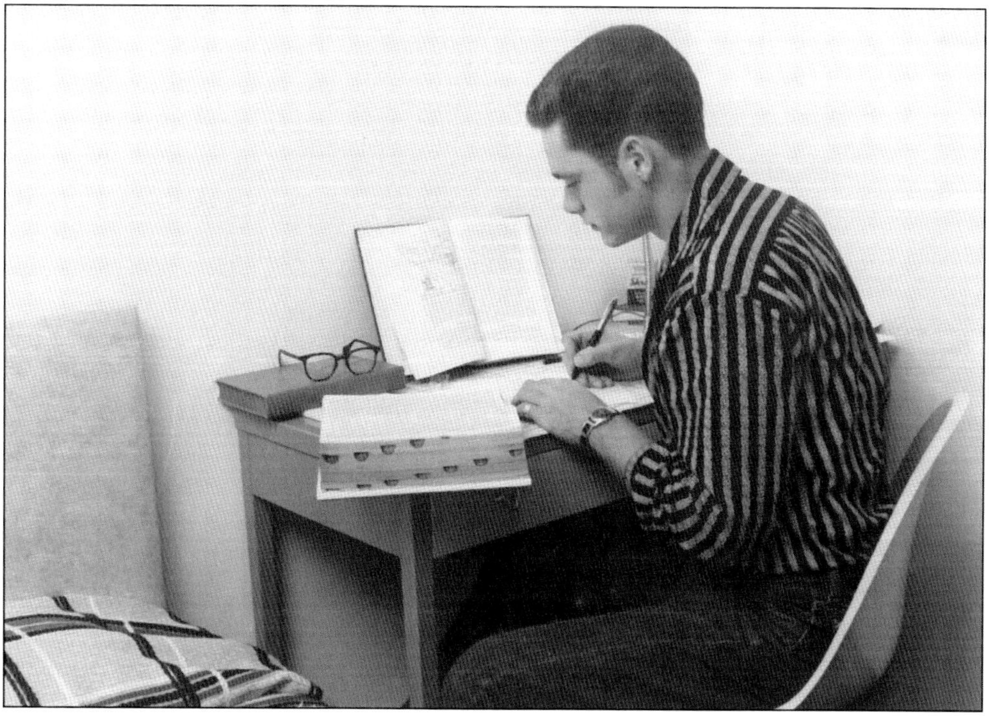

MALE STUDENT IN DORM. Michael Couglin '60 writes a history paper in his dorm room in Whelan Hall during the 1956–1957 academic year. The desk seems small and the conditions spartan compared to today's student housing.

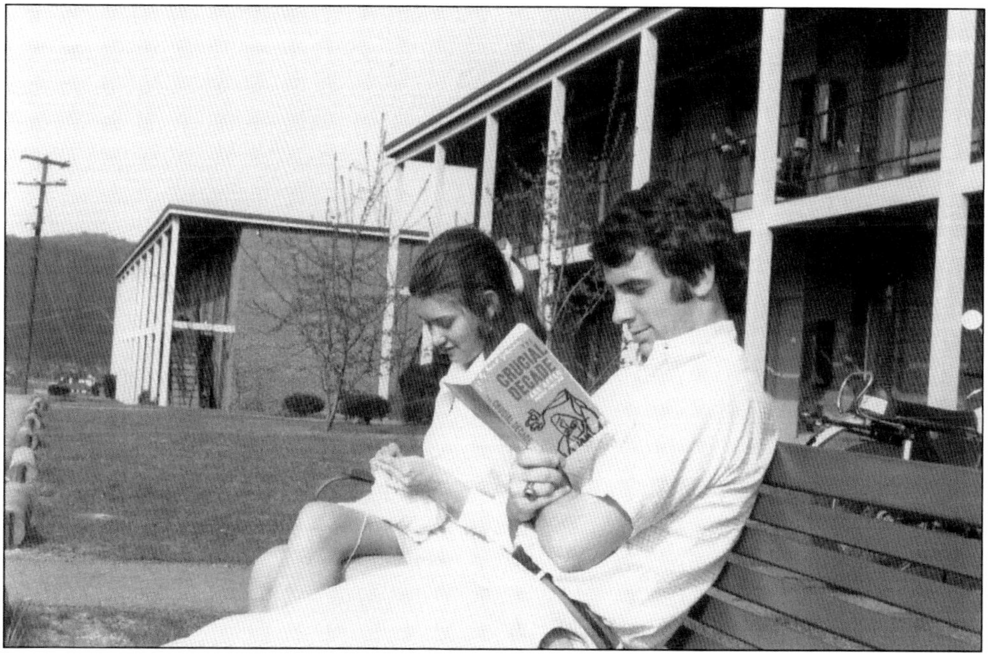

STUDENTS AT WORK. Two students relax in front of the Hill Apartments. The man is reading Eric F. Goldman's *The Crucial Decade—and After: America, 1945–1960*, while the woman knits. The clothing, hairstyles, and book date the picture to around the late 1960s.

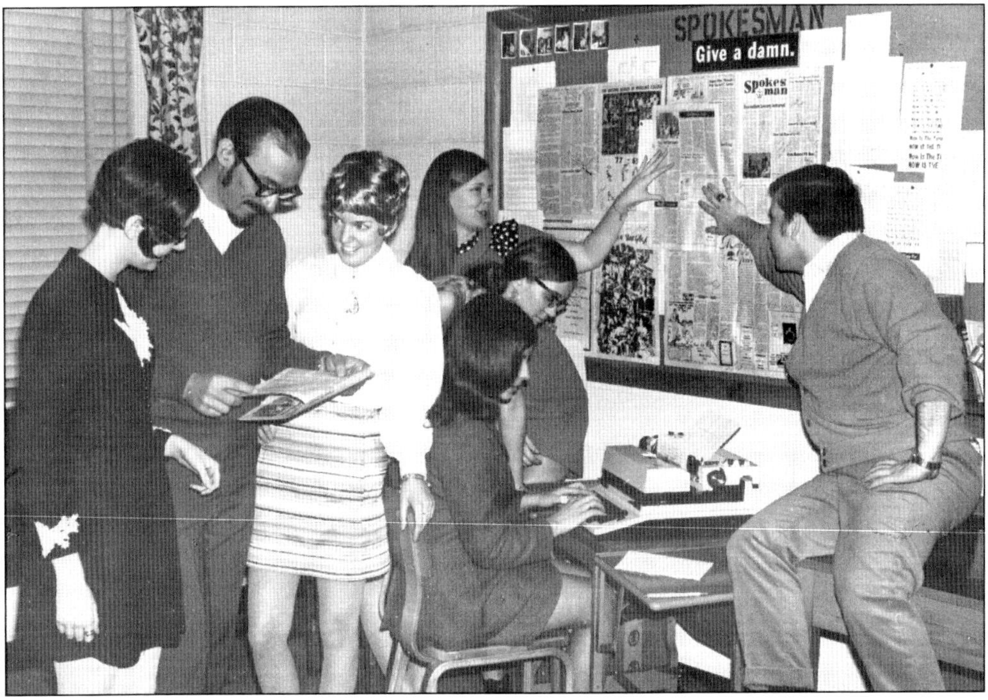

Keeping Students Informed. Wheeling College students turned out the first edition of the student newspaper, *The Spokesman,* on November 22, 1955. The name refers to a helmsman of a riverboat—appropriate, since Wheeling is located on the Ohio River. For several years, the paper stopped publication due to insufficient student interest and lack of a moderator, but it was revived and called *Nova,* then *The Spokesman,* and, now, *The Cardinal Connection.*

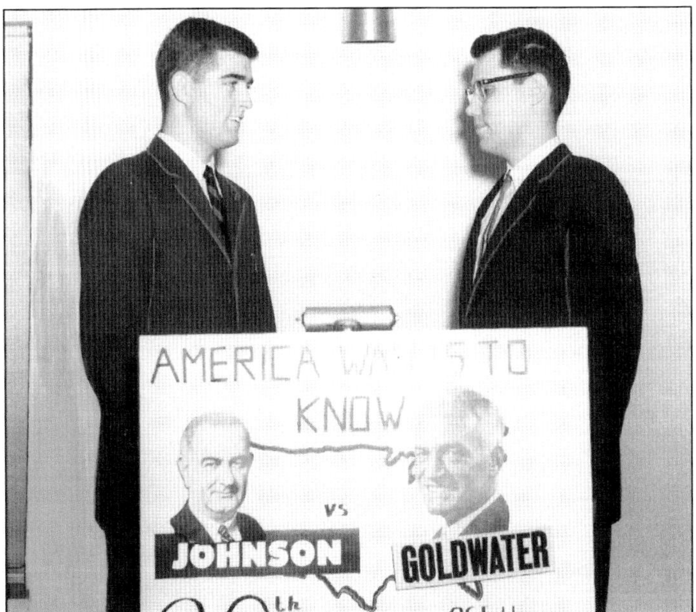

1964 Election Debate. Students organized a student debate several days before the 1964 election in which Jack Powers (left, as Pres. Lyndon Johnson) debated John Letzkus (as Sen. Barry Goldwater); two other students played the parts of the vice-presidential candidates. Students then voted in a mock election, with 78 percent favoring Johnson. Since 1964, both students and faculty have held similar debates during presidential campaigns.

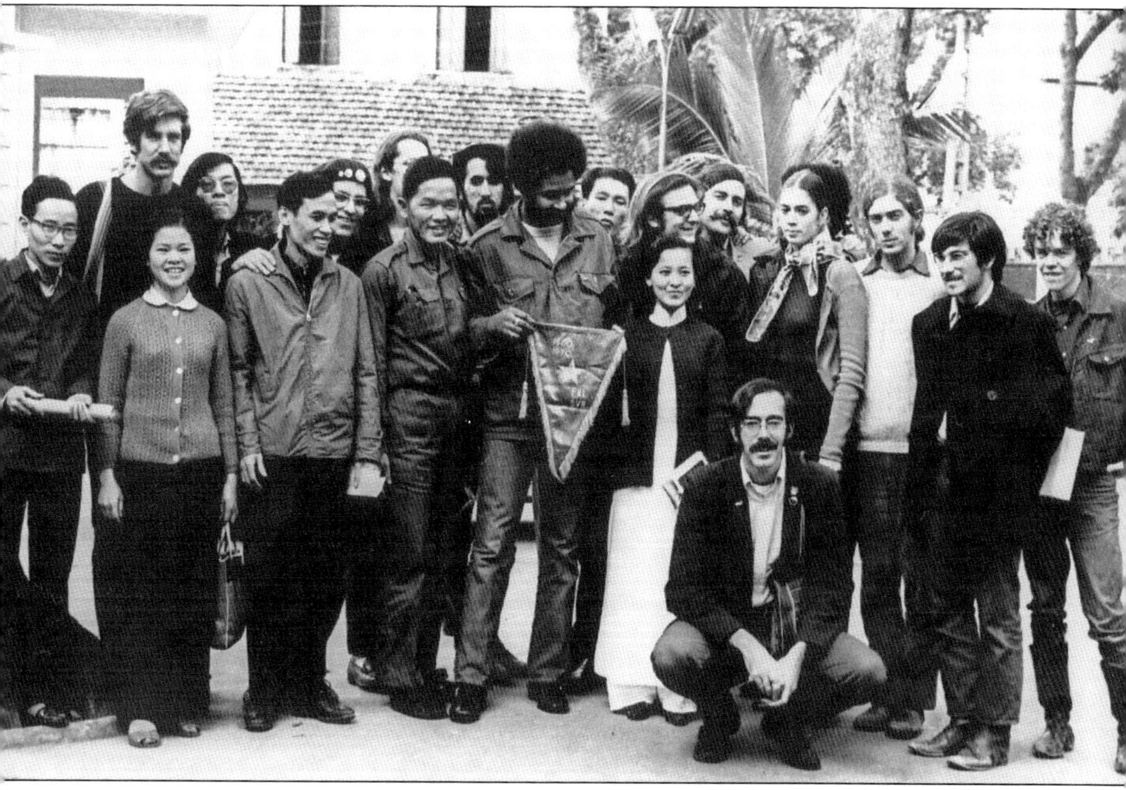

Trip to North Vietnam. In 1970, James Doherty (squatting) was one of ten student leaders chosen by the US National Students Association to visit Vietnam during the war. The group received briefings in Washington, DC, before visiting North Vietnam in December. Upon his return, Doherty wrote a lengthy article for the college newspaper. While he did not support North Vietnam, he also believed that the United States' policy was mistaken and called for a quick end to the war.

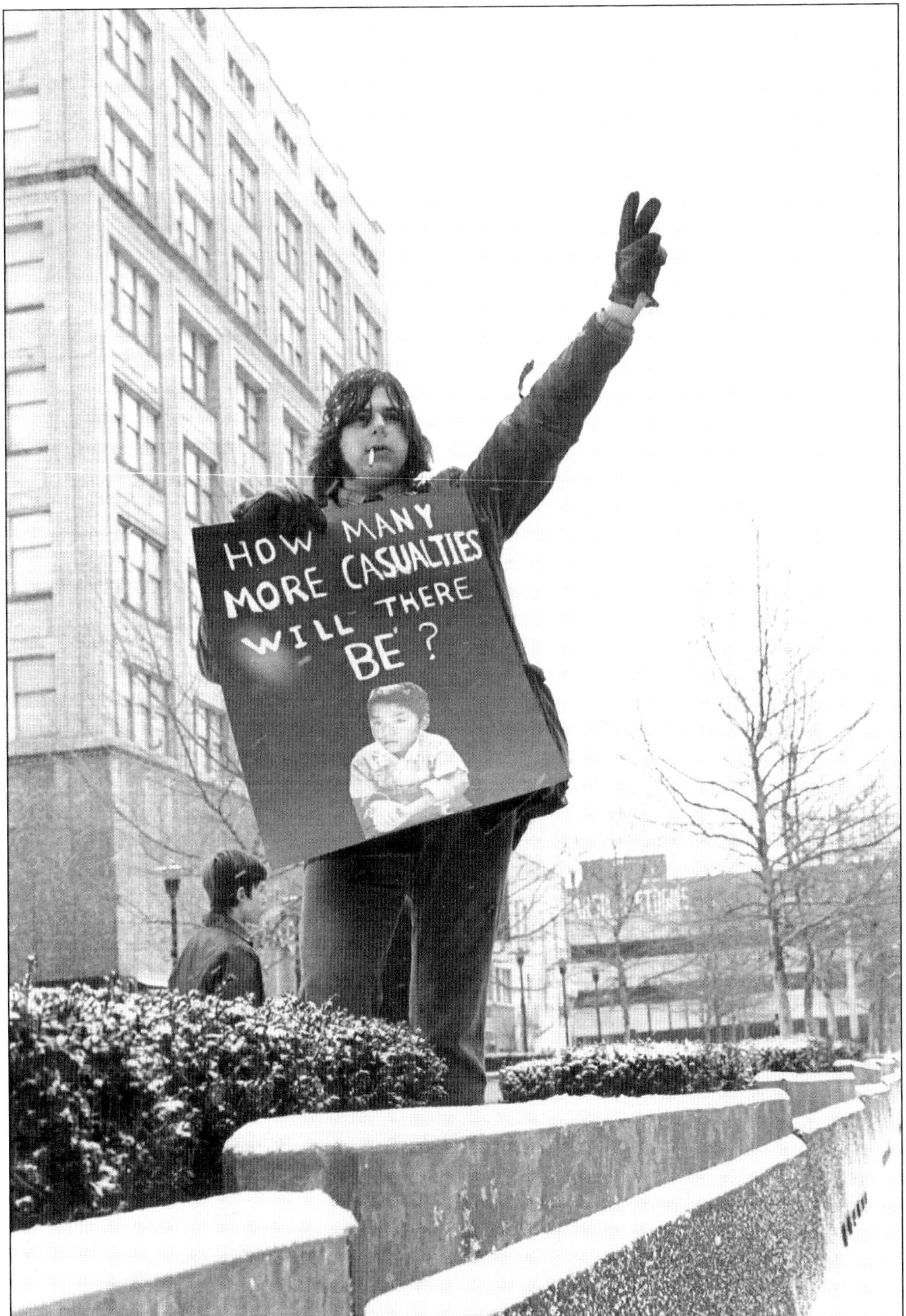

PROTESTING THE VIETNAM WAR. Larry Dorsch and more than 50 other Wheeling College students protested the war in Vietnam in February 1971. Because they had not secured a parade permit ahead of time, they were told to disperse, and they did so without trouble.

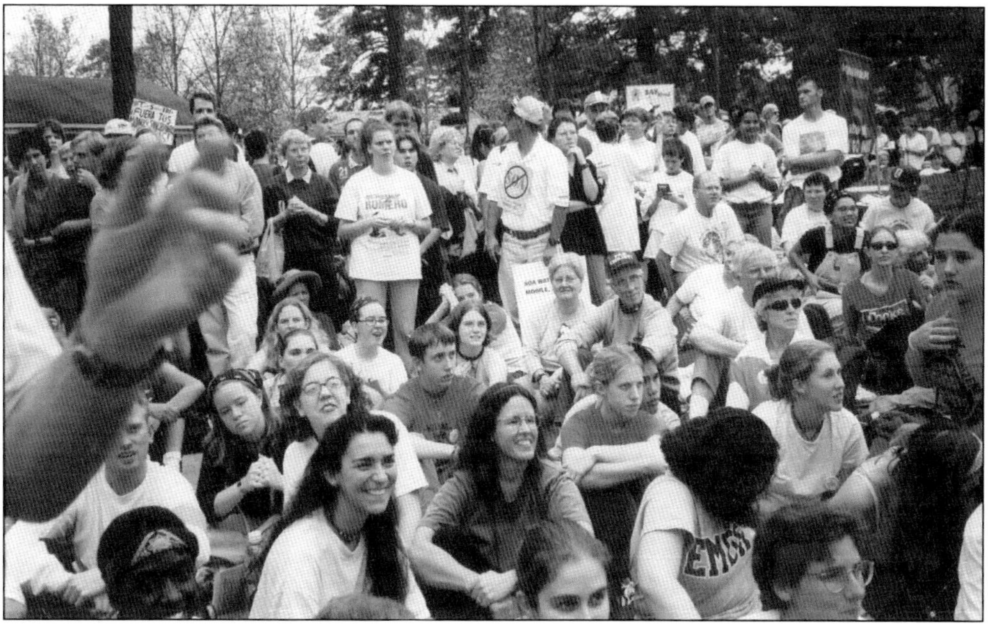

SOA Rally. One club connected to Campus Ministry, JAPOT (Justice and Peace in Our Time), organizes a yearly trip to Fort Benning, Georgia, to join a protest against the School of the Americas (now called the Western Hemisphere Institute for Security Cooperation), where the US Army trains Latin American military members. The protests began after the killing of six Jesuits in El Salvador in 1989, reportedly by soldiers trained at Fort Benning.

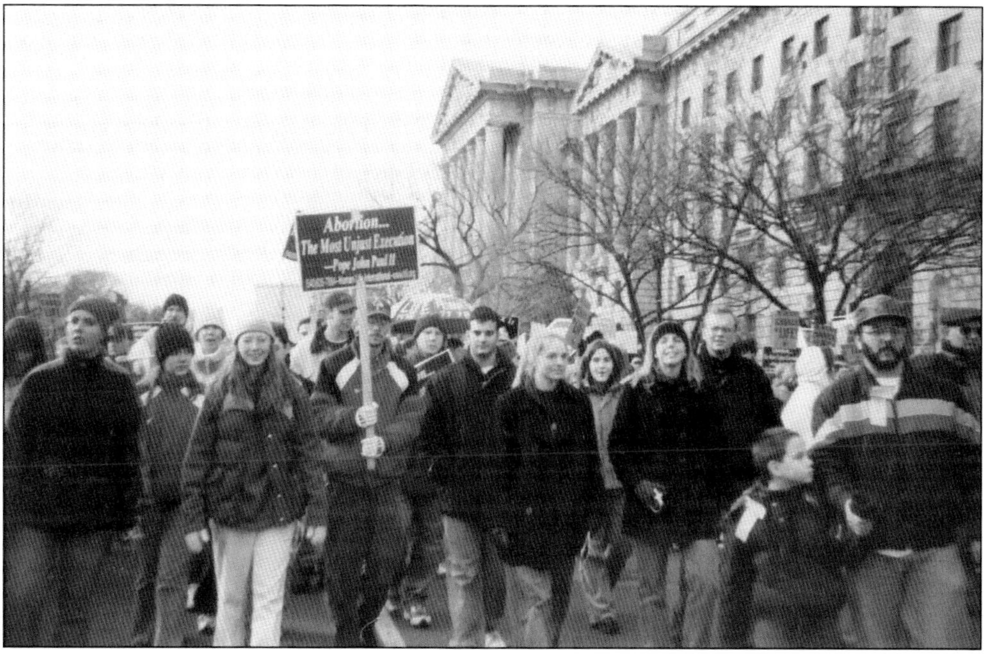

March for Life Rally. For more than 15 years, students from Wheeling Jesuit have attended the annual March for Life in Washington, DC, which demands an end to abortion. Usually, 30 to 40 students make the trip to the January 22 march. The Student Life Club, which organizes the trip, is connected to Campus Ministry. (Courtesy of Campus Ministry.)

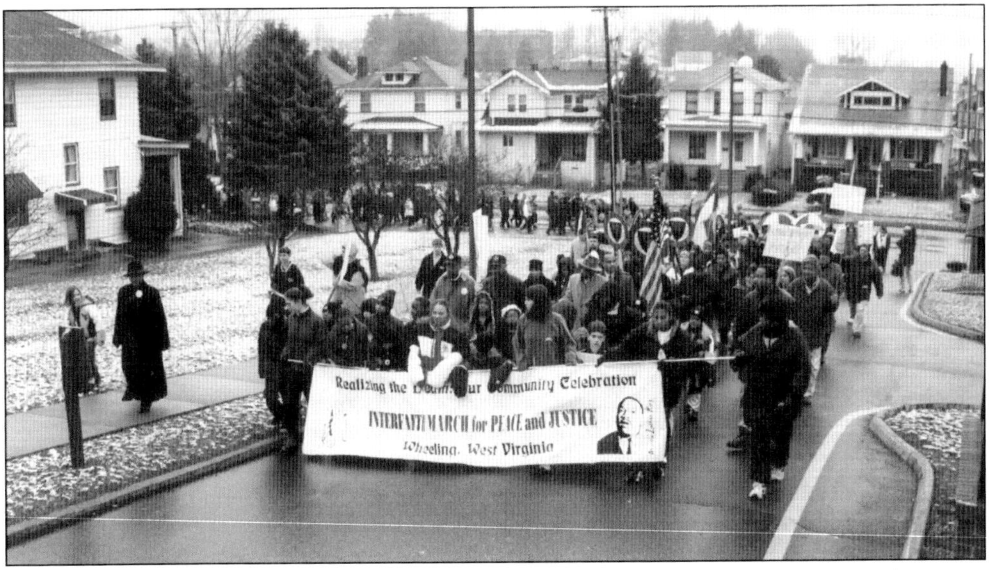

MARTIN LUTHER KING MARCH. Each year, on Martin Luther King Day, marchers come from two different directions to meet on the college's campus to commemorate the work of Dr. King. In this photograph, the two marches have converged and are entering the main entrance to the campus.

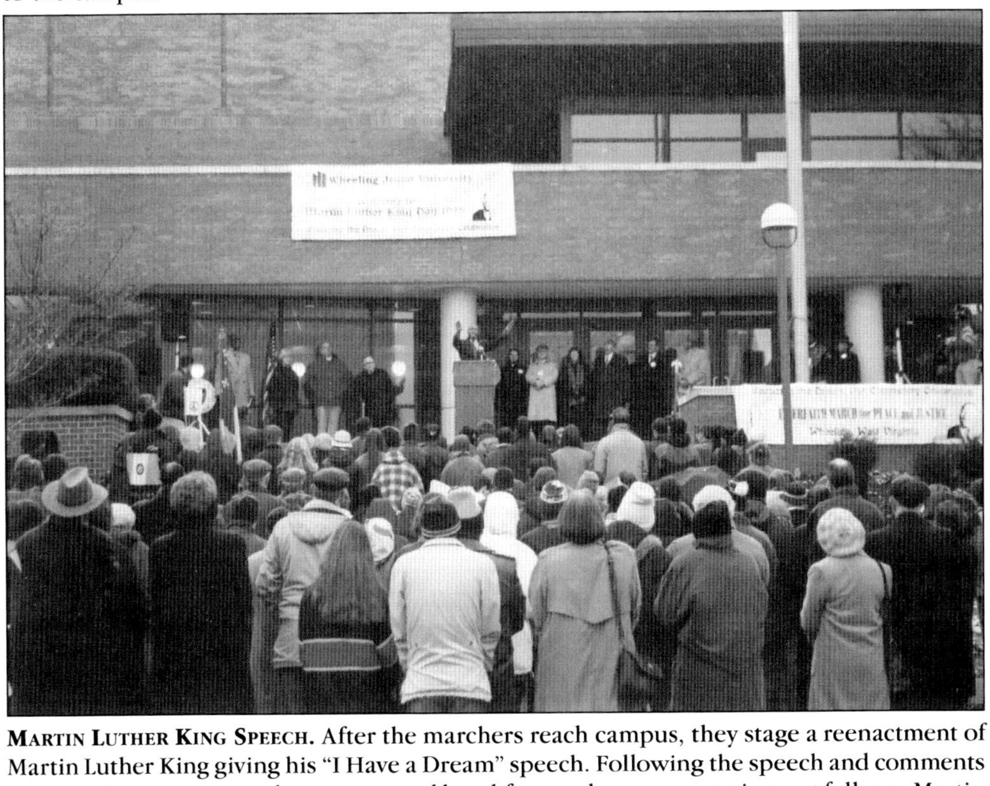

MARTIN LUTHER KING SPEECH. After the marchers reach campus, they stage a reenactment of Martin Luther King giving his "I Have a Dream" speech. Following the speech and comments by local dignitaries, marchers are served breakfast, and some entertainment follows. Martin Luther King Day activities provide one of the most important opportunities for town-gown cooperation and understanding.

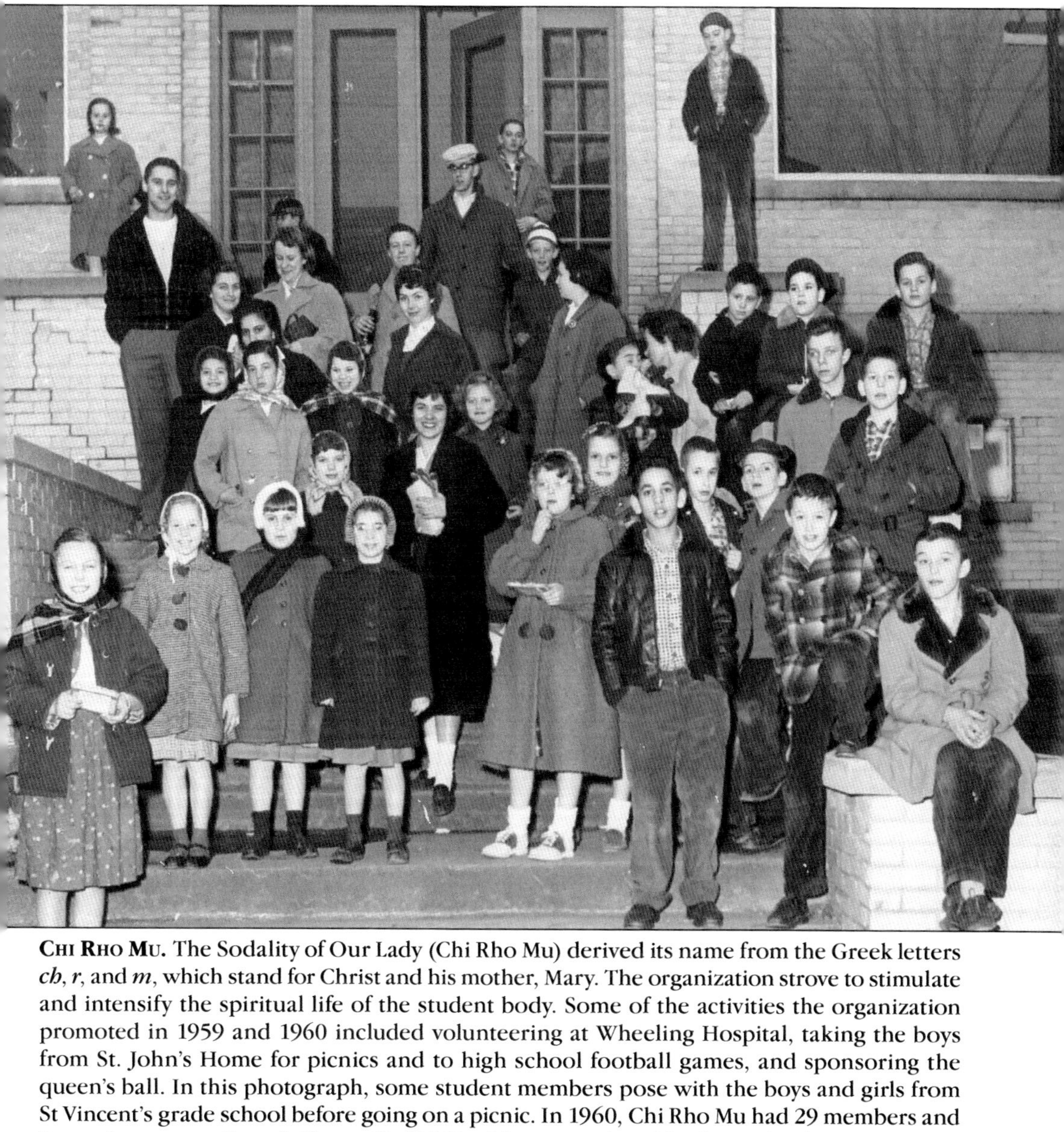

CHI RHO MU. The Sodality of Our Lady (Chi Rho Mu) derived its name from the Greek letters *ch*, *r*, and *m*, which stand for Christ and his mother, Mary. The organization strove to stimulate and intensify the spiritual life of the student body. Some of the activities the organization promoted in 1959 and 1960 included volunteering at Wheeling Hospital, taking the boys from St. John's Home for picnics and to high school football games, and sponsoring the queen's ball. In this photograph, some student members pose with the boys and girls from St Vincent's grade school before going on a picnic. In 1960, Chi Rho Mu had 29 members and its moderator was Joseph Kerns, SJ. Chi Rho Mu was replaced by S.I.U. (Students In Union), but the focus remained on service.

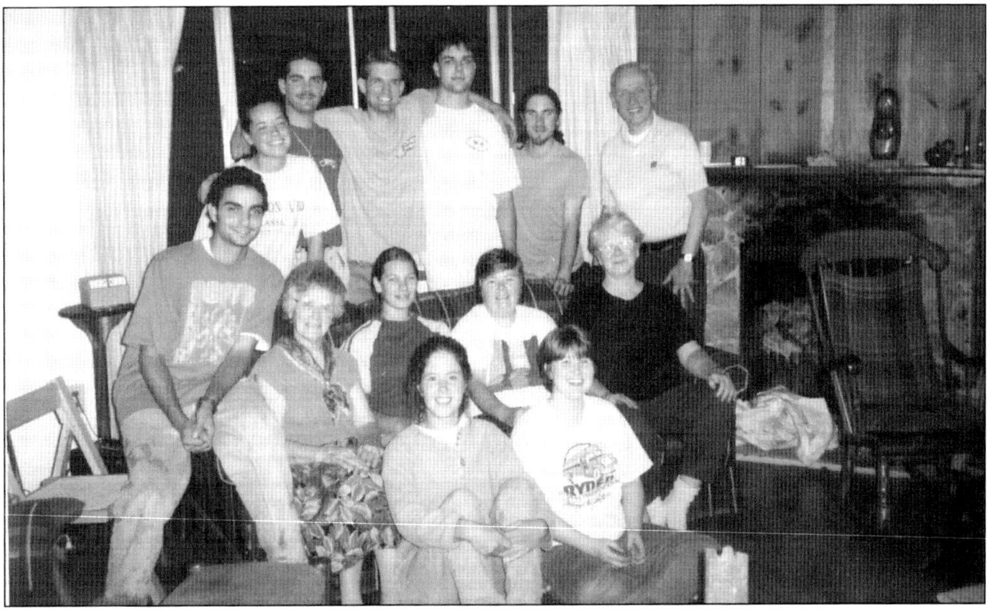

Appalachian Experience. Following the signing of the Appalachian Pastoral Letter *This Land is Home to Me* in 1975, the Appalachian Experience Club was created. The club organizes two trips a year to southern West Virginia, during the fall and spring breaks. Students spend time helping those in need by doing tasks such as splitting wood, painting, cleaning, and so forth, while learning to appreciate Appalachian culture.

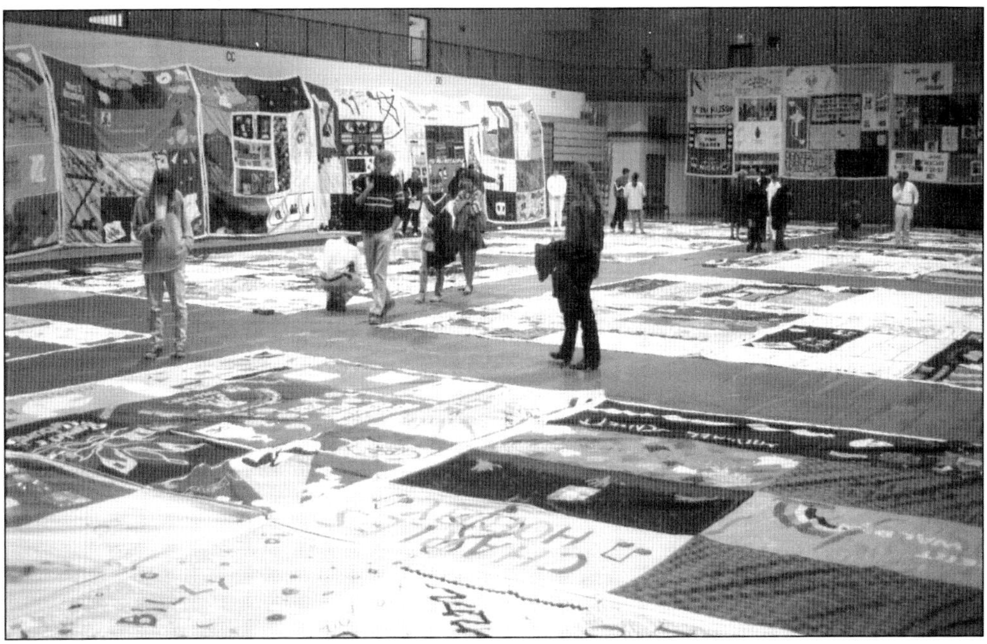

AIDS Quilt. In the spring of 1994 and 1995, Carol Orts, vice president of the university and student government, arranged for the display of the Names Project AIDS Memorial Quilt in the McDonough Field House. The event raised more than $8,000 to be used for the care and shipment of the quilts. The main goals of the exhibition are to raise both awareness of AIDS and the level of compassion for those suffering from it.

COMMUTERS. Wheeling Jesuit, now largely a residential university, once had difficulty making commuters feel fully integrated into student life and activities. Campus Ministry plays a crucial role in this regard because of its numerous programs on and off campus. Madelaine Keys (first row, left), of Campus Ministry, stands with the members of the 1984 Commuter Council at a party for commuters.

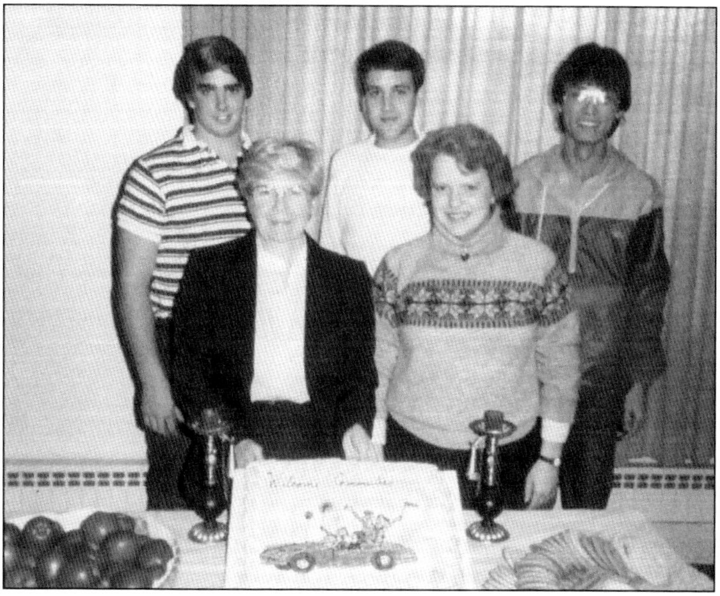

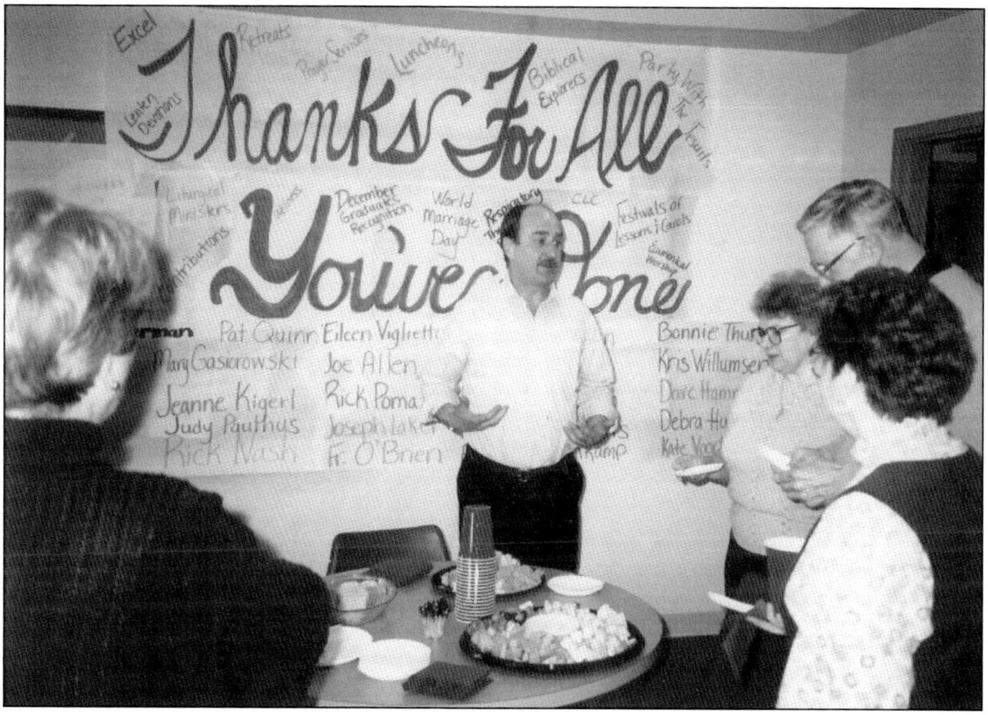

CAMPUS MINISTRY PARTY. Campus Ministry attempts to involve faculty and staff in as many student activities as it can and always remembers to organize a party to thank those who have been involved in their programs. Some of the programs are written on the white board behind Dr. Richard Pomazal, who is chatting with Sr. Sandra DeNardis (biology), and Walter Buckius, SJ. (Courtesy of Campus Ministry.)

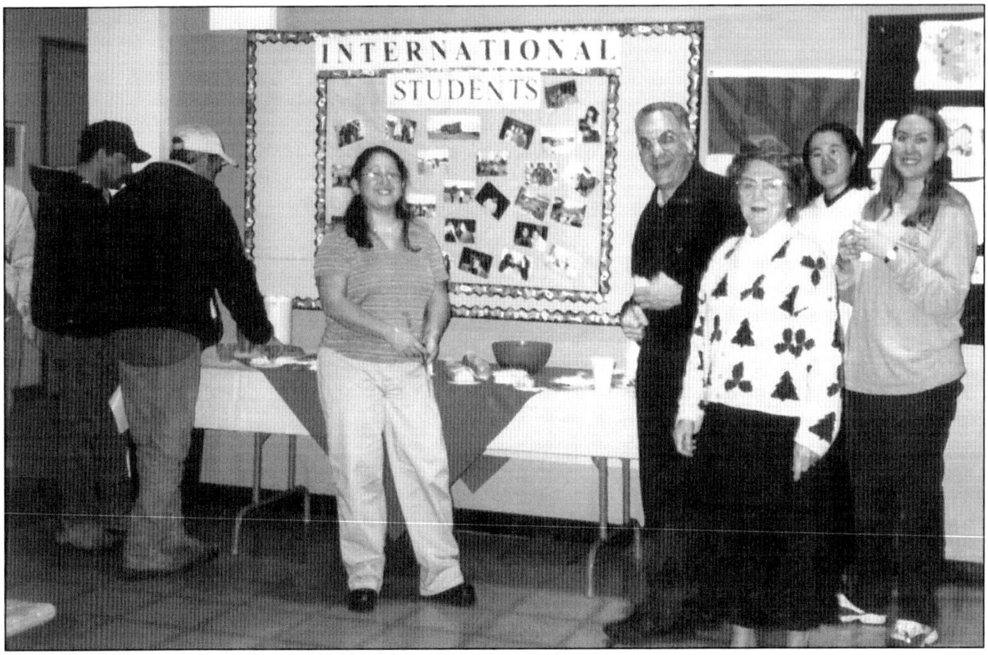

INTERNATIONAL STUDENTS CLUB. The creation of the English as a Second Language Institute in 1983—through efforts of Dr. Robert Lado, professor of linguistics at Georgetown—has done much to internationalize the campus. The International Club is open to all students on campus, and monthly receptions are held to introduce foreign students from different countries.

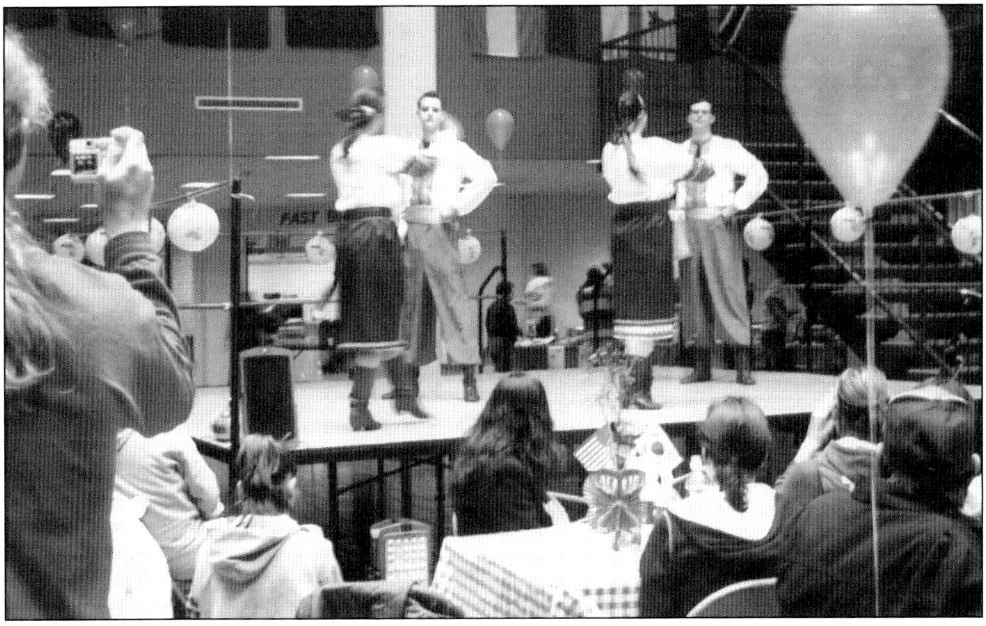

STUDENT FAIR. Each spring, the International Club organizes an international food and entertainment fair. Members prepare dishes from their respective countries for people to sample. The students provide entertainment, although folk dancers from Pittsburgh are also often invited to participate. The fair has proved to be increasingly popular and attracts many attendees from the community.

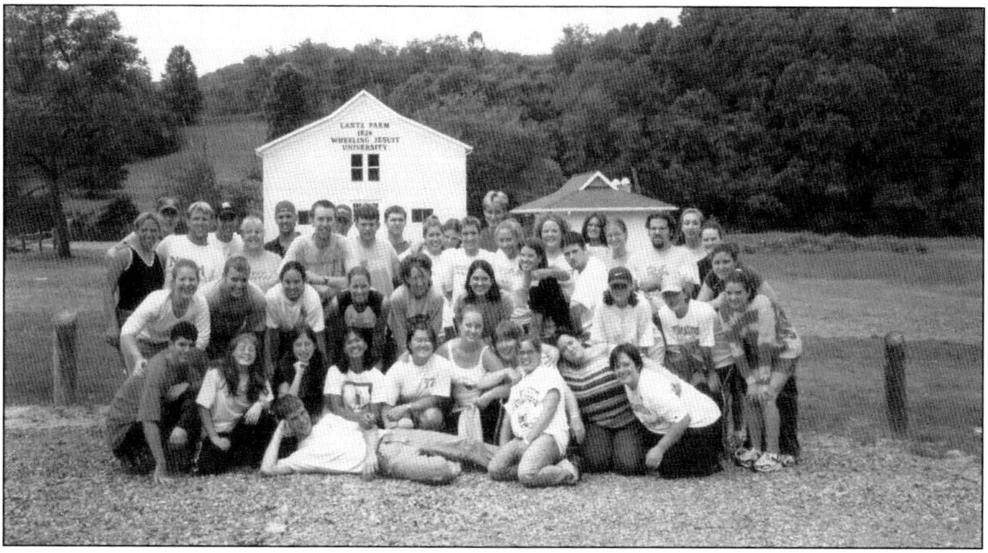

Lantz Farm Retreats. Campus Ministry conducts a number of spiritual retreats each year. After the Lantz family donated their 545-acre farm to Wheeling Jesuit in 1998, the university created a center there where retreats have been held. Many are based on the class to which students belong. These 50 freshmen are participating in a retreat. (Courtesy of Campus Ministry.)

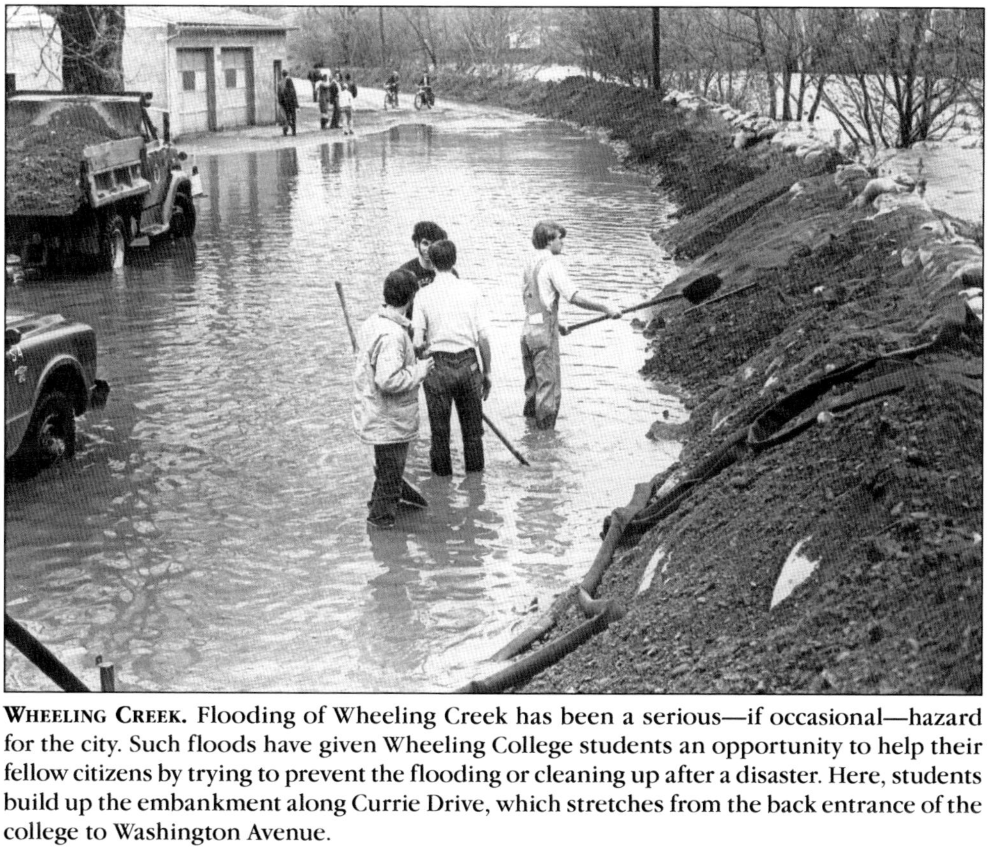

Wheeling Creek. Flooding of Wheeling Creek has been a serious—if occasional—hazard for the city. Such floods have given Wheeling College students an opportunity to help their fellow citizens by trying to prevent the flooding or cleaning up after a disaster. Here, students build up the embankment along Currie Drive, which stretches from the back entrance of the college to Washington Avenue.

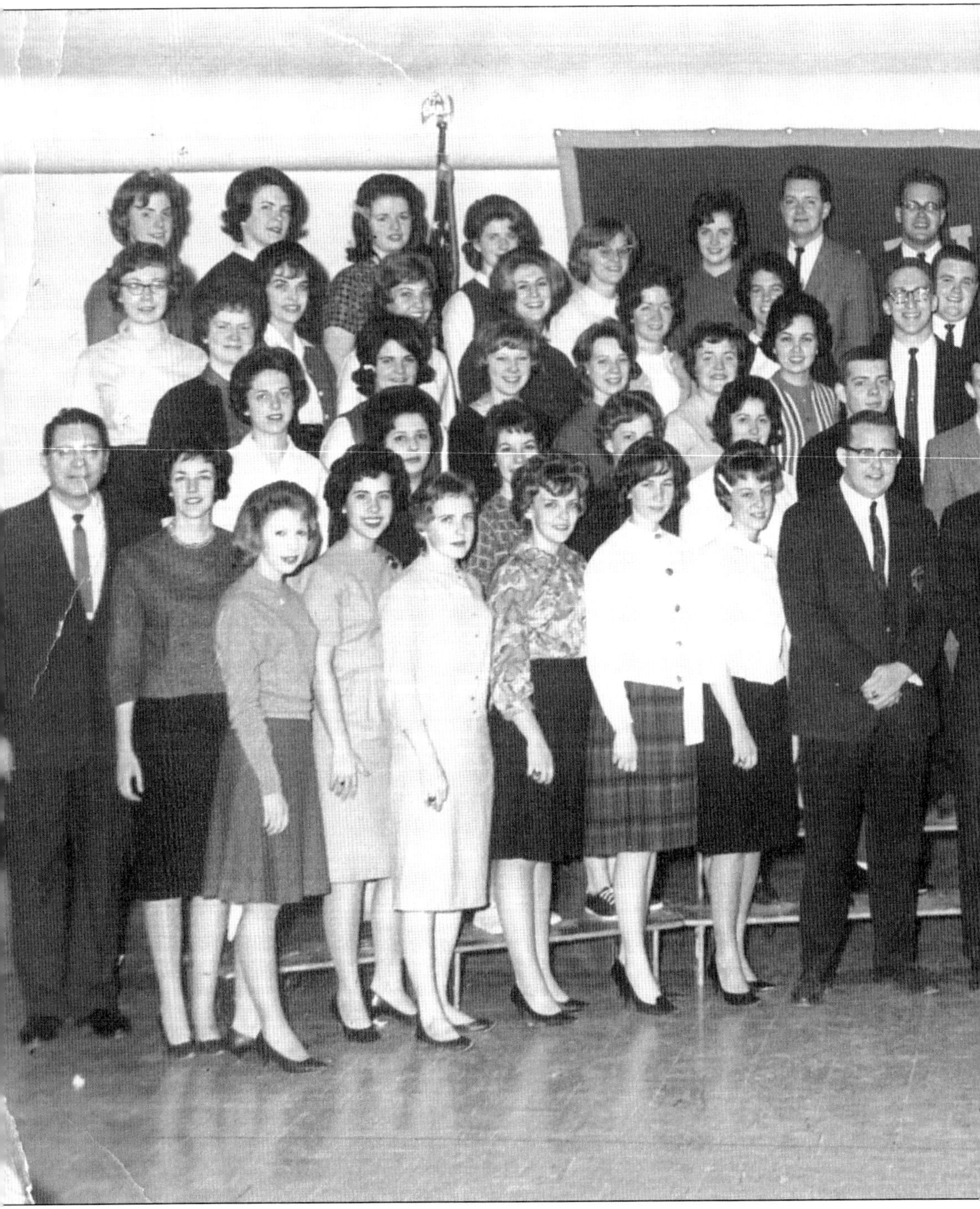

Glee Club. Fr. Edward Gannon, SJ, organized the Glee Club in the second year of the college's existence, and by 1961, the club had 71 members. J. Loran Mercer, on the far left in the first row, was the musical director in 1961, and Fr. G. Gordon Henderson, SJ, was the faculty

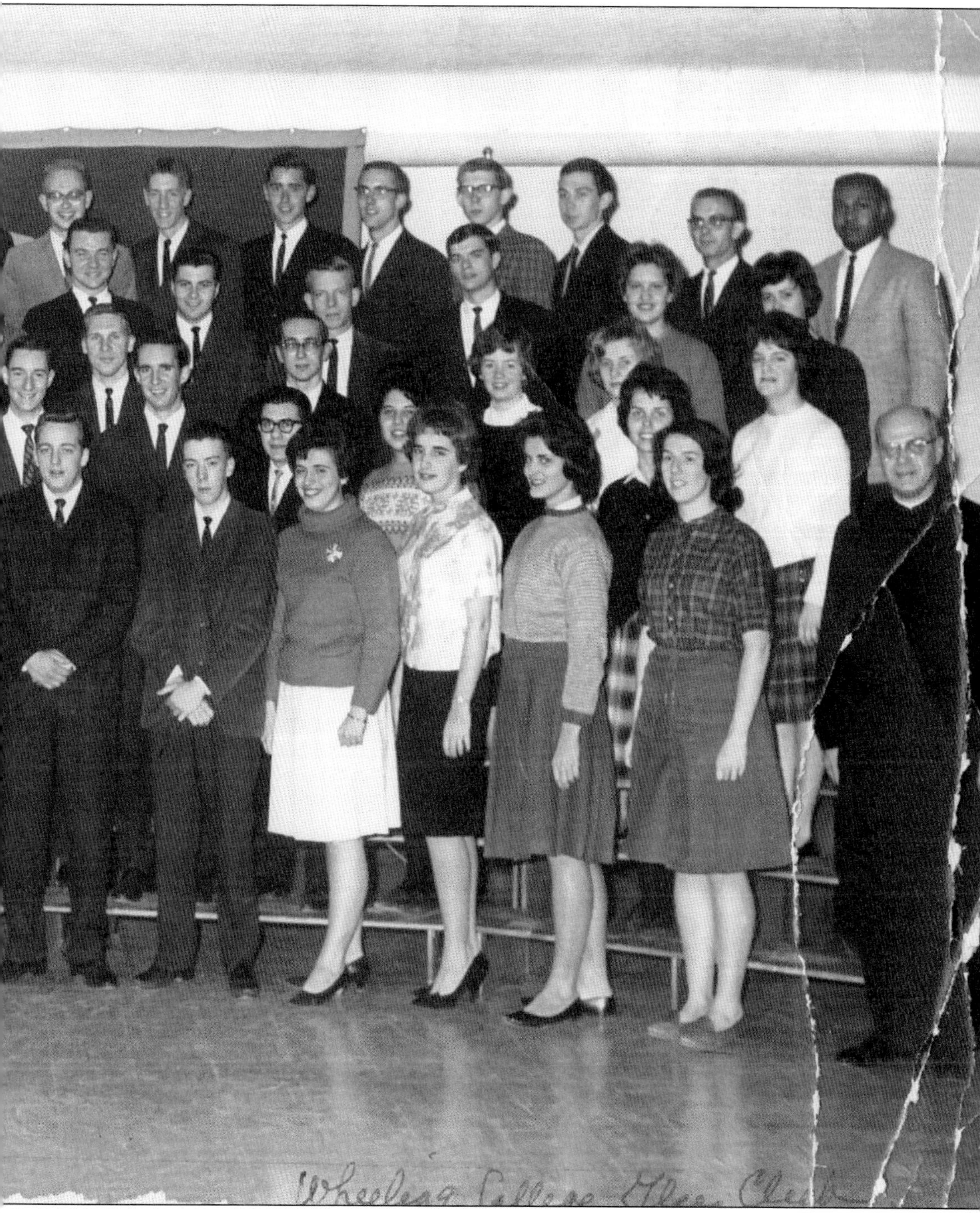

moderator. Mercer was the head of the music department at Warwood High School. The club was very popular during the college's first decade. Today, a smaller group of about 20 students make up the Wheeling College Singers. (Courtesy of Don Mercer.)

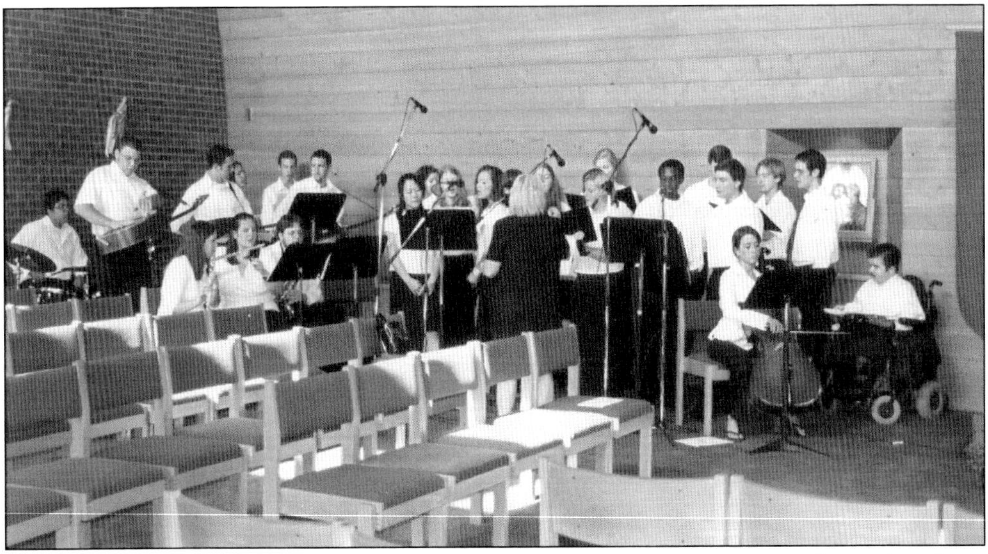

CAMPUS MINISTRY MUSICIANS. Wheeling Jesuit usually holds three Masses on Sunday, and students with musical talent are encouraged to provide instrumental music or their voices to lead the congregations. Many of these students are also members of the Wheeling College Singers, but the two groups have separate audiences. This group is rehearsing in the chapel.

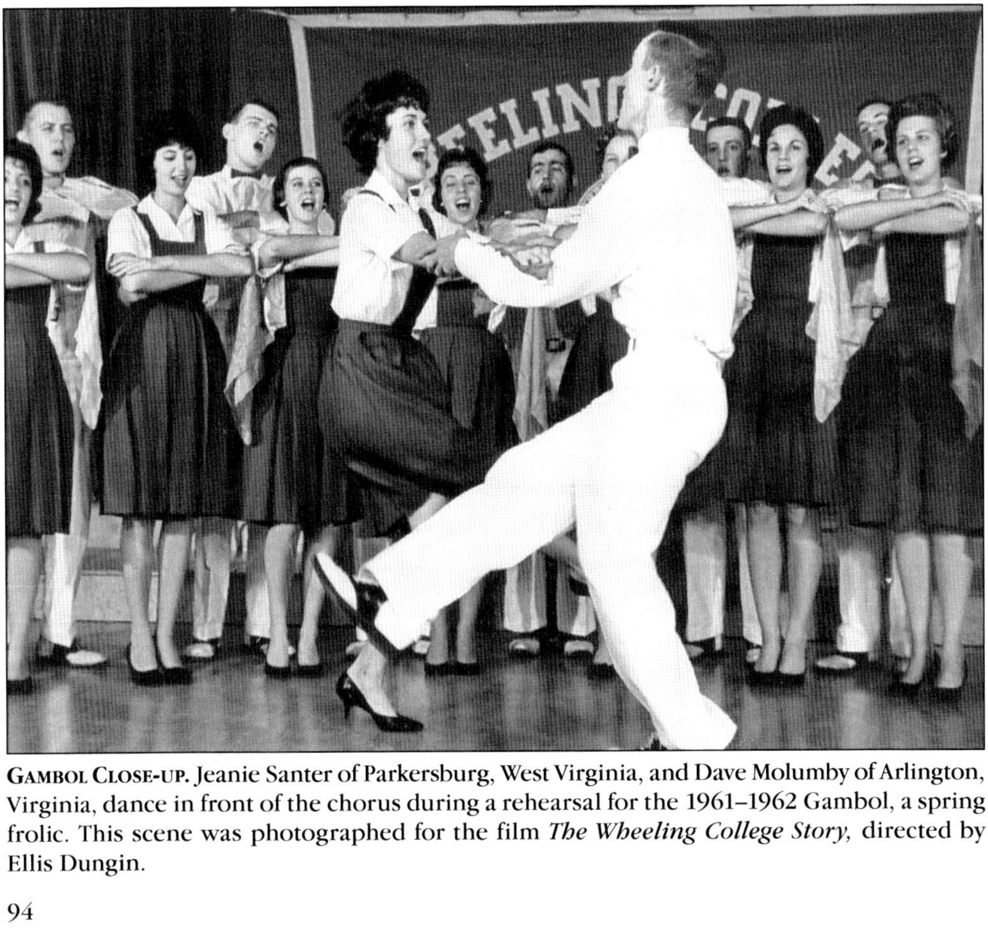

GAMBOL CLOSE-UP. Jeanie Santer of Parkersburg, West Virginia, and Dave Molumby of Arlington, Virginia, dance in front of the chorus during a rehearsal for the 1961–1962 Gambol, a spring frolic. This scene was photographed for the film *The Wheeling College Story,* directed by Ellis Dungin.

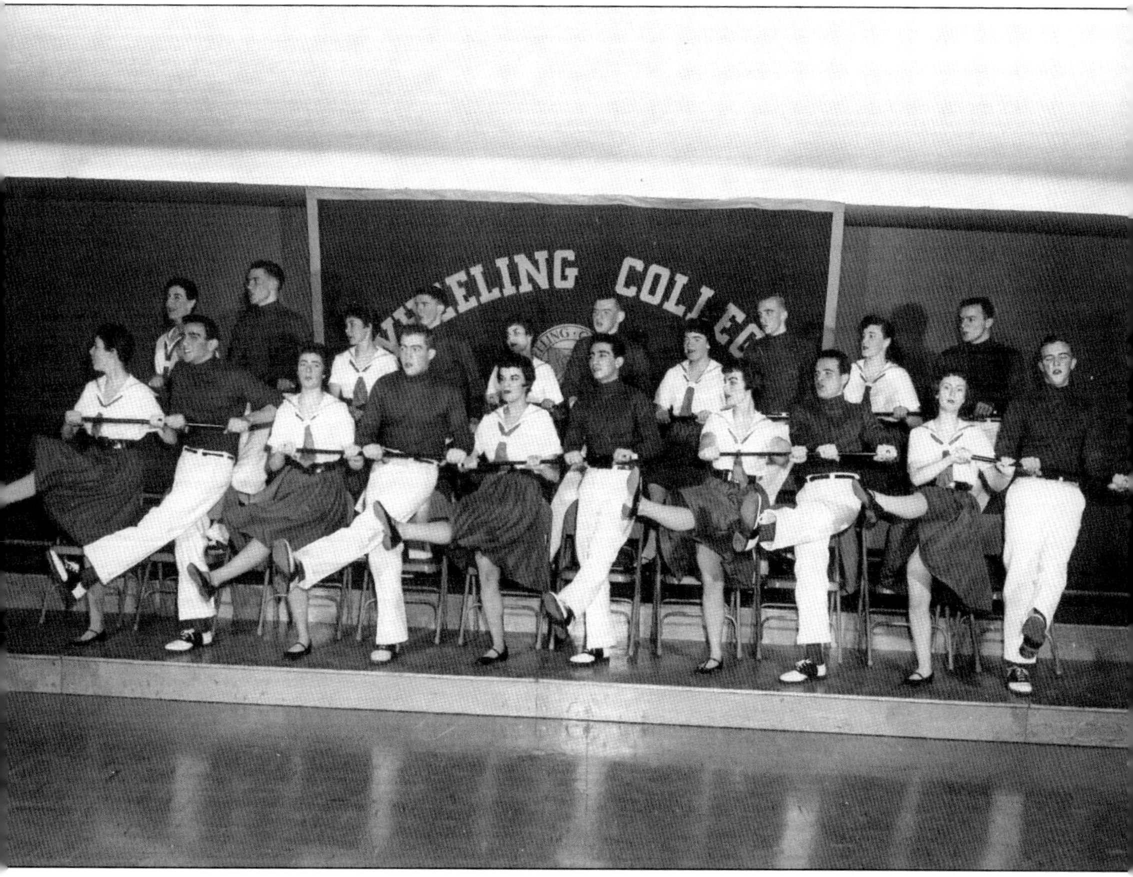

Gambol Chorus. In this late 1961 Gambol production, the chorus is kicking through the tune "Carolina in the Morning." Gambol productions always required a large number of students, both as entertainers and as stagehands.

PROGRA

Masters of Ceremonies . . . J. L. Lyons

Accompaniment . . . Bernie Gle

1. OPENING CHORUS .... Ed Anthony, Mary Ann Becker, Mary Kay Beltz, Pente Camilletti, Don Canestraro, Tom Carrigan, Barbara Creamer, Tony Ellis, Bob Kammer, Tom Kendo, Beverly Kennen, Mary Knowles, Carolyn Lee, John Murphy, Phyllis Nickerson, Terry Nudd, John Padden, Bob Palmer, Ellen Pockl and Rita Wojcik.

2. THE TENDER TRAP .... Ed Anthony and Ellen Pockl

3. CAROLINA IN THE MORNING .... The Chorus

4. COMMERCIAL LTD. .... J. D. Graziano, Rose Ann Ellem and Jerry Goebel

5. I WHISTLE A HAPPY TUNE .... Pente Camilletti

6. MIXTUM GATHERUM .... Tom Carrigan, Bill Thalman, Don Canestraro and J. L. Lyons.

7. THE BIRTH OF THE BLUES .... Pente Camilletti, Phyllis Nickerson, Ellen Pockl and Rita Wojcik

8. THE ROAD TO MANDALAY .... George Oryszkewycz

9. BILL

10. PAS

11. TWO

12. THE

13. BAL

14. I'M

15. TEA

16. WHE

17. FIVE

18. HOT

ANNOUNCEMENT OF ELECTION W

RECEPTION AND DANCE IN TH

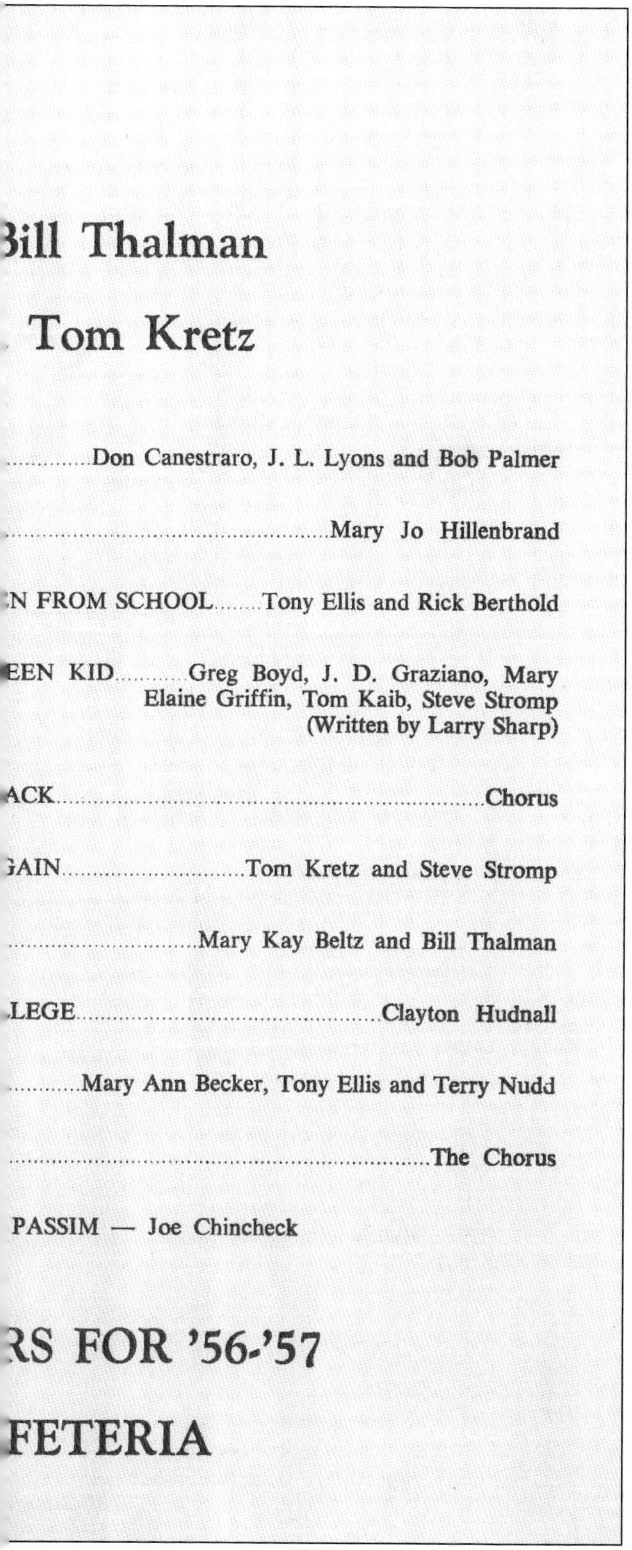

3ill Thalman

. Tom Kretz

..............Don Canestraro, J. L. Lyons and Bob Palmer

....Mary Jo Hillenbrand

:N FROM SCHOOL........Tony Ellis and Rick Berthold

EEN KID............Greg Boyd, J. D. Graziano, Mary
Elaine Griffin, Tom Kaib, Steve Stromp
(Written by Larry Sharp)

ACK...Chorus

;AIN..............................Tom Kretz and Steve Stromp

..............................Mary Kay Beltz and Bill Thalman

.LEGE..Clayton Hudnall

............Mary Ann Becker, Tony Ellis and Terry Nudd

....The Chorus

PASSIM — Joe Chincheck

{S FOR '56-'57

FETERIA

Gambol Program. The first Gambol production took place on May 15, 1957. Organized and directed by Fr. Edward Gannon, who taught philosophy and fine arts at Wheeling College from 1956 to 1973, early Gambol productions were variety shows that combined singing, dancing, and comedy routines. At the end of the performance, Fr. Lawrence Troy, then dean of the college, announced the winner of the Student of the Year award and the class officers for the next academic year. The nature of the Gambol changed from a variety show to a musical when Rev. Charles Braun took over Gambol productions in the mid-1970s.

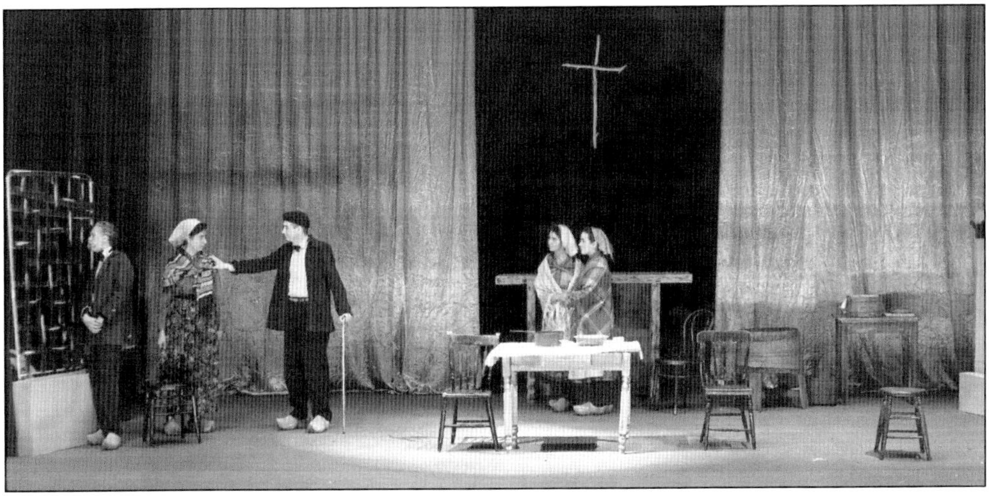

Smallest of All. In November 1957, the Caviar Club presented the premiere performance of a play by Sr. Francis Marie, PC, called *Smallest of All*, about Bernadette Soubirous of Lourdes, at the Virginia Theater in downtown Wheeling. The following spring, the cast of 21 took the three-act play on a tour of nine different communities in West Virginia. Director Fr. Gerald Kernan, SJ, and Rev. Thomas McDonnell, the auxiliary bishop of Wheeling-Charleston, accompanied them.

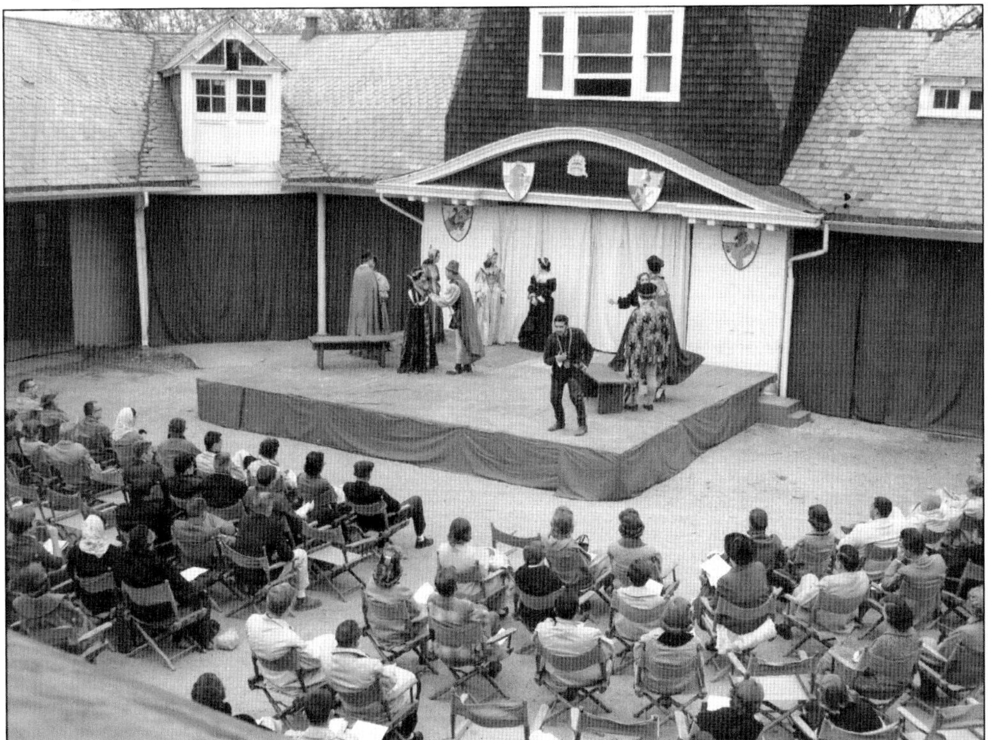

Othello. Fr. Gerald Kernan, SJ, associate professor of English, directed the college's first production of a Shakespeare drama in the fall of 1959. Student actors only had five weeks to prepare for the performances, which were staged in Oglebay Park. The stage's platform was built atop beer kegs. The play ran for two successive weekends to sparse audiences.

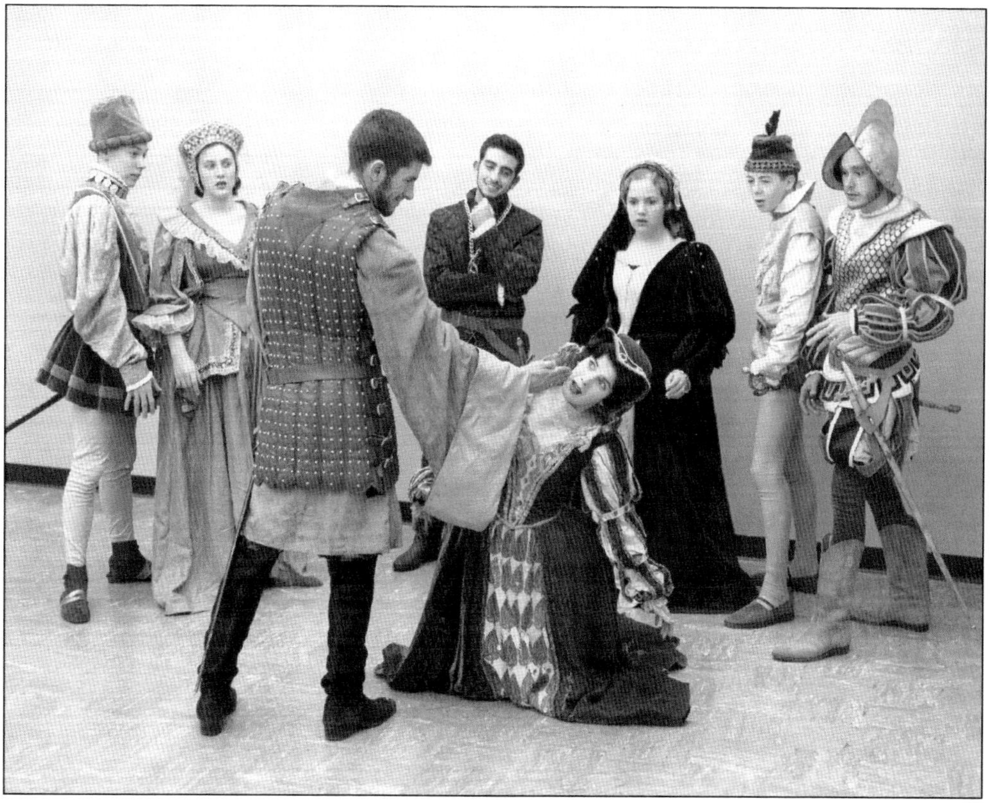

***Othello* Rehearsal.** The Jesuits have a long history of encouraging drama, and Wheeling founded the Caviar Club to recruit students to perform on stage. The club put on three one-act plays in the spring of 1956. The next spring, it staged Thornton Wilder's *Our Town,* which called for a cast of 50 (at a school with 200 students). *Othello*, performed in the fall of 1959, was the club's most ambitious production. The Caviar Club still thrives today.

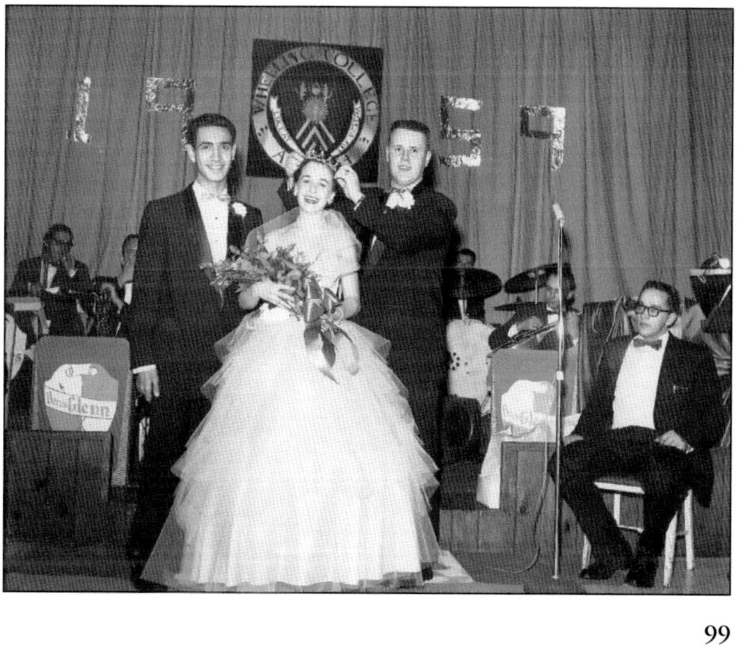

The Colonial Ball. Ellen Pockl '59 is pictured here being crowned Queen of the Colonial Ball by William Thalman, chairman of the ball committee. Pockl's escort, Ed Anthony '59, stands to the left. Bernie Glenn '59 and His Esquires provided the music. The ball was held in the Pine Room at Oglebay Park.

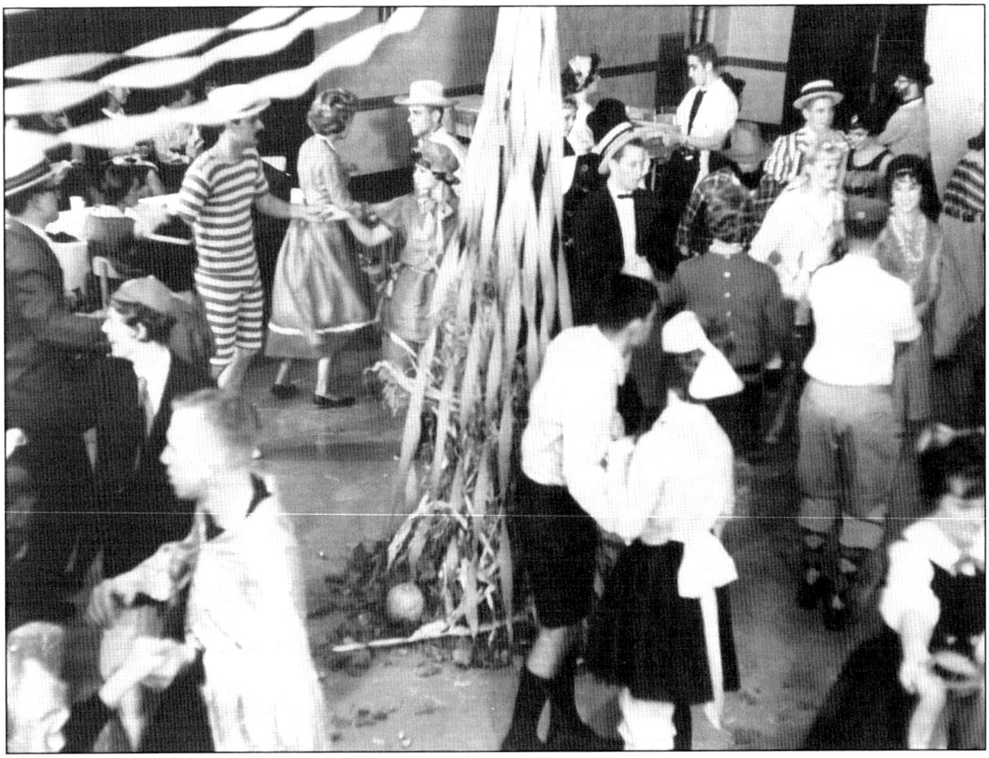

Sadie Hawkins Dance. A popular fall event, usually held on the first Saturday of November, is a dance at which women ask men for a date. Sadie Hawkins was a character introduced by the cartoonist Al Capp in 1937 in his comic strip *Li'l Abner*. Many of the dancers dress up as if they are part of Capp's hillbilly world.

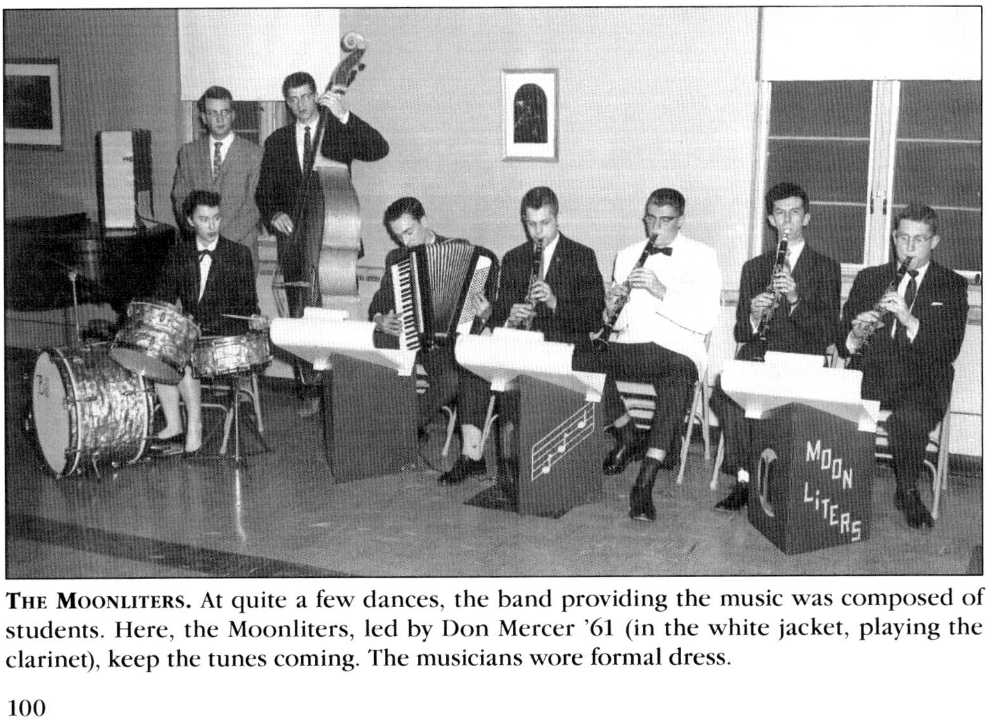

The Moonliters. At quite a few dances, the band providing the music was composed of students. Here, the Moonliters, led by Don Mercer '61 (in the white jacket, playing the clarinet), keep the tunes coming. The musicians wore formal dress.

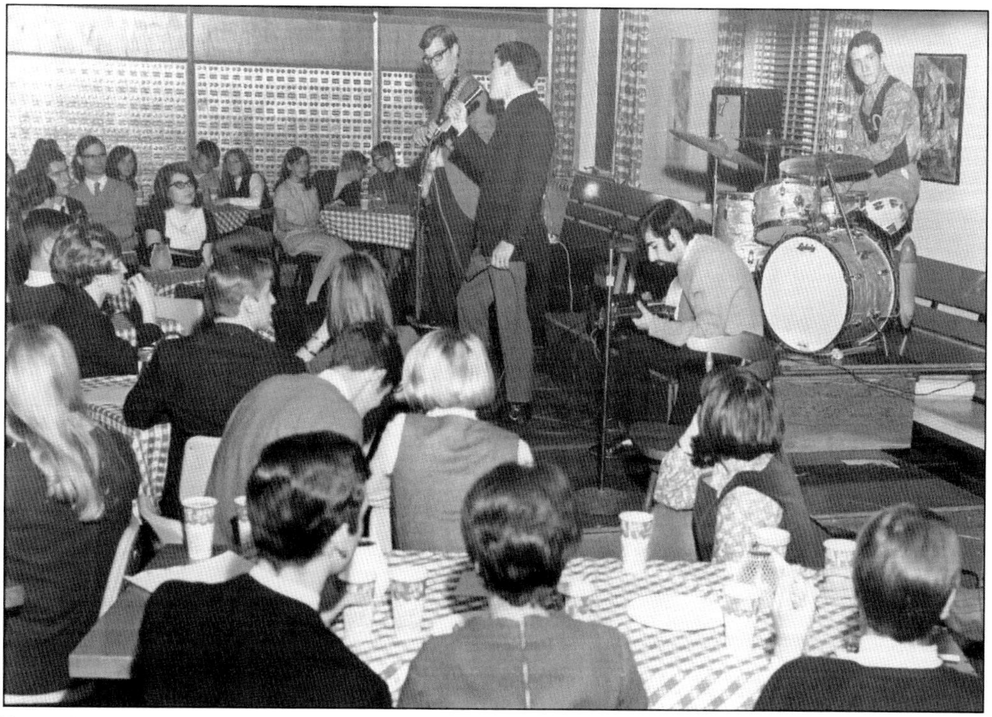

Rock Band. It was popular in the late 1960s to create a nightclub setting in which the audience sat at tables to hear student rock musicians. The mailboxes in the background mark the location of the event—the snack bar in Swint Hall. The dress of the musicians is more casual than in the past, but still quite clean-cut.

The Rathskeller. The Rathskeller, which was established in the early 1970s, is a student-operated bar that has a faculty moderator who tries to ensure that it is properly run and that all alcohol policies are followed. Wheeling College students still go to off-campus bars (e.g., the Alpha, and in times past, Macs and the Cardinal Inn), but the presence of "The Ratt" on campus has helped to reduce drinking and driving.

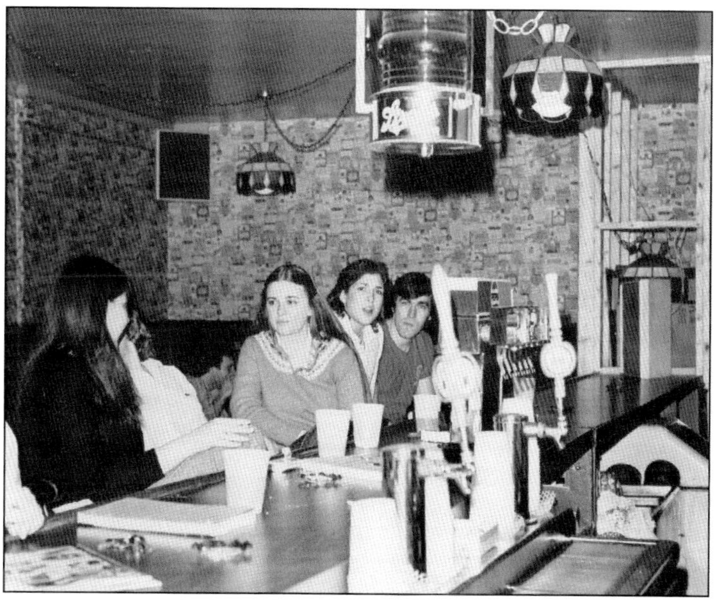

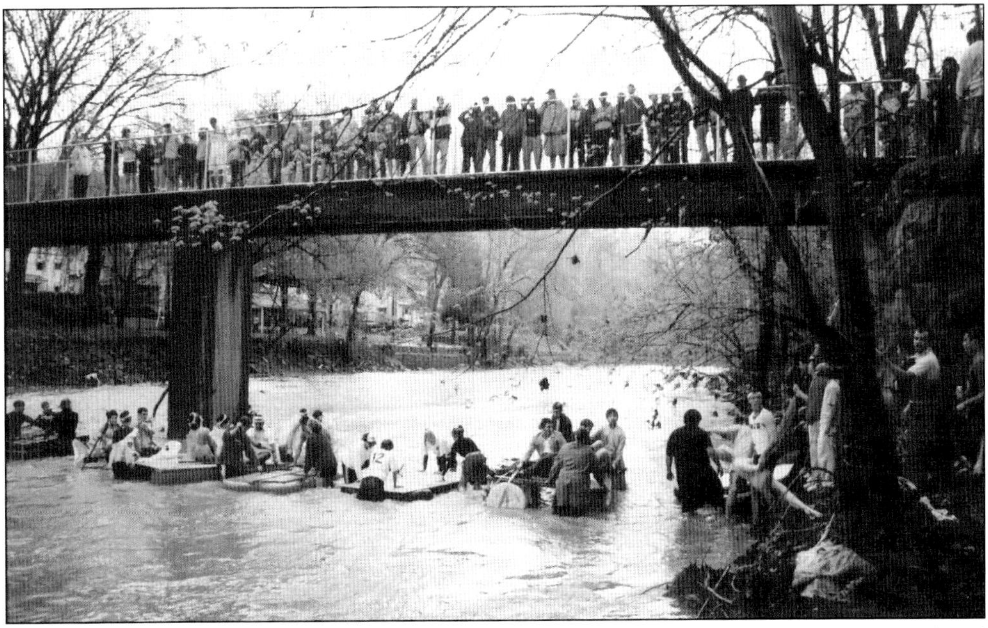

Last Blast Raft Race. The last big party of the year for students takes place on the weekend before final exams. The kickoff event is the annual raft race in Wheeling Creek, which goes from the footbridge at the back entrance of campus to about 500 meters downstream. Students line the footbridge to watch the start of the race. Student teams construct the rafts of rubber inner tubes, foam, plastic bags, boards, tape, and such. The winners get bragging rights.

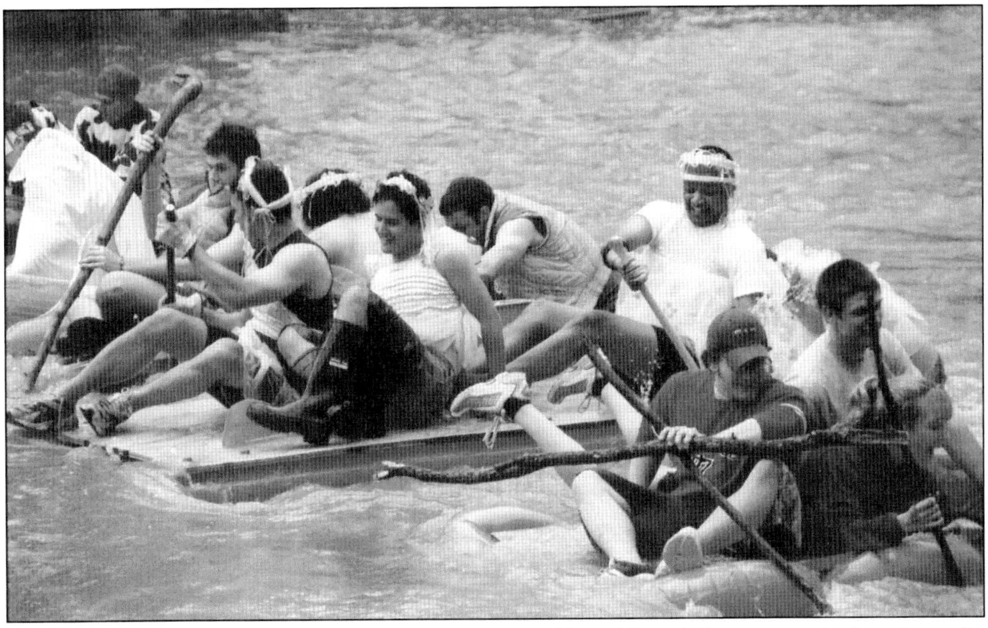

Last Blast Raft Race Close-up. The water is usually cold and deep enough that the rafts do not constantly bump along the bottom, and everyone involved seems to have great fun. Outrageous dress is expected, and some crews are more eager to create mayhem on the creek than to be first across the finish line. After the race is a picnic, followed by a rock music concert in the evening.

Five

Sporting Life and Students

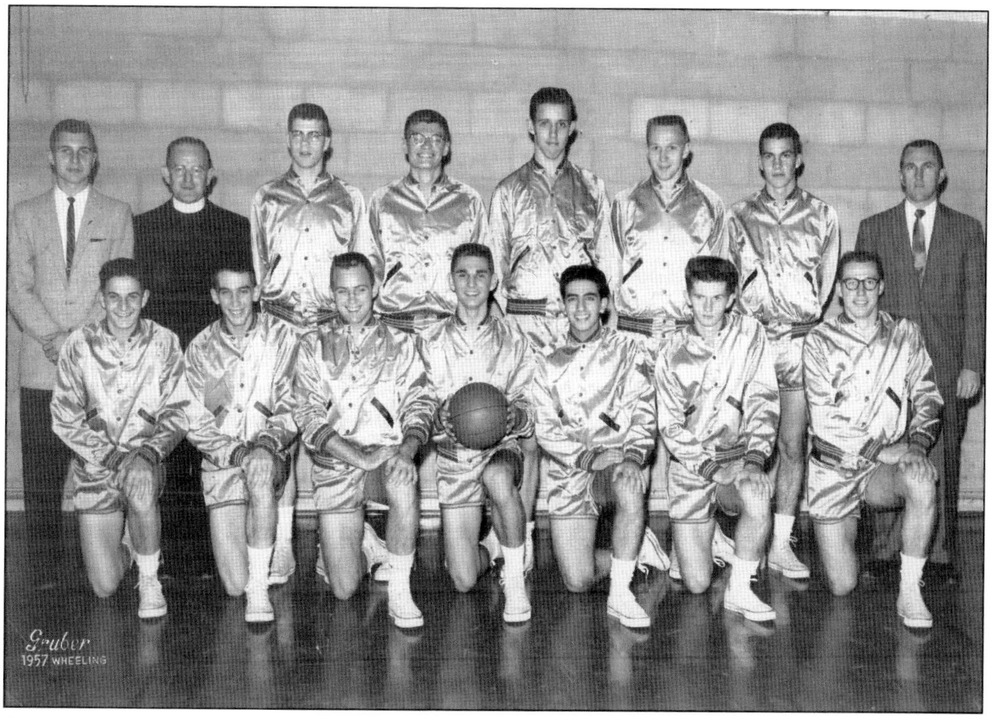

First Basketball Coach. Ed Coyne is standing on the far right. A Wheeling businessman, Coyne coached the Wheeling College Cardinals for five years in his spare time. He led varsity teams to 25 wins versus 40 losses. Here, Coyne is pictured with the 1956–1957 team.

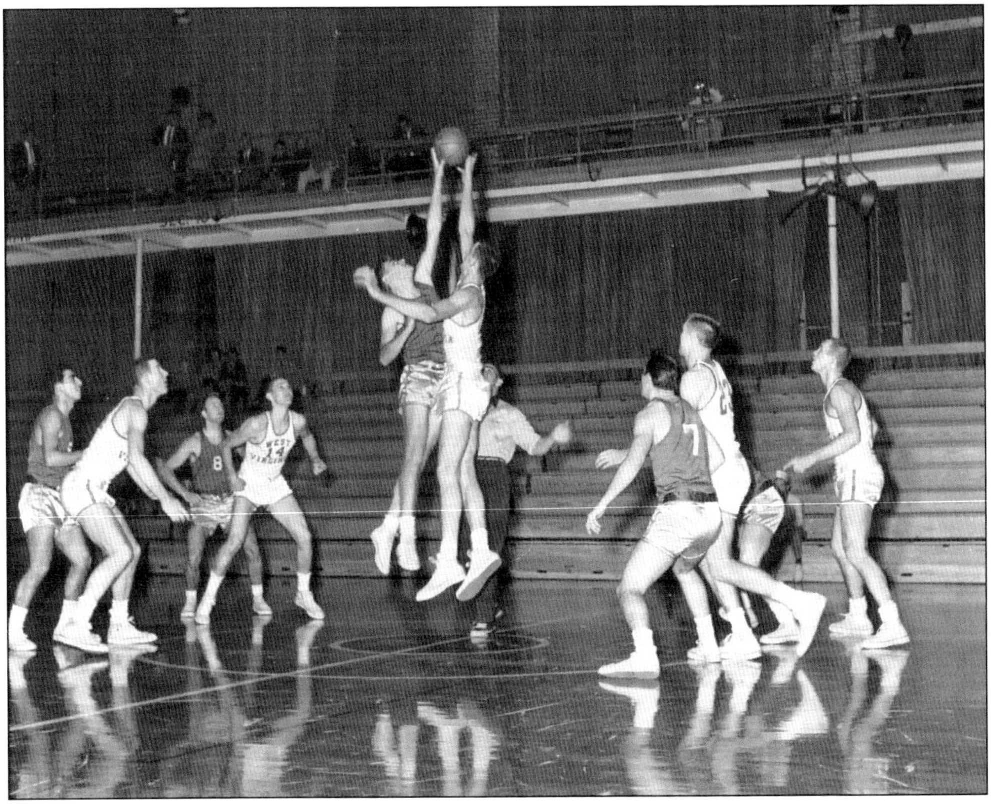

First Men's Basketball Game. Wheeling College's first intercollegiate basketball game took place in Morgantown against the West Virginia University freshman team on December 1, 1955. West Virginia defeated the Cardinals 92-71. Future NBA star Jerry West, who played for WVU, is No. 14 in the picture. Wheeling's team was made up of freshmen and sophomores. Their most significant victory that year was against Duquesne University, 69-65.

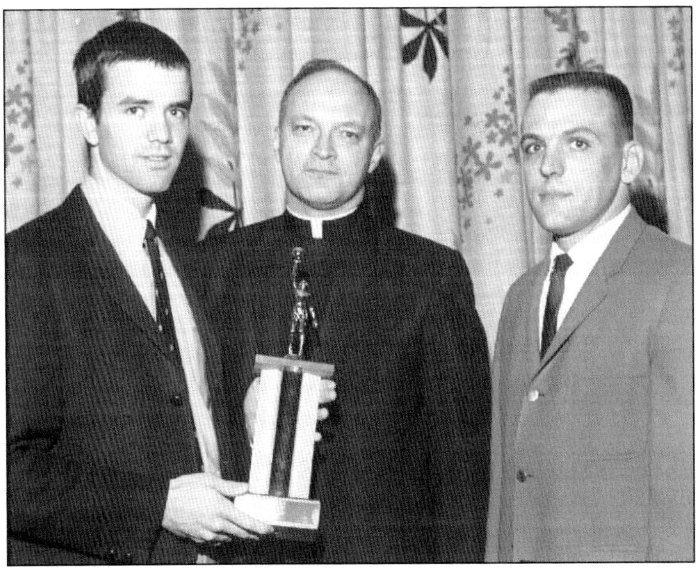

Second Basketball Coach. Joe Blaha was a local man who graduated from West Liberty State College in 1959. A high school coach for three years, Blaha coached the Wheeling Cardinals from 1961 to 1971, during which his teams recorded 82 wins and 135 losses. After leaving coaching, Blaha became a Wheeling businessman. Pictured are Jed O'Connell (left), Pres. Frank Haig, SJ (center), and Blaha.

PAUL BAKER. Baker visited the university in December 1997 to autograph his book *Moments in Time* and reminisce about his eight years coaching at Wheeling in the 1970s. He had a win-loss record of 128-107 and coached standouts such as scorers James "Dickey" Kelly, Ron Gaddy, and Paul Mullholland and rebounders like Mike Barnes, Al Walker, and Eddie Graham.

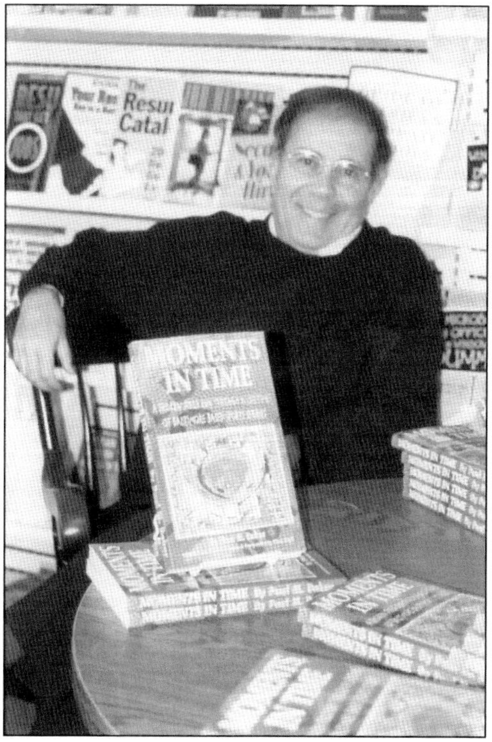

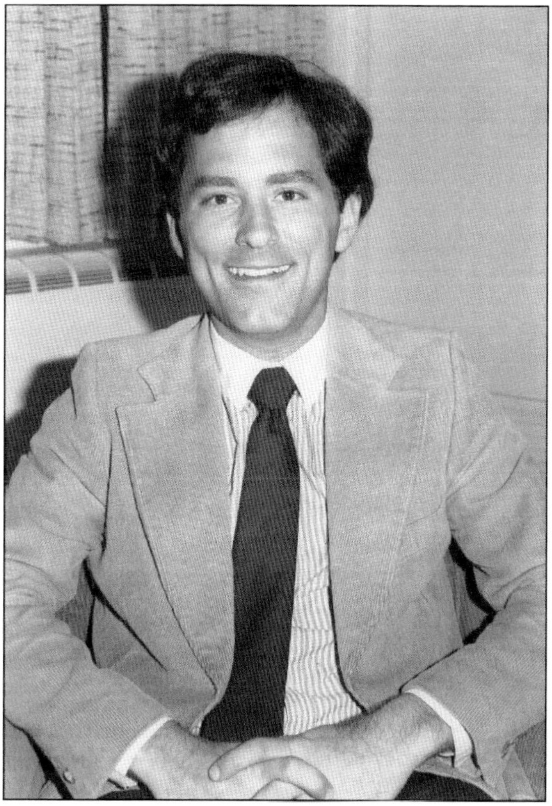

JAMES O'BRIEN. For five years, O'Brien coached the Cardinal teams to a 74-69 win-loss record. Standout players included Jeff Kepros, Bryant Houston, Paul McIntyre, and Tom Conroy. After leaving Wheeling, O'Brien coached at several universities and then with the Boston Celtics. During the past decade, he has been head coach for three NBA teams—the Boston Celtics, the Philadelphia 76ers, and the Indiana Pacers.

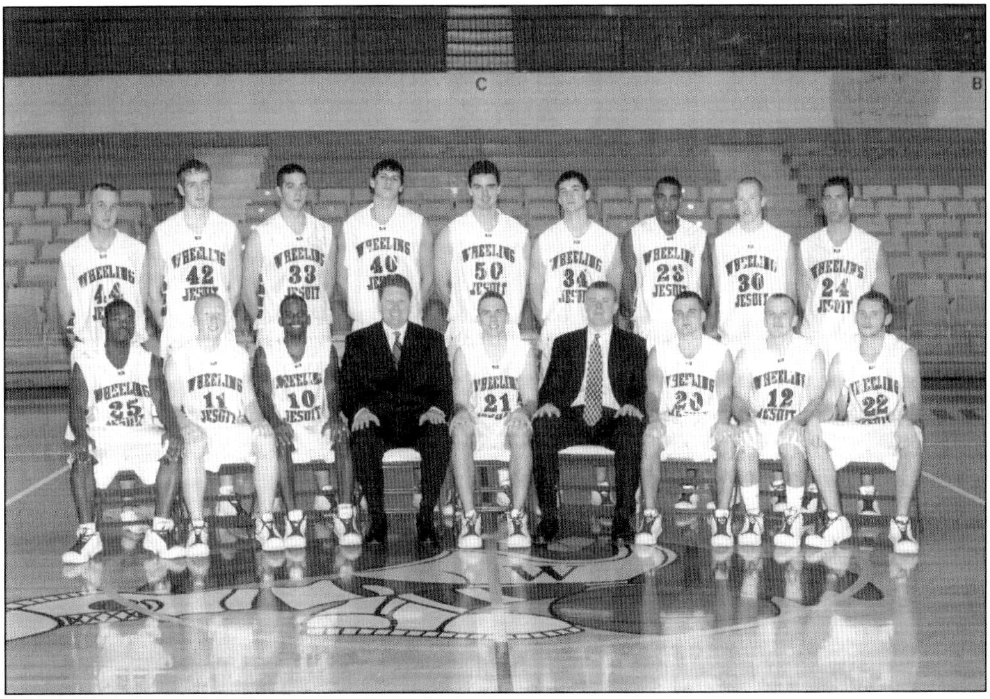

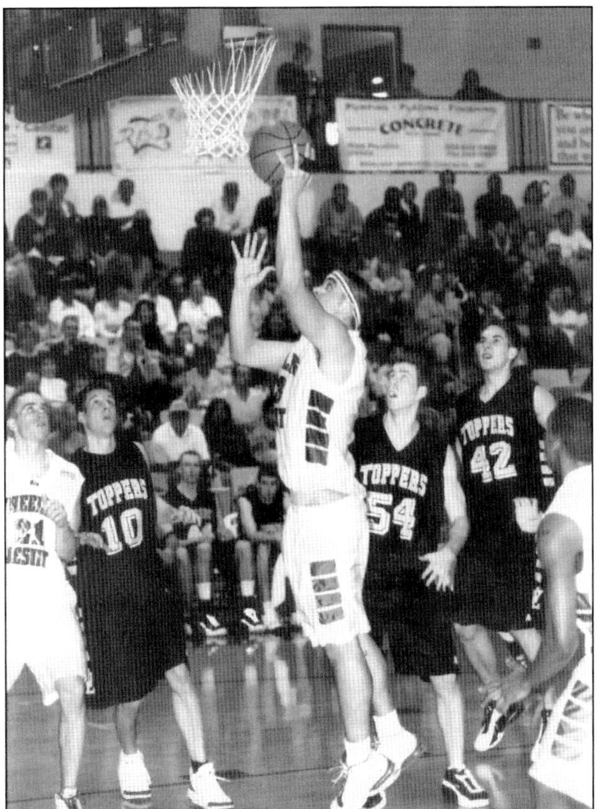

JAY AND DAN. Jay DeFruscio was Jim O'Brien's assistant and took over the top job in 1987. As head coach for 15 of his 20 years at Wheeling Jesuit, DeFruscio led teams to 251 wins against 182 losses. He then became assistant coach for the Indiana Pacers under O'Brien. In this picture of the 2001–2002 squad, DeFruscio is seated fourth from left, while his assistant Danny Sancomb is sixth from left. Sancomb took over as Wheeling's head coach after DeFruscio's departure.

STRONG RIVALS. Wheeling Jesuit and West Liberty State University have a strong rivalry, especially between the basketball teams. West Liberty's campus is located about eight miles north of Wheeling. One can expect packed field houses whenever these two teams play (usually three times a year). The games attract not only students, but also people from the community.

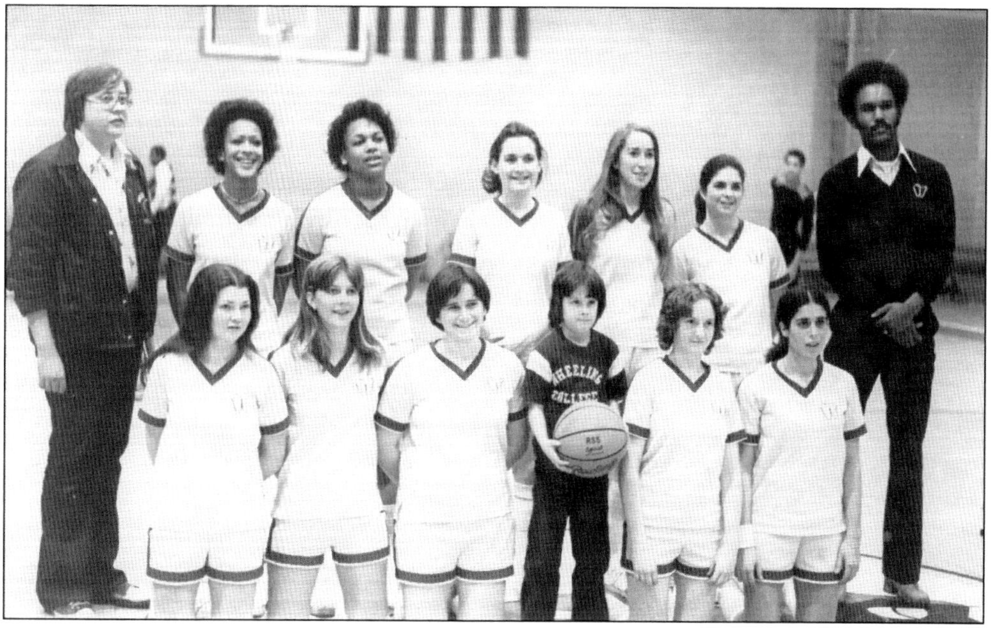

Women's Basketball. In 1976, intercollegiate basketball started for women at Wheeling Jesuit because of the efforts of students like Debbie DiFalco and the support of administrators like Kitty McCready, the registrar, who was appointed director of women's athletics. The head coach was Ron Kelly (far right), and his assistant was Mike Veneman (far left). The women's team struggled at first but steadily improved.

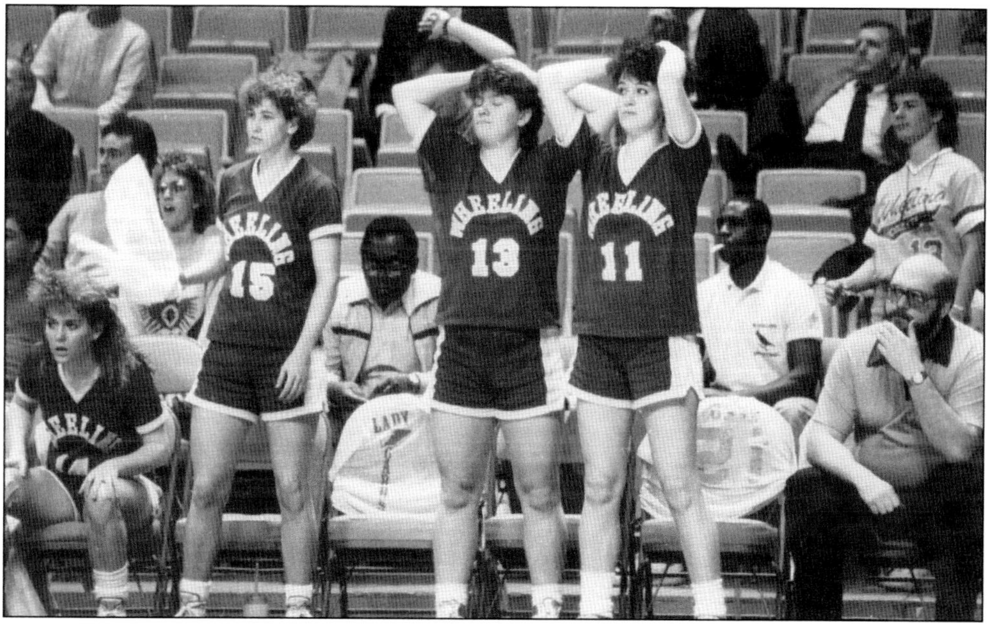

Defeated by Wesleyan. Disbelief and dismay are written on the faces of, from left to right, Sharon Nester, Amelia Reed, Cheryl Petras, and Frances MacDonald as Wheeling Jesuit goes down 58-55 at the hands of West Virginia Wesleyan in the West Virginia Conference Semifinals in Charleston. In 1988, the women had posted a 21-10 record, had beaten archrival West Liberty three times, and had defeated Wesleyan by 15 points earlier in the season.

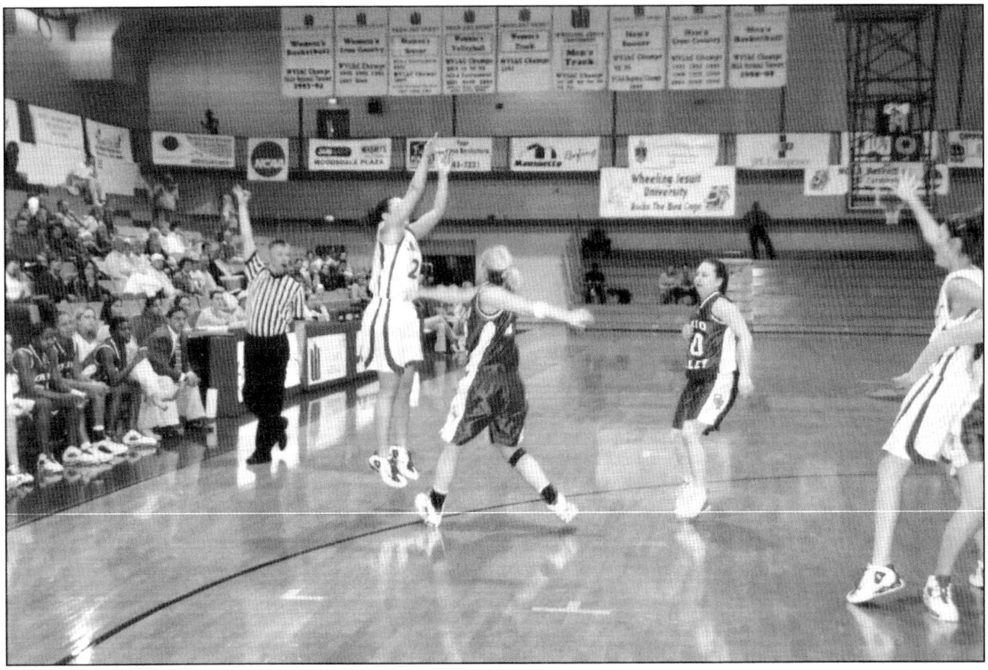

Wheeling College vs. Ohio Valley, 1993. The WJU women's basketball program has become increasingly successful and popular on campus. Two coaches, Dan Hustead and Joe Key, created winning programs. The uniforms that the women wear have also become more colorful.

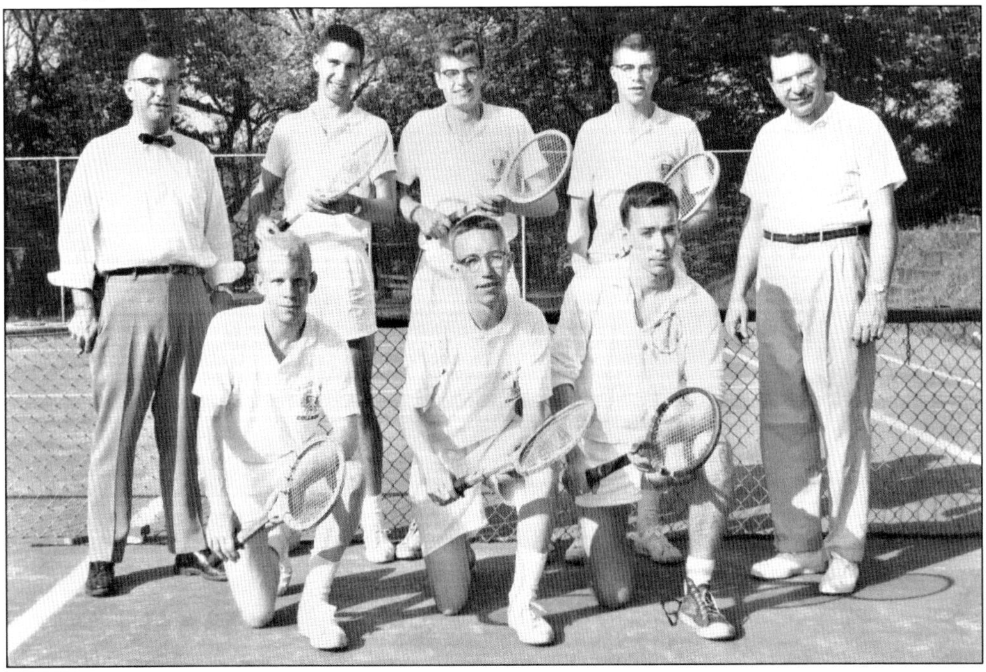

First (Men's) Tennis Team. The 1958 tennis team lost all four of its regularly scheduled matches but still won the West Virginia Conference tournament. Tennis is now one of the 16 intercollegiate sports programs at the university that have both men's and women's teams. The women's team began in 2005.

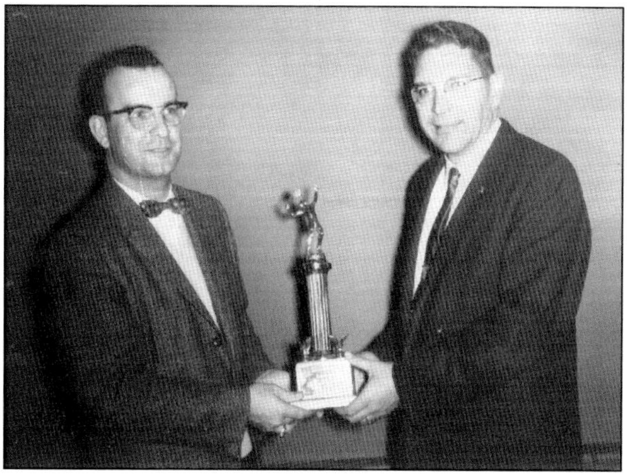

First Athletic Trophy. Moderator Dr. Robert Grob (left) and coach J. Loren Mercer hold the first sports trophy won by any team at Wheeling College. Don Mercer '60, Loren's son, won the state championship in tennis by defeating Sam Bacote of West Virginia. *The Spokesman* said the trophy was on display in Swint Hall and that "every few minutes . . . Dr. Grob checks to make sure no one has lifted the prize." Ironically, no one knows where the trophy is currently located.

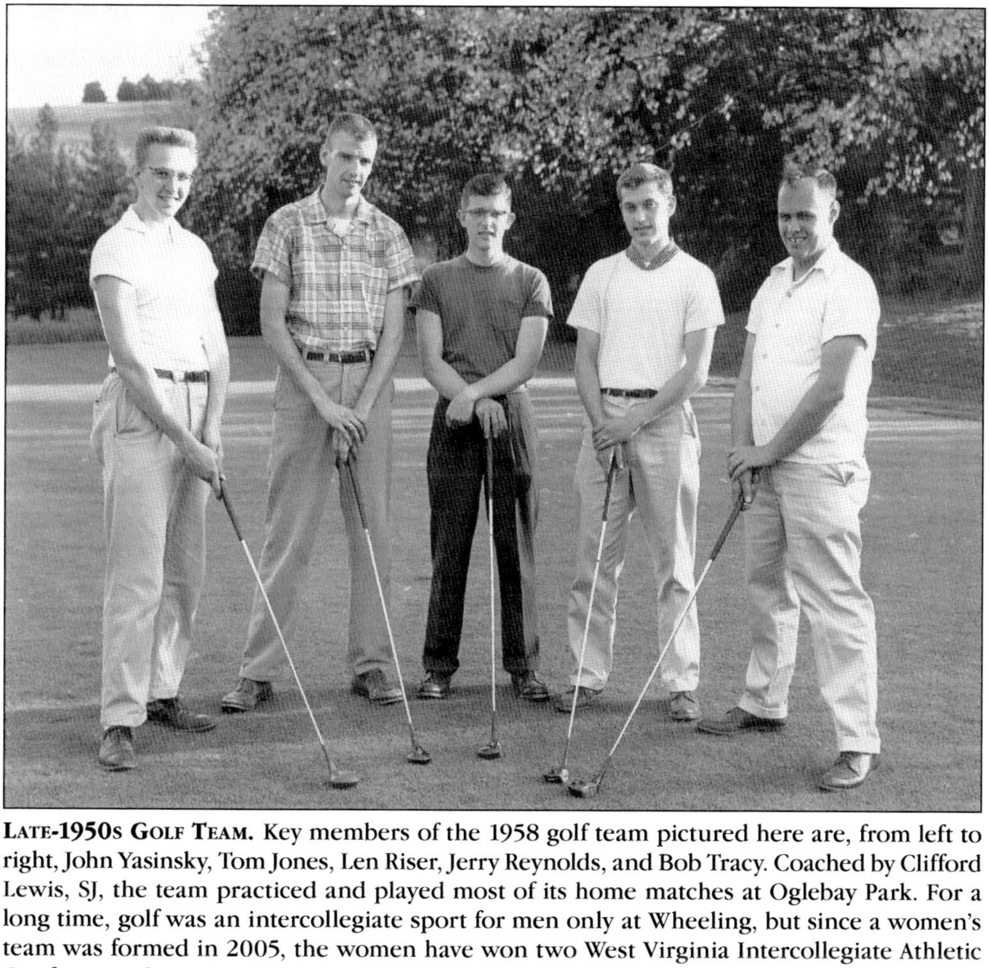

Late-1950s Golf Team. Key members of the 1958 golf team pictured here are, from left to right, John Yasinsky, Tom Jones, Len Riser, Jerry Reynolds, and Bob Tracy. Coached by Clifford Lewis, SJ, the team practiced and played most of its home matches at Oglebay Park. For a long time, golf was an intercollegiate sport for men only at Wheeling, but since a women's team was formed in 2005, the women have won two West Virginia Intercollegiate Athletic Conference championships.

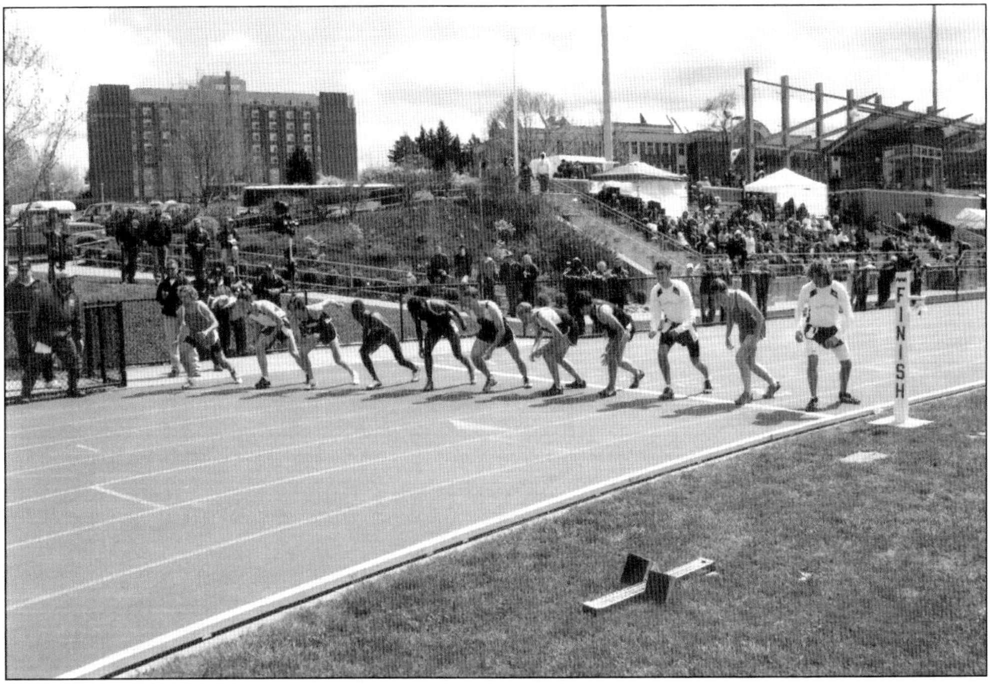

Men's Track and Field. Wheeling Jesuit entered track-and-field competition for both men and women in 1994. Two years later, an Olympic-quality track was laid on the LaRosa athletic field. Mark Swiger took over as cross-country and track coach in 1997 and built a credible team over the next eight years. Track and field offers many student athletes an opportunity to compete in intercollegiate athletics.

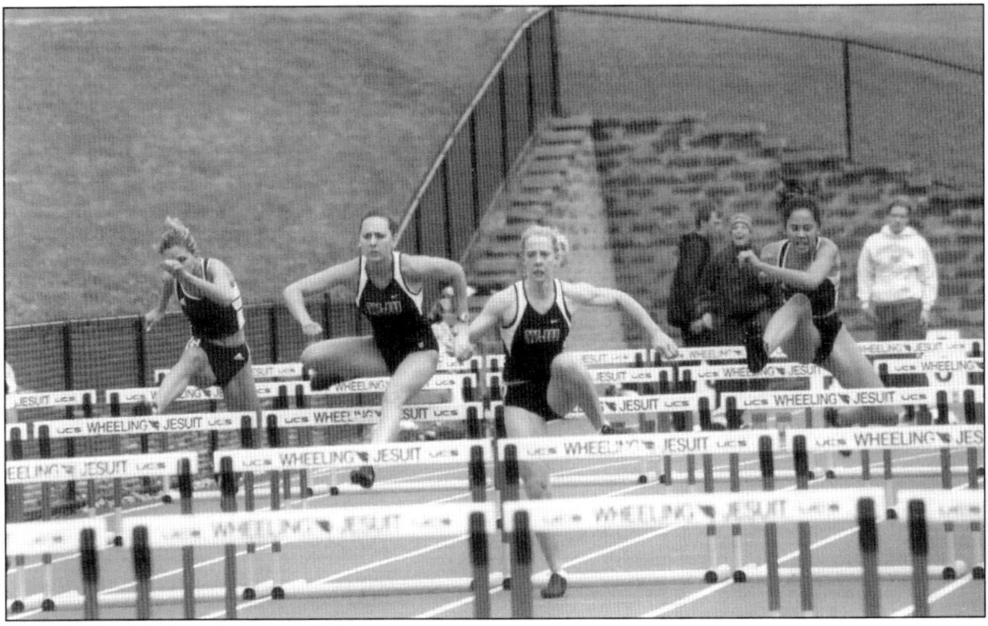

Women's Hurdles. Track and field and cross-country have opened up numerous possibilities for female athletes at Wheeling Jesuit, and the track team has twice won the WVIAC championship (and come in second seven times).

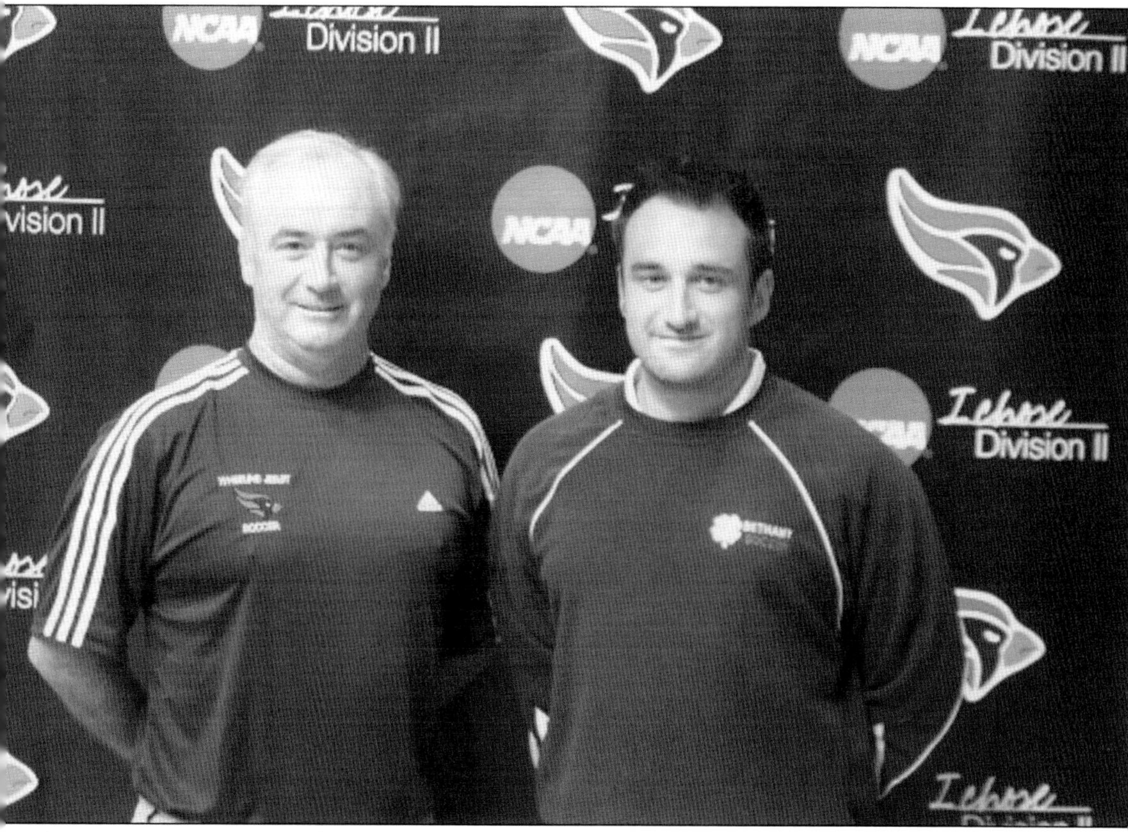

SOCCER COACH. Jim Regan has been head coach of WJU men's soccer teams since 1982 and has guided the Cardinals to conference championships. His teams have recorded well over 300 wins. For approximately 10 years, he coached both the men's and women's soccer teams at Wheeling. Here, he poses with his son Sean, who played for the Cardinals for four years.

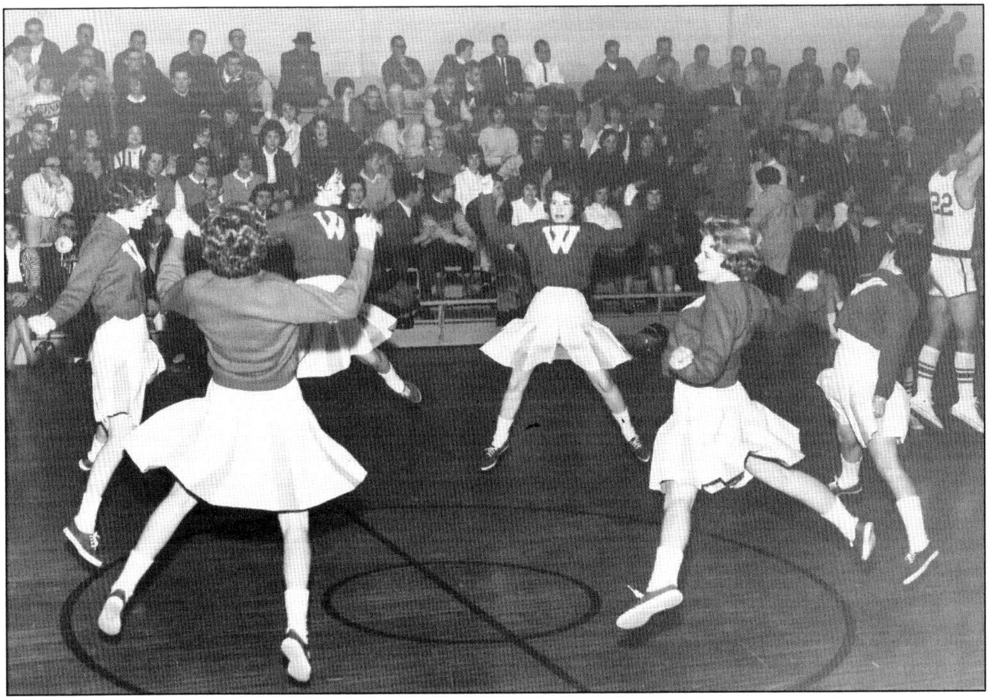

CHEERLEADERS. Cheerleaders from the 1962–1963 basketball season perform before a fairly large crowd. Until the 1970s, cheerleading was the most prestigious athletic program for women. Today, cheerleading routines have become more elaborate and daring, but in 1963, this style was typical.

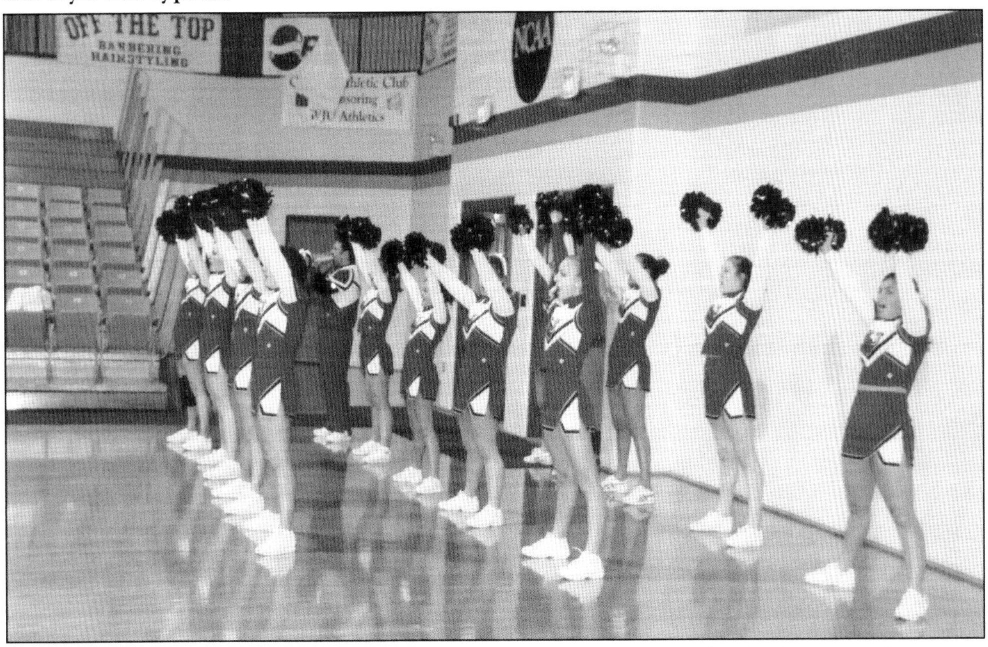

CHEERLEADERS OF TODAY. Cheerleading at Wheeling Jesuit is now for both men and women, and they engage in far more gymnastics than in earlier times. This photograph shows 12 women and one man at a basketball game.

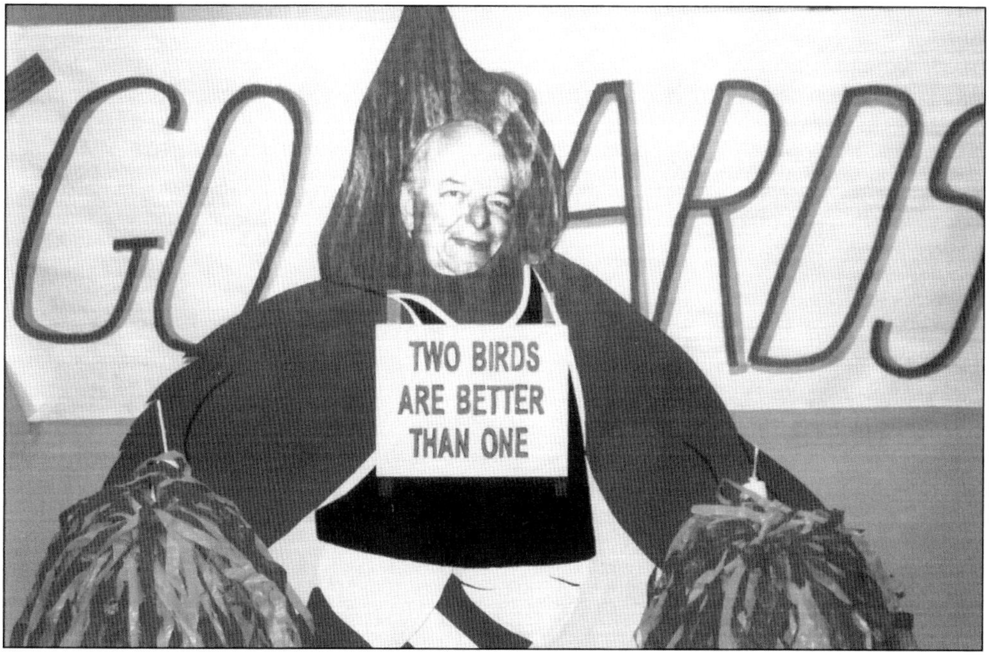

Byrd and the Cardinal. The cardinal has been the name for most of the university's sports teams since students took a vote in 1955 on the Wheeling College mascot. They chose the cardinal and the school colors, crimson and gold, at the same time. In this picture, a student has put a photograph of Sen. Robert Byrd's face in the hole of a large wooden board depicting a cardinal, making an obvious pun on the senator's name.

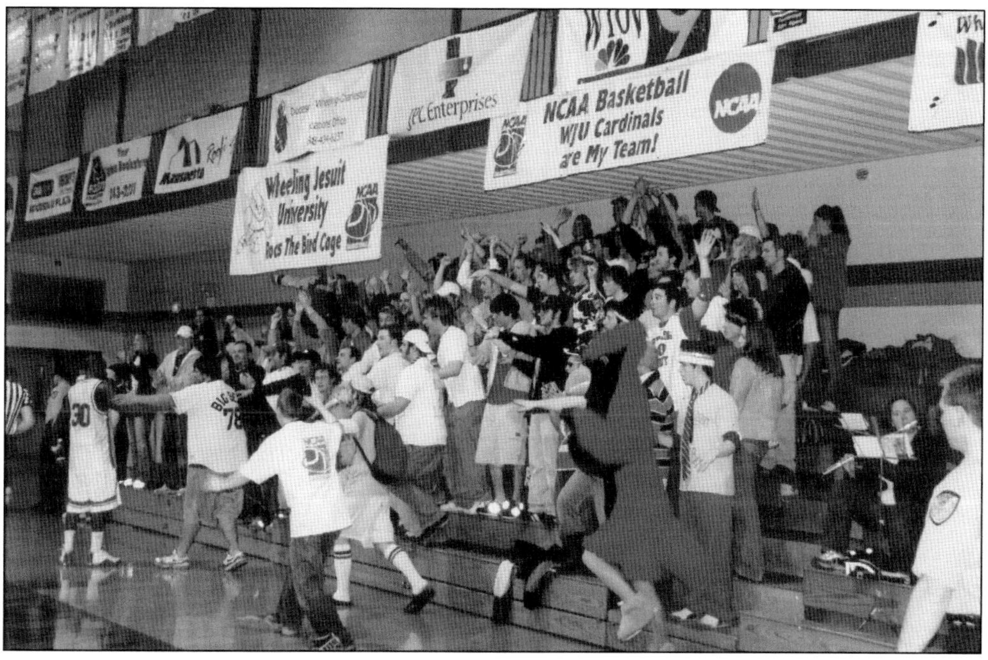

Pep Club. In recent years, a pep band and a cohort of approximately 75 students will sit and stand in the bleachers behind the basket at the far end of the field house to cheer on the Cardinals at home games.

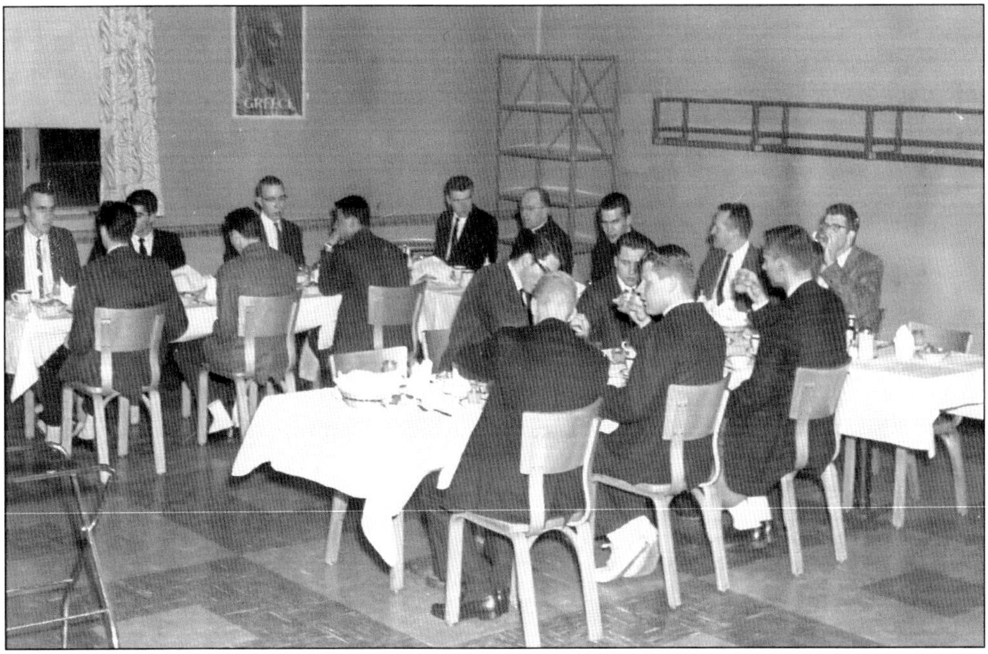

EARLY BASKETBALL BANQUET. The earliest sports banquets were modest affairs that attracted athletes, coaches, and a few administrators and faculty due mainly to the limited number of intercollegiate sports programs on campus. This picture of the 1960 banquet shows only Fr. McGoarty, SJ (back row, fifth from left), and coach Ed Coyne (back row, seventh from left) with members of the basketball team.

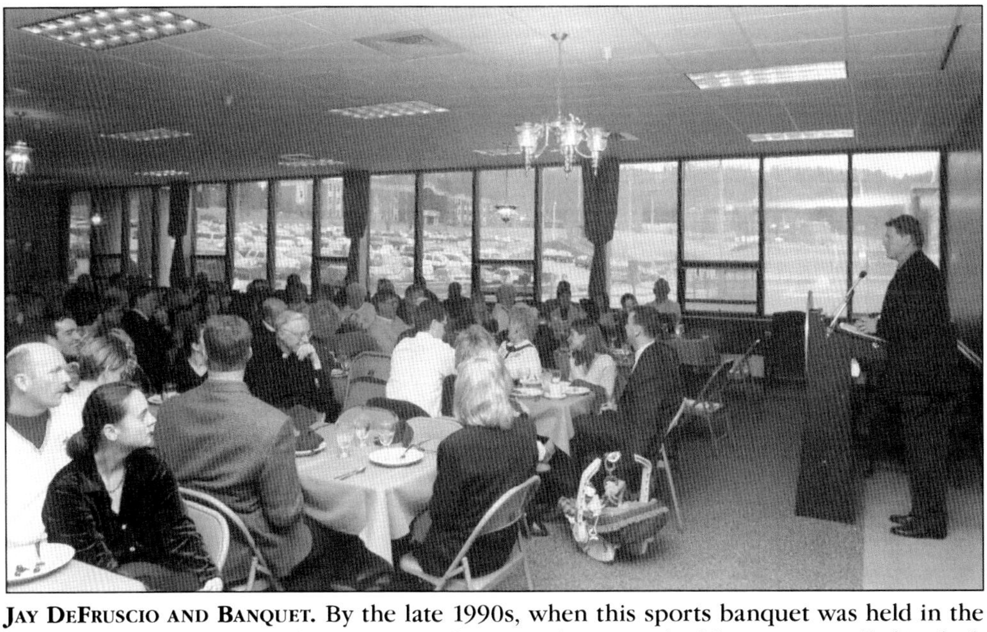

JAY DEFRUSCIO AND BANQUET. By the late 1990s, when this sports banquet was held in the Ericson Alumni Center in the McDonough Center, banquets had become a really big deal. Many athletes and coaches from lots of teams, Jesuits, faculty, administrators, alumni, and family members attended the events to eat good food in plush surroundings, listen to speeches, and see honors conferred on extraordinary athletes.

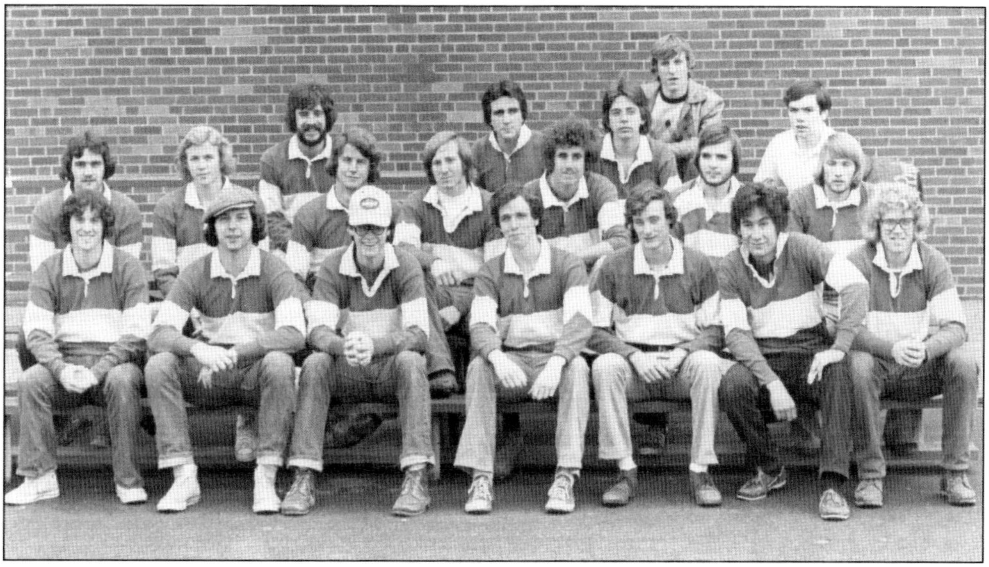

Rugby Club. The Rugby Club was founded in 1966 with the aid of Tom Vogel, a recent graduate who was a proctor (dorm counselor). The club received only minimal financial support from the college, but it generated strong excitement on campus and provided an outlet for students who wanted to play a contact team sport that would involve travel to different colleges in adjacent states. The college newspaper devoted a major story to the Rugby Club's exploits in almost every issue from the 1960s through the 1980s. The club lasted until 2000, but the wide availability of other contact sports since the 1990s reduced support for the team. This is a picture of the 1978 Rugby Club.

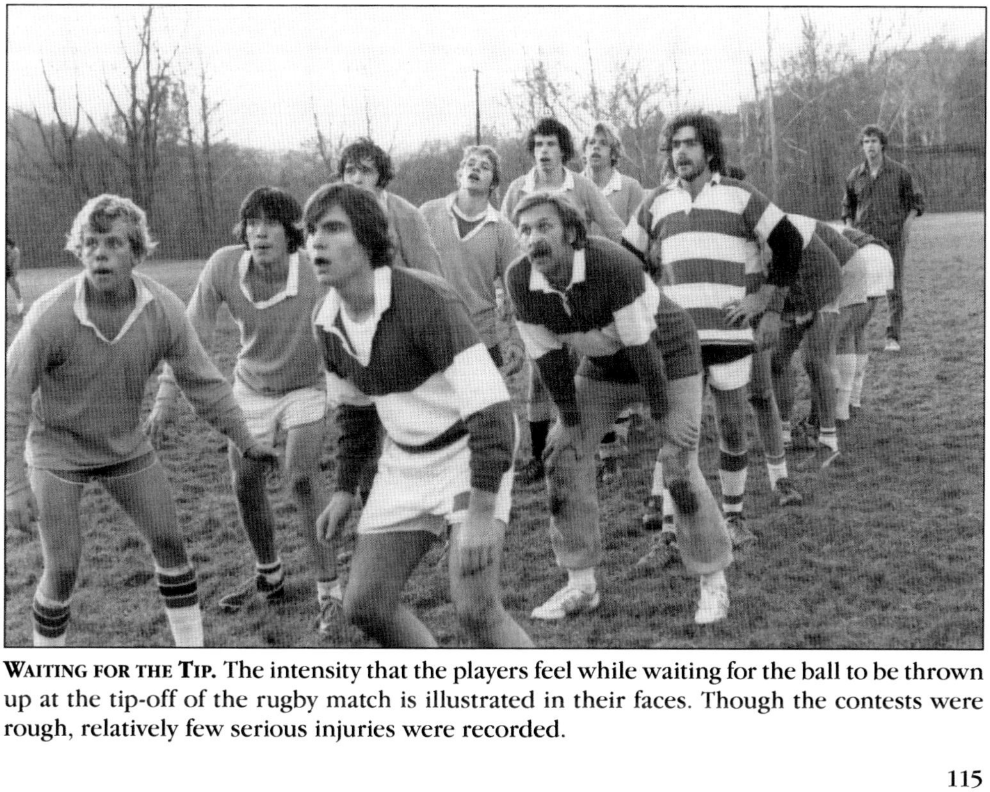

Waiting for the Tip. The intensity that the players feel while waiting for the ball to be thrown up at the tip-off of the rugby match is illustrated in their faces. Though the contests were rough, relatively few serious injuries were recorded.

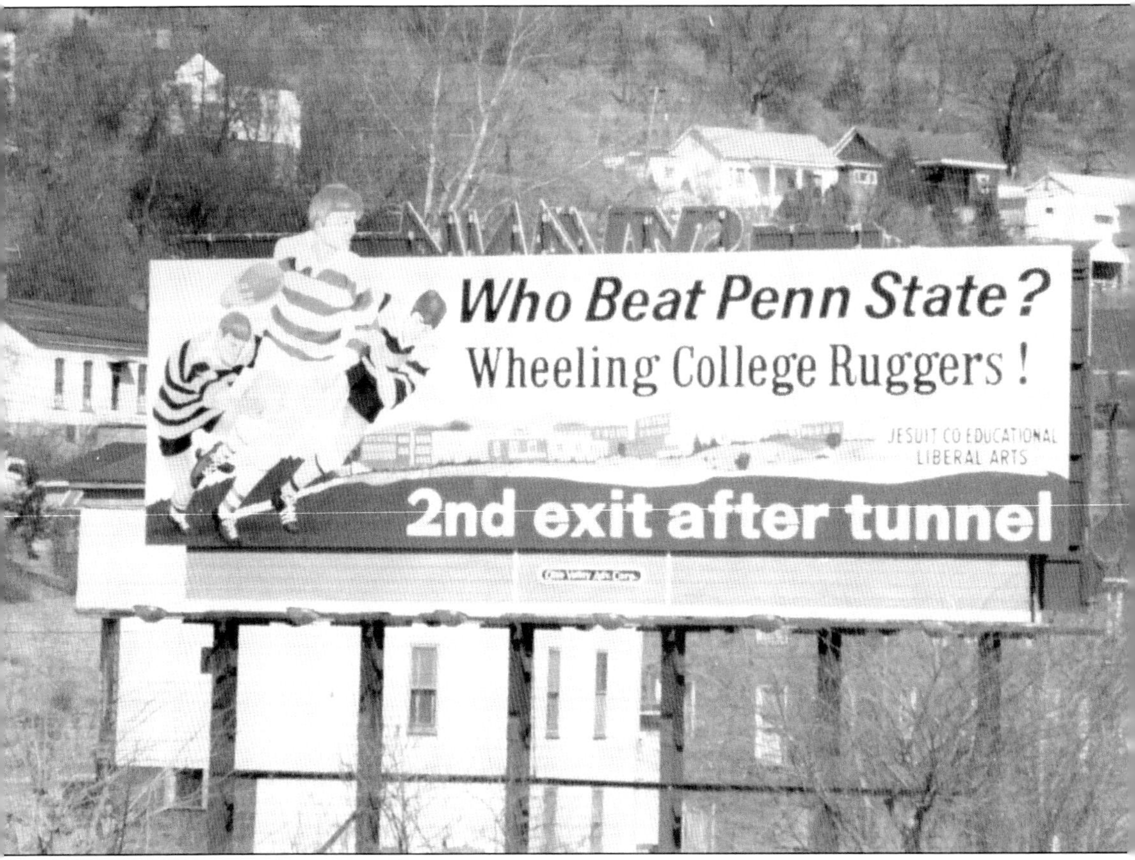

BEATING PENN STATE. On February 27, 1970, this lighted billboard reminded people traveling east on I-70 about the Wheeling College rugby team's most celebrated win. Both the A and B teams defeated Penn State's squads. The billboard got front-page coverage in both Wheeling and State College, Pennsylvania, the home of Penn State. A second billboard erected near the Wheeling College displayed the rugby schedule for the semester.

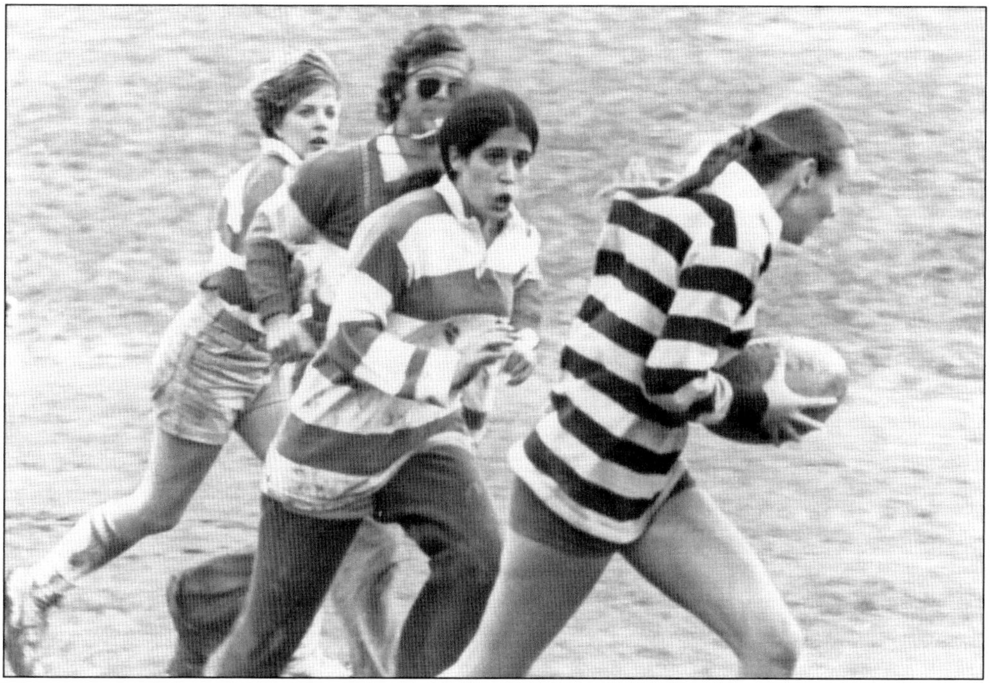

WOMEN'S RUGBY. In the mid-1980s, women like Debbie DiFalco and Christine O'Brien pushed hard for women's sports teams. For a few years, they led the effort to play such sports as basketball and rugby. Basketball survived, but women's rugby soon ended. Women's rugby was revived in the 1996–1997 academic year, but interest soon waned again.

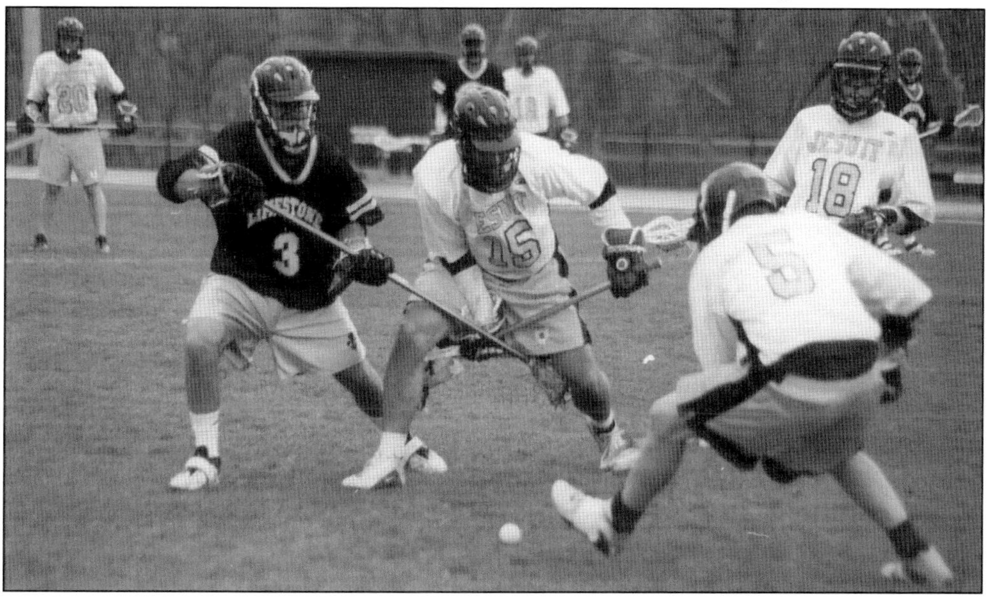

LACROSSE. Lacrosse began in 1979 as a club sport for men and was finally given intercollegiate status in the fall of 1990. The men have generally played a schedule of 15 games during the spring season. For a number of reasons, lacrosse competed with rugby for players. There is now also a women's lacrosse team at the university. Here, the men play Limestone College, which is located in Gaffney, South Carolina.

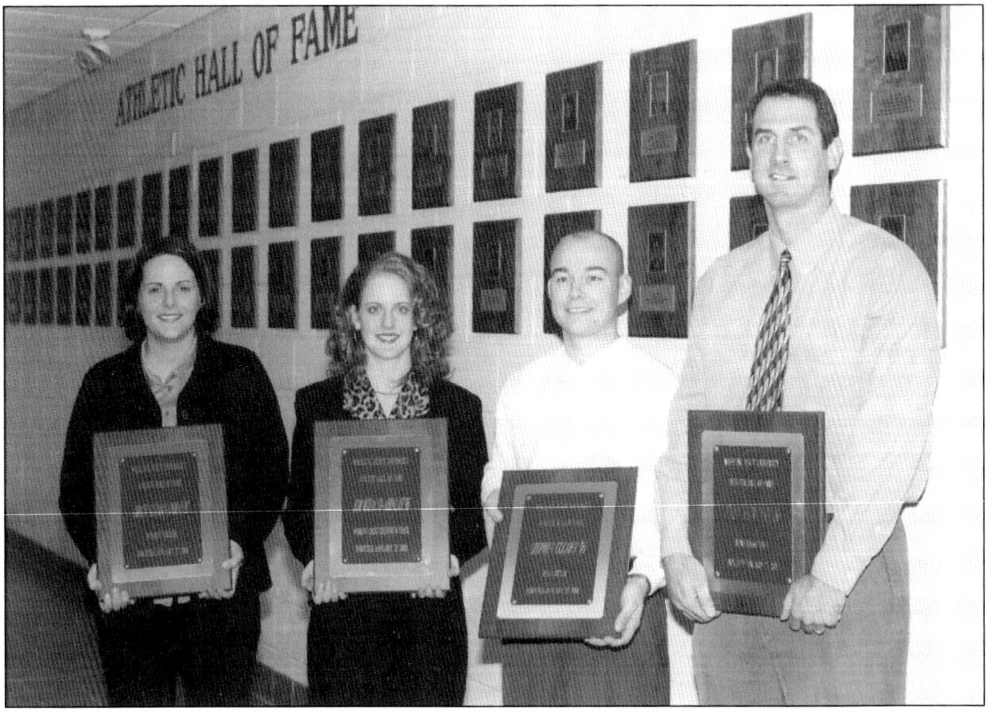

Hall of Fame. Wheeling created an Athletic Hall of Fame in 1987. Since then, 74 individuals have been honored with plaques on the wall outside of the basketball court. Seven coaches, one faculty member, two administrations, and sixty-four athletes have been selected. Pictured here are, from left to right, Chrissy Sassaman Findlay '98 (soccer), Kim Mihalyo Abdalah '95 (cross-country and track), Stephen Cleary '95 (soccer), and Paul McIntyre '86 (basketball).

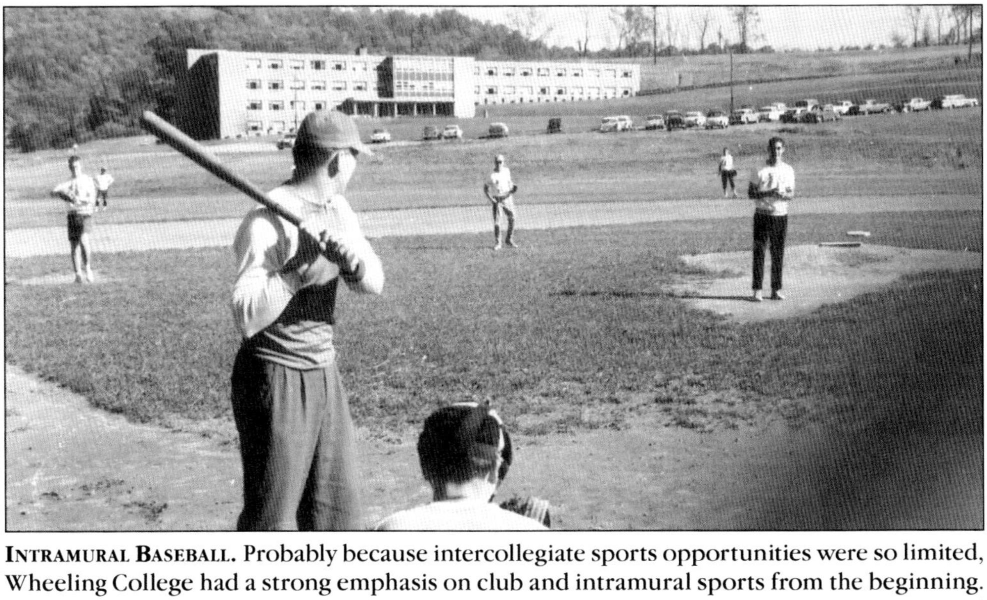

Intramural Baseball. Probably because intercollegiate sports opportunities were so limited, Wheeling College had a strong emphasis on club and intramural sports from the beginning. Students started teams in order to play touch football, basketball, volleyball, ping-pong, and baseball. Wrestling, archery, bowling, and martial arts clubs have also existed on campus. Intramural sports remain popular today.

Six

The Alumni

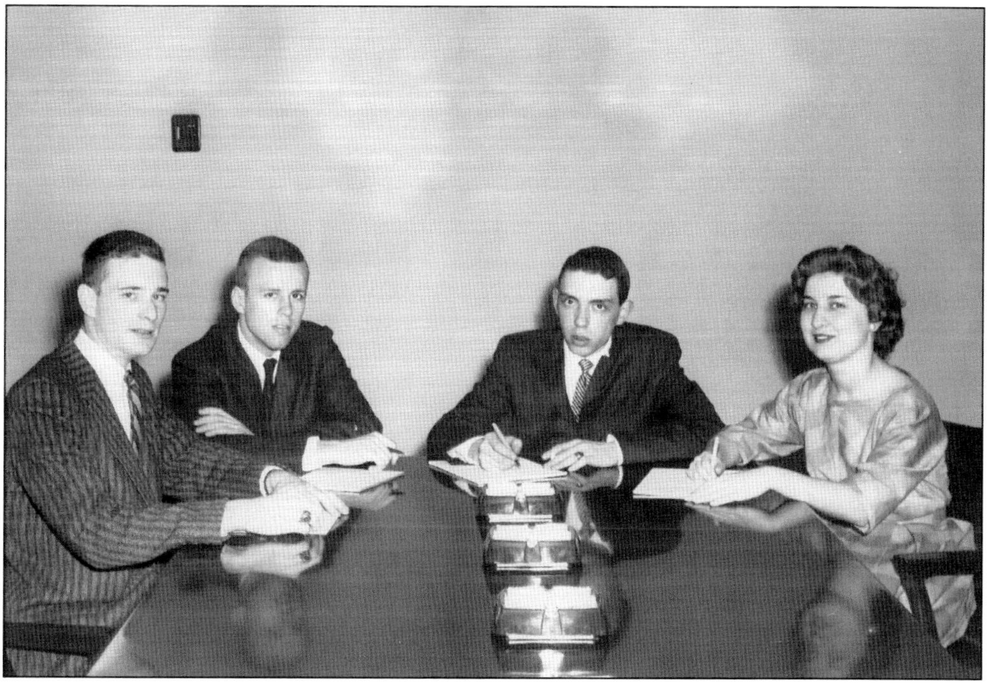

Alumni Officers. The Wheeling Jesuit Alumni Council currently has 37 members and 100 class agents. The council recommends alumni for four different awards for achievement each year and helps plan reunions. Alumni chapters in eight cities hold two events per year to raise funds and recommend students, among other activities. In 1961, four of the five newly elected class alumni officers are, from left to right, Peter May, Dan Haller, Sam Carcione, and Barbara Yeager.

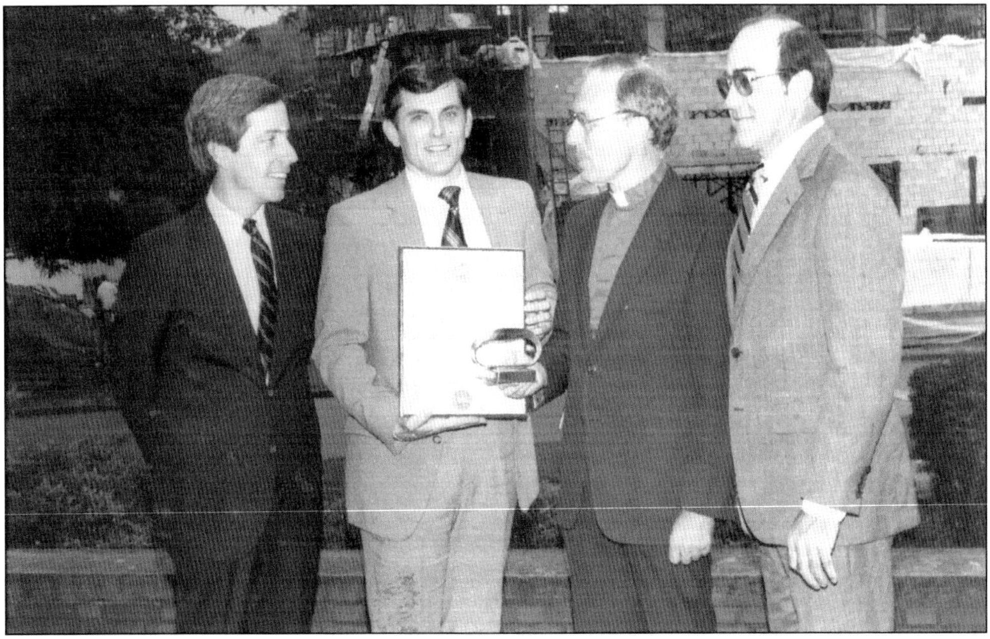

CASE/US STEEL AWARD. In 1984, William Gallagher, president of the Alumni Association, received the CASE/US Steel Alumni Award for Sustained Giving for the best percentage of giving by alumni among colleges and universities. Gallagher holds the certificate, and Fr. Thomas Acker holds the trophy. At left is Pat Joyce, and at right is Tom Vogel. (Courtesy of the Wheeling-Charleston Diocese Archives.)

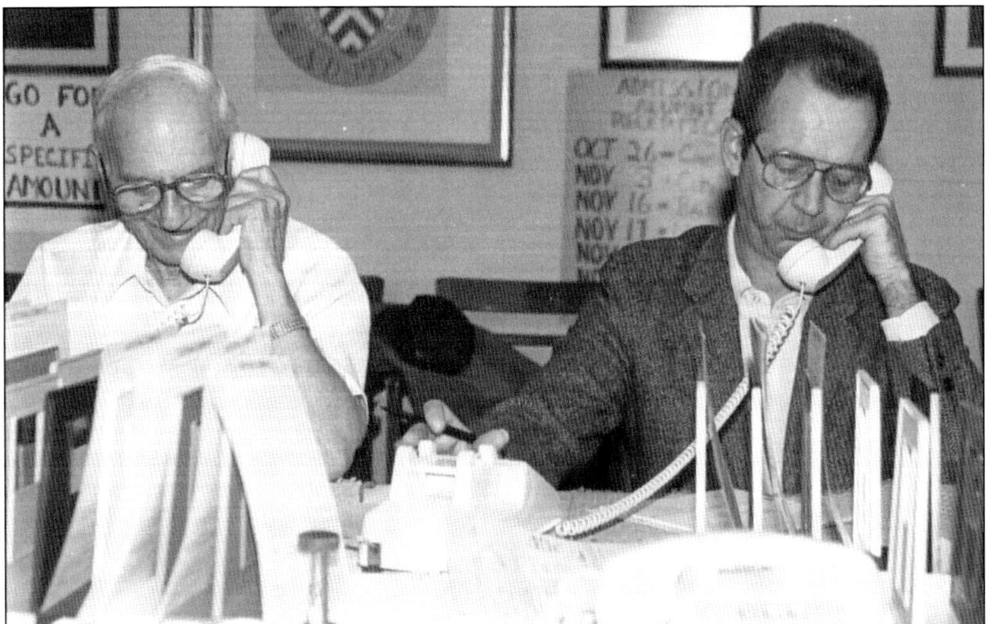

PHONE-A-THON. One of the important ways that colleges and universities convince alumni and friends of the institution to donate is by holding phone-a-thons. Every year, the college makes a weeklong effort to raise money by calling alumni. Here, Bob Teufel (left), husband of the college receptionist, Madelaine, and Tom Carrigan, director of alumni, sell the college.

Keeping Alumni Informed. In 1958, the administration began publishing a four-page flyer called *This Is Wheeling College*. Under Fr. Charles Currie, SJ, the college shifted to a newspaper format and published the *Wheeling College Chronicle* once per month. Pres. Thomas Acker, SJ, turned *Wheeling Jesuit College Chronicle* into a slick, professional-looking quarterly. The *Chronicle*'s Spring 1995 cover shows Fr. James O'Brien, longtime teacher of philosophy, conversing with an unidentified man on campus.

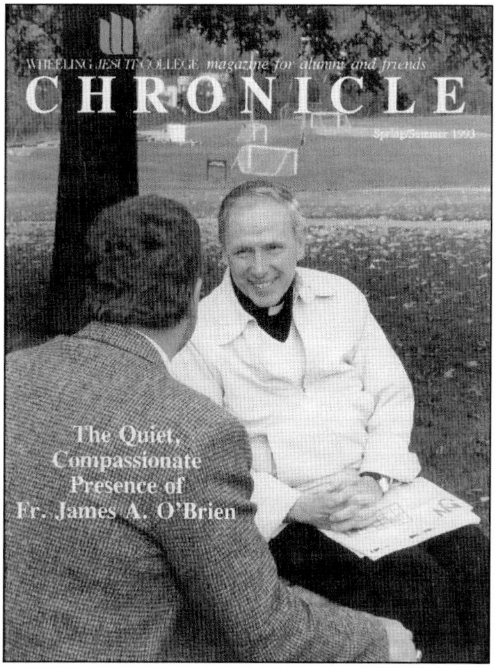

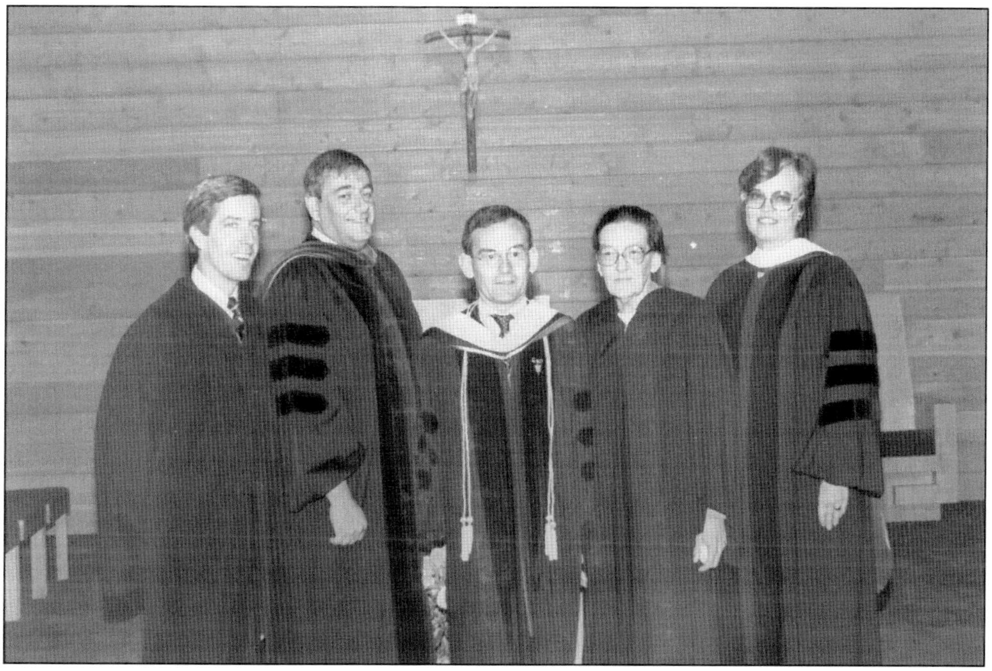

Alumni Honors. At the fall honors convocation in 1985, three alumni were given awards: Ed Shahady, a doctor and chair of the Department of Medicine at the University of North Carolina; John Gasiorowski, an associate professor of social science at Wheeling; and Rev. Margaret Phillimore, vicar of St. Luke's Episcopal Church in Wheeling, who is represented in the picture by a friend. Pictured, from left to right, are Pat Joyce, Ed Shahady, John Gasiorowski, Phillimore's unidentified friend, and Dr. Jeane Kammer, academic dean and a Wheeling College graduate. (Courtesy of the Wheeling-Charleston Diocese Archives.)

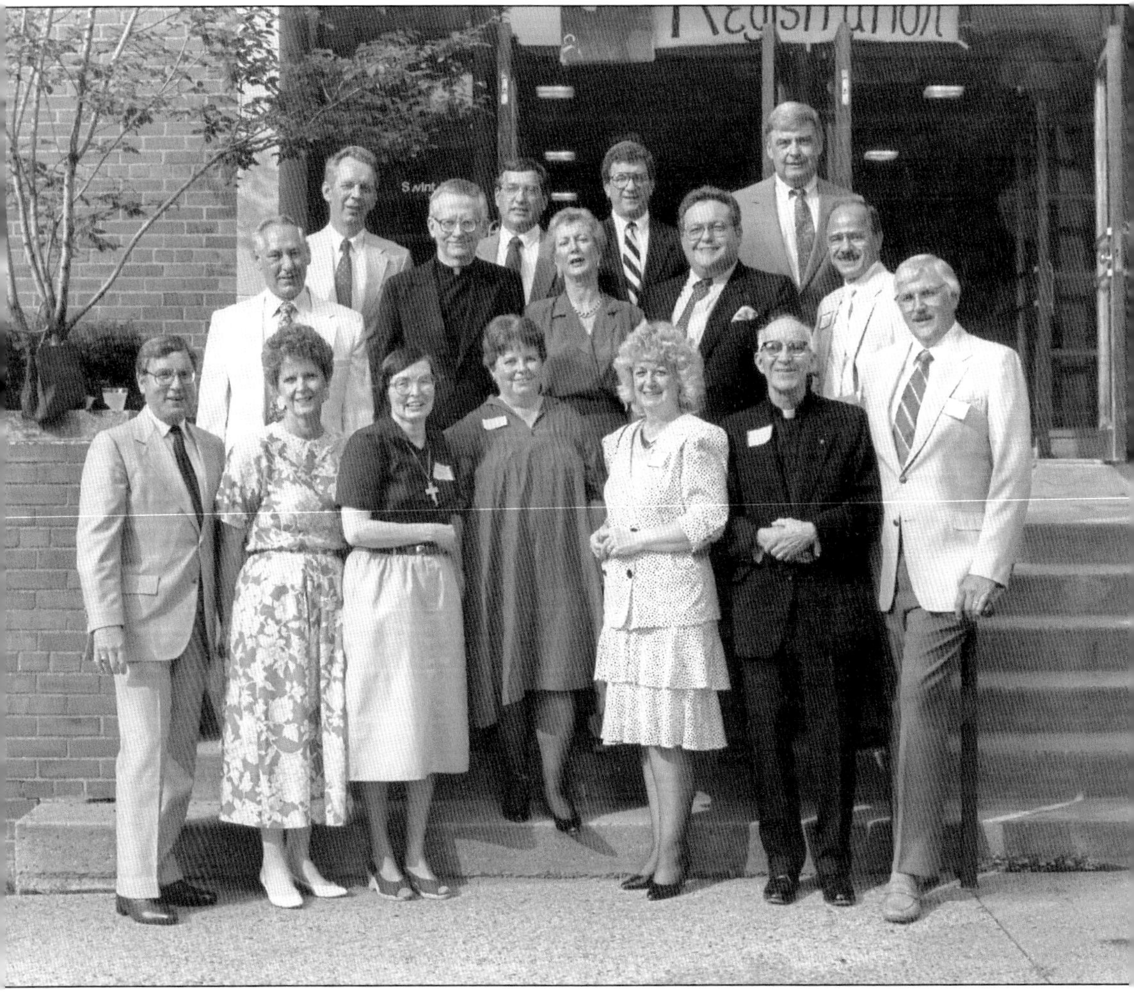

ALUMNI REUNIONS. Wheeling holds alumni reunions every year, but each class is invited back to campus every fifth year. This picture shows the alums of the first graduating class, who returned in 1989. Third from left in the first row is Sr. Joanne Gonter, who spent her career teaching chemistry and music at the Mount de Chantal Visitation Academy. She became the school's alumni director and eventually headed the academy. With the closure of Mount de Chantal in May 2008, Sister Gonter retired and relocated to the Georgetown Visitation Academy in Washington, DC, but she continues to direct Mount de Chantal's alumni affairs.

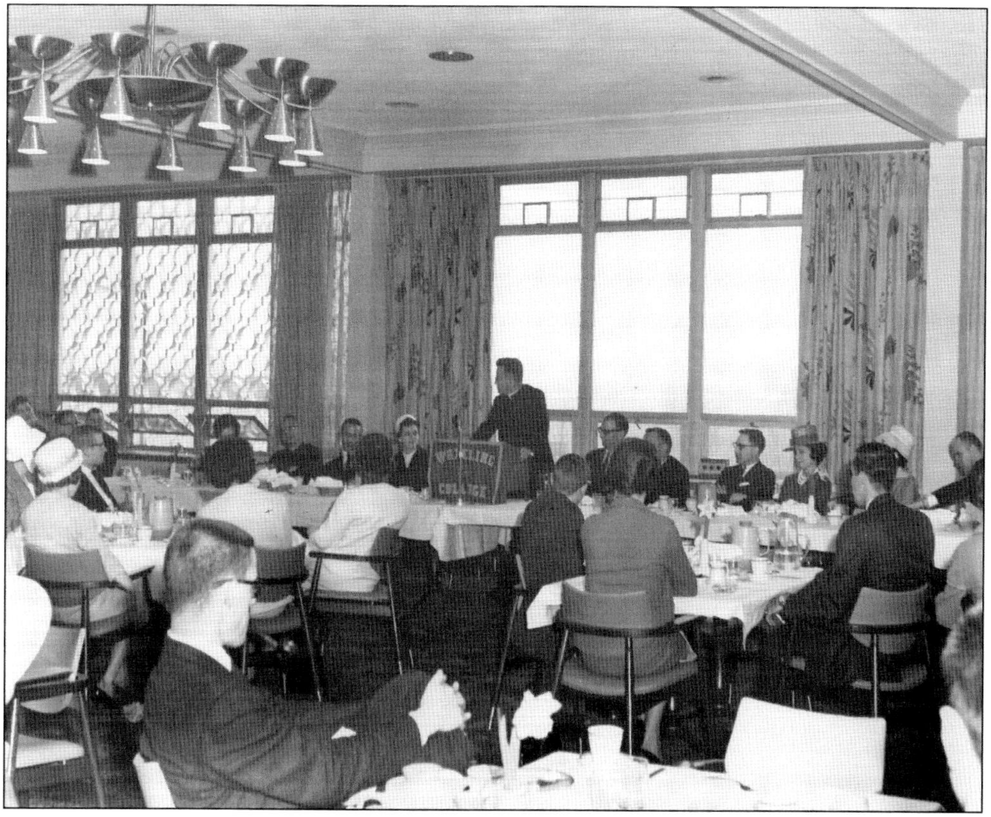

Communion Breakfast at a Reunion. Alumni reunions are held in the middle of the summer at Wheeling Jesuit, when the weather is usually hot and dry. At the end of every alumni weekend, participants go to a late afternoon Mass, followed by a reception, dinner, and party on Saturday, and a farewell breakfast on Sunday morning. In this image from the 1960s, Fr. William Troy addresses a Sunday morning breakfast.

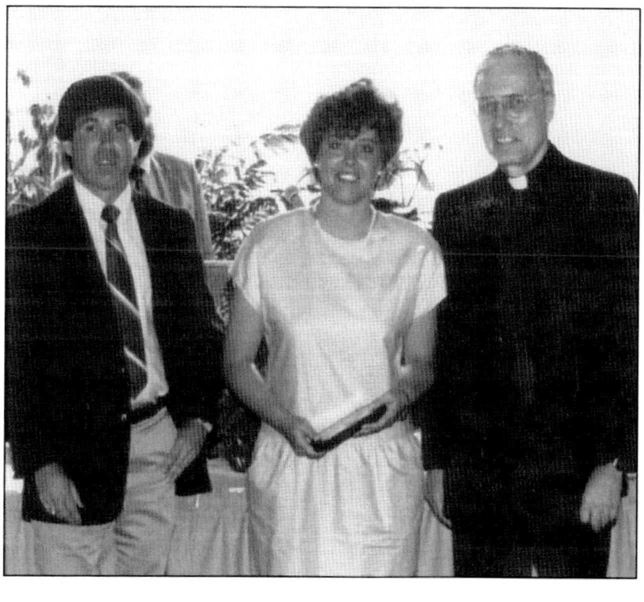

Edward Younkins '73. Younkins (left) acquired an MBA from Duquesne, then a PhD from the University of Mississippi. He has taught at Wheeling, his alma mater, throughout his career and was instrumental in the creation of both the evening division and the MBA programs at WJU. Younkins has written or edited six books, as well as numerous articles. His latest book is called *Flourishing and Happiness in a Free Society*.

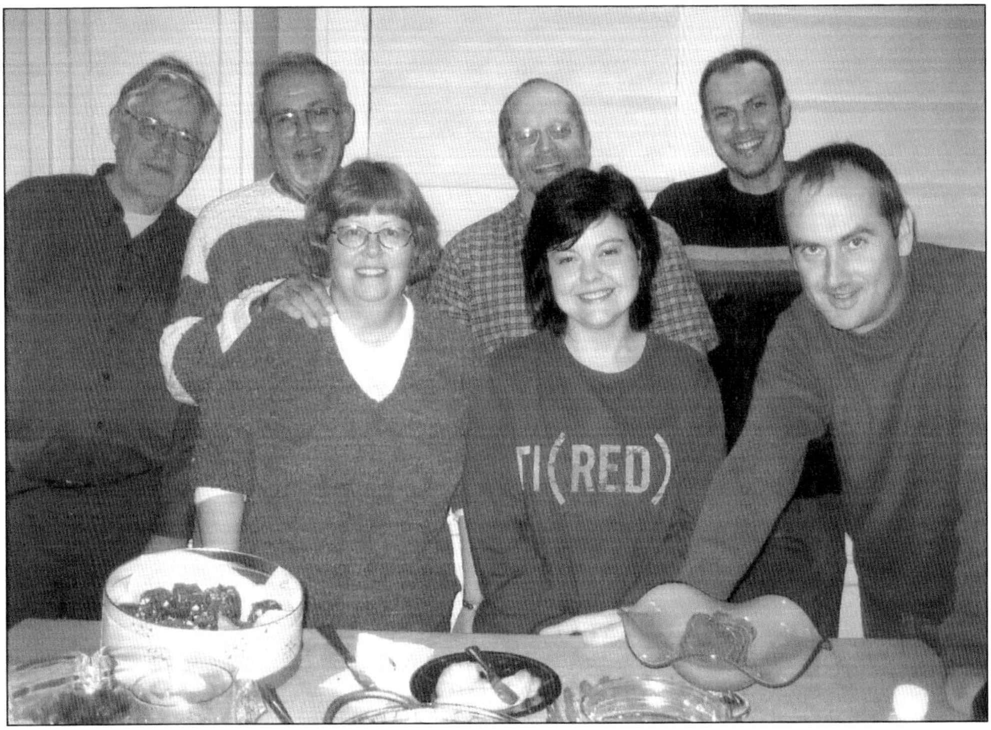

Rosanna Gatens '75. Gatens (first row, far left) acquired a master's degree from Duquesne in 1982 and a doctorate from the University of Pittsburgh 10 years later; both degrees focused on German history. Between 1985 and 2002, she taught history at Wheeling and Belmont Colleges. Since 2002, she has served as the director of the Center for Holocaust and Human Rights Education at Florida Atlantic University in Boca Raton, Florida.

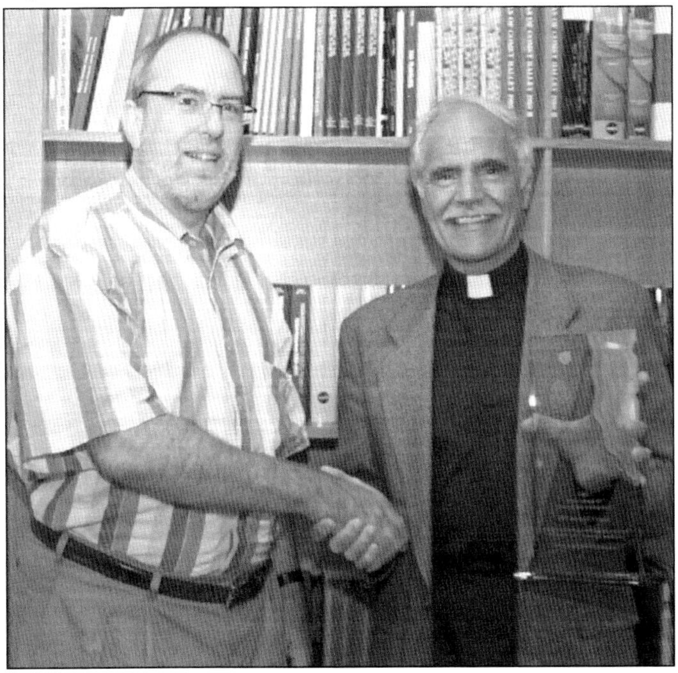

Mark Gresham '84. After graduation, Gresham (left) went to Japan to teach English and then worked for several Japanese firms. He is now the director of Japan for Cambridge University Press and president of United Publishers Services Limited. An avid photographer, Gresham supplied the pictures for the book *Japan Textures: Sight and Word*; Prof. A. Robert Lee provided the text. Gresham is pictured with Fr. Julio Giulietti.

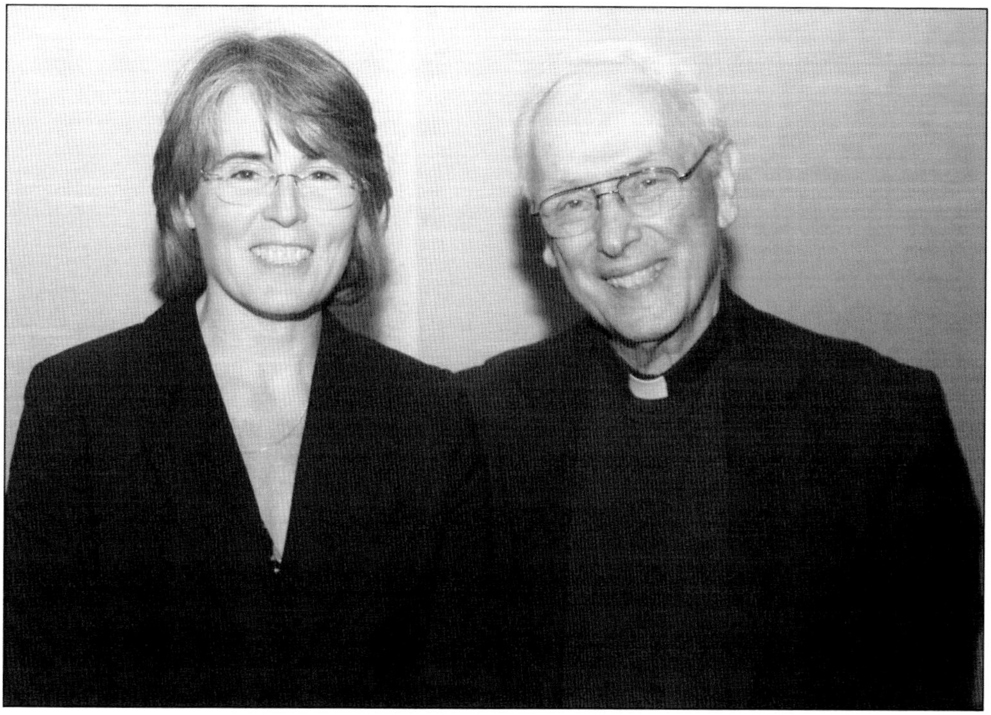

MARGARET "MIMIE" (O'HARA) HELM '84. Helm is currently the chair of the Wheeling Jesuit board of directors. Following graduation, she served in the Jesuit Volunteer Corps, helping to change the curriculum in Baltimore public schools. Helm entered the corporate world in marketing and sales at C&P Telephone, Bell Atlantic, and Verizon. She has served on the executive committee of St. Vincent de Paul of Baltimore.

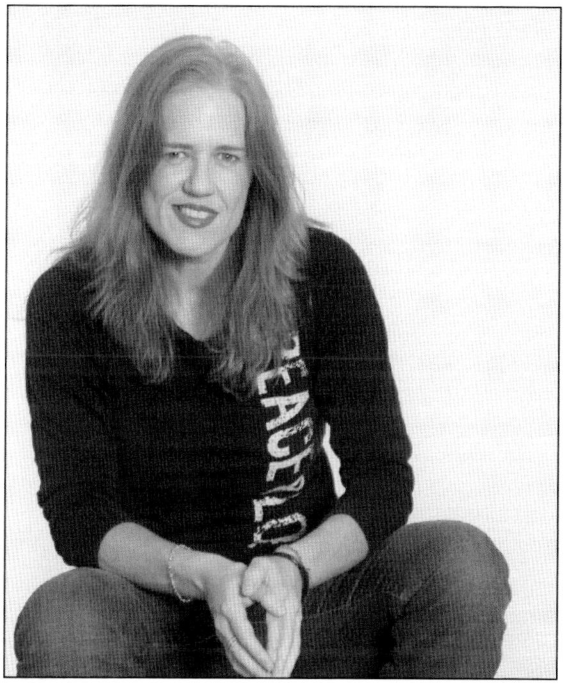

KATHERINE "KATIE" TORPEY '91. Torpey acquired a master's degree from the UCLA film school and settled into a career of writing for television and film. She wrote the original script for the film *The Perfect Man*, has written many other scripts, and received the prestigious UCLA Diane Thomas Screenwriting Award for her accomplishments. She recently finished an autobiography entitled *Just Breathe*.

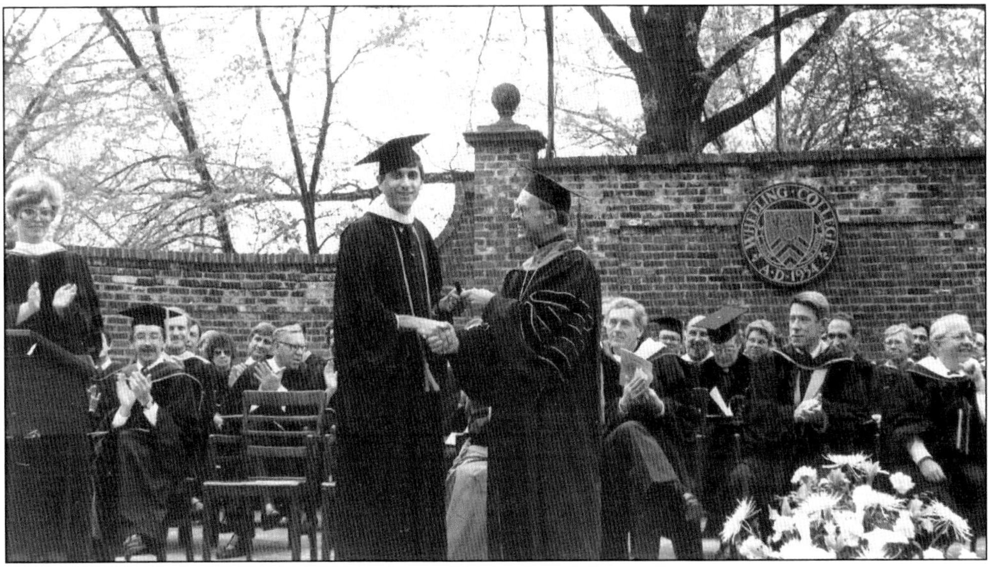

TERRENCE MCCORMICK '84. Pictured here at his graduation from Wheeling College, McCormick received the Archbishop John Swint Medal, which is given to the male student who best exemplifies the ideals of the institution, from Pres. Thomas Acker. McCormick has spent his career in children's services and joined St. John's Home, where he is now executive director, in 1992. (Courtesy of the Wheeling-Charleston Diocese Archives.)

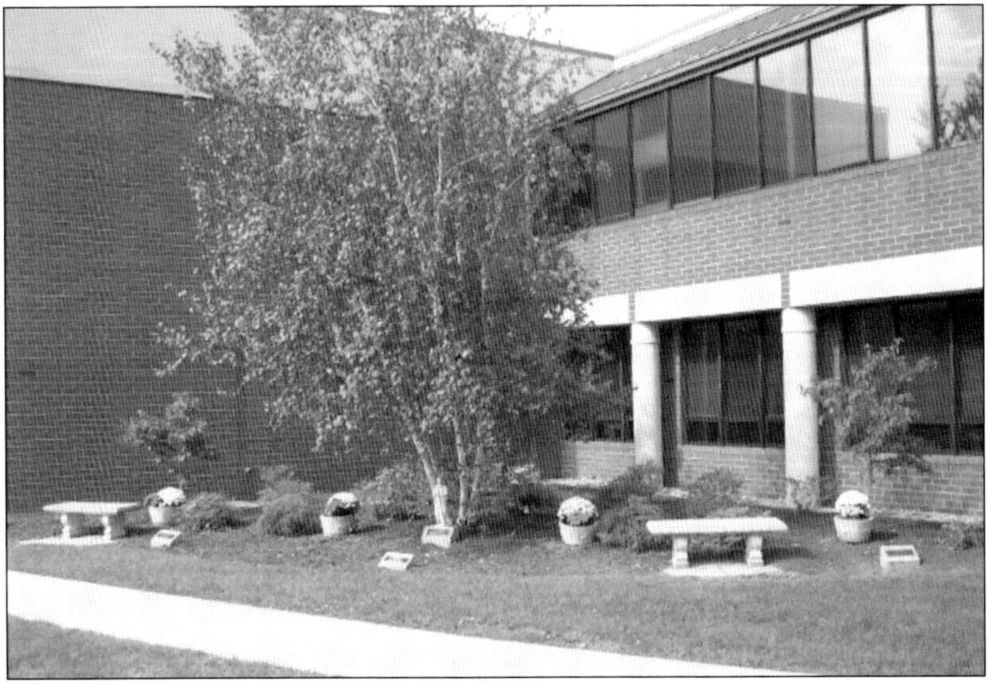

RITZ GARDEN. On campus, a common way to memorialize loved ones is by planting trees with an accompanying plaque. There are more than 24 of these memorial spots at Wheeling Jesuit; the most elaborate is the Ritz family garden in front of the McDonough athletic center. Jim and Marie Ritz established the garden to remember not only Jim's brother Tom, a Wheeling graduate and longtime campus physician, but other relatives as well.

BIBLIOGRAPHY

Diocese of Wheeling-Charleston website. www.dwc.org.

Dunham, Tom. *Wheeling in the 20th Century*. Bloomington, IN: 1st Books Library, 2003.

Fetherling, George. *Wheeling: A Brief History*. Wheeling: Polyhedron Learning Media, 2008.

Pyne, Tricia T. *Faith in the Mountains: A History of the Diocese of Wheeling-Charleston 1850–2000*. Strasbourg, France: Editions du Signe, 2000.

Rutkowski, Ryan. *Catholic West Virginia*. Charleston, SC: Arcadia, 2010.

West Virginia Register Wheeling College pictorial supplement, October 12, 1956.

Wheeling Jesuit University. *The First 50 Years of Wheeling Jesuit University*. Wheeling: Wheeling Jesuit University, 2005.

Wheeling Jesuit University website. www.wju.edu.

The author also used various other sources to collect information for this text:

The student newspaper, called various names in the last 57 years, including *The Spokesman, Nova,* and *The Cardinal Connection.*

The student yearbook, *The Manifest*, which has been published almost every year since the founding of the school.

The newsletter/newspaper/magazine published by Wheeling Jesuit for alumni and friends of the college, called *The Wheeling College Chronicle* or *Wheeling Jesuit University Chronicle.*

Unpublished manuscripts about the history of the college by Clifford Lewis, SJ; Marc Connelly, SJ; Francis Gormley, SJ; and Dr. Paul Orr, the university's archivist, who is currently writing a history of the institution.